PRAISE FOR THE HAPPY CHRISTIAN

"*Happy* is a cheap word nowadays. . . . . alistic, joyful, triumphant Christian life . . . . us. His book overflows with earthy, dee. . . . . s but all of us need."

—J. I. Packer, Professor of Theol. . . . . . College,
Vancouver, Canada, and author of *Knowing God*

"Christians and non-Christians alike are besieged by bad news and a world of difficulty. Christians, though, should respond in a way that reflects the hope they have found in Christ. In *The Happy Christian*, David Murray instructs us on how to face the challenges of this cynical age with a rooted joy and a resounding happiness. *The Happy Christian* will instruct, inspire, and encourage believers to live our their faith with true joy."

—Ed Stetzer, president of Lifeway Research Division,
contributing editor for *Christianity Today*

"If anyone else had written a book with this title I wouldn't have picked it up. The fact that it was written by Dr. David Murray made me not only pick it up but study it in depth. This is not a 'feel good' book but a book about the genuine joy and happiness that we can know as beloved followers of Christ in a broken world."

—Sheila Walsh, author of *Loved Back to Life*

"David Murray has written a timely corrective to both the excesses of the 'prosperity gospel' and the gloomy spirit that overcomes so many Christians. Biblically compelling and pastorally encouraging, this easy-to-read book makes an important point that Christians need to hear. Read *The Happy Christian* and remember that through the love of Christ you are blessed by God!"

—Dr. Richard Phillips, senior minister of Second Presbyterian
Church, Greenville, South Carolina; author of *Jesus the Evangelist*;
board member, Alliance of Confessing Evangelicals

"David Murray insists that Christians not only can but must be happy. And surely he is right! A word of caution, though. Murray is both a biblical scholar and pastor—and he knows all too well that trite 'fix-it' approaches fall apart all too easily. *The Happy Christian* is a robust and welcome defense of how the gospel acts (should act, I dare say) in the lives of those who have been transformed by it. A great read—transforming and uplifting."

—Derek W. H. Thomas, Robert Strong Professor of Systematic
and Historical Theology (RTS Atlanta); senior minister,
First Presbyterian Church, Columbia South Carolina

"This is one shockingly and happifyingly helpful book! With winning honesty, tenderness, and grace, David Murray gives the recipe for sturdy, God-grounded happiness. Many of us have seen how hollow is the common, self-hypnotizing idea of 'positive thinking' and grown understandably cynical; David Murray shows us a far better way, a way that is biblical, beautiful, and built to last."

—MICHAEL REEVES, AUTHOR OF *DELIGHTING IN THE TRINITY*; DIRECTOR OF
UNION AND SENIOR LECTURER, WALES EVANGELICAL SCHOOL OF THEOLOGY

"There's a sort of gloom and doom in the air. You don't have to go far to get a whiff of it, as matter of fact, you probably know it well. David Murray understands that there is a problem when our hearts and minds are set on the negative things of this world and he has a wonderful solution: the Bible. 'The Bible has an uplifting and positive message,' he says. And he is right. 'Jesus leads us through the dark valleys and beside green pastures.' If we set our minds on all we have in Christ, how could one not be filled with the joy of the Lord? With a fascinating mixture of science and biblical truth, Murray sets out to help us see how we practically seek the joy found in Christ. *The Happy Christian* reminds me that the joy of the Lord truly is my strength."

—TRILLIA NEWBELL, AUTHOR OF *UNITED: CAPTURED BY GOD'S VISION FOR
DIVERSITY* AND *FEAR AND FAITH: FINDING THE PEACE YOUR HEART CRAVES*

"While interacting with secular researchers, popular authors, and theologians both ancient and modern, in his newest book David Murray opens up the Scriptures and offers immensely practical means for cultivating the abundant life Jesus promises to his people. Thankfully, I can also attest that David not only teaches these truths, but lives them, which causes their authenticity to ring through the pages."

—PASTOR BARRY YORK, RPTS PROFESSOR OF PASTORAL THEOLOGY

"Our culture of negativity, cynicism, and skepticism has poisoned millions, including many in the church, producing a dark and joyless spirit. Thankfully, Dr. Murray's gospel-rich, biblically driven, practical, and pointed book is medicine for the soul that guides the reader into the joy of the Lord in all spheres of life."

—JOE THORN, AUTHOR, LEAD PASTOR OF REDEEMER
FELLOWSHIP IN ST. CHARLES, ILLINOIS

"David Murray here opens out ten arguments to show how a Christian's gloom may be converted into happiness. Believers will welcome this practical guidance on how our feelings may, by biblical discipline, become increasingly joyful. This book is good medicine for sad saints."

—MAURICE ROBERTS, RETIRED PASTOR
AND AUTHOR OF *THE HAPPINESS OF HEAVEN*

"I am so very happy to commend my friend David Murray's new book on happiness. David follows in a long line of Reformed experiential theology and Christian living, which is a rich inheritance to draw from in contemporary pastoral ministry. Saturated in Scripture, guided by history, and sensitive to the insights of contemporary psychological and physiological research, David offers a care for souls that is so needed by believers today."

—REV. DANIEL R. HYDE, PASTOR OF OCEANSIDE UNITED
REFORMED CHURCH, CARLSBAD / OCEANSIDE, CALIFORNIA

"What does it mean to be happy? The light of nature allows us to observe, desire, and appreciate the benefits of certain kinds of happiness. Only the light of Scripture enables us properly to define, obtain, and cultivate true and lasting happiness. David Murray's difficult task in this genuinely stimulating and sometimes provocative book is to accept and acknowledge the former source of illumination while being governed by and relying upon the latter. He has no appetite for the fixed grin and glassy stare of a carnally manufactured positivity. Instead, David seeks to train our hearts in Christian cheerfulness, genuine gladness, and believing hopefulness, to enjoy and employ the 'solid joys and lasting treasures' of the true children of God. Some might take issue with the balance of his foundations and the choice or proportion of his materials, but all Christians would do well to consider the structure and style of the building David erects. It is a good and bright place to live, and many of us need to start construction."

—PASTOR JEREMY WALKER, AUTHOR OF
THE BROKEN-HEARTED EVANGELIST

"Jesus came to give abundant life and his own joy to his people. I praise God for David Murray, and I pray the Christlike happiness taught in this book will be your way of life."

—DR. JIM HAMILTON, PROFESSOR OF
BIBLICAL THEOLOGY, SOUTHERN SEMINARY

"A happy countenance is a good thing but is too often lacking in Christian lives. *The Happy Christian* is a book that addresses this present need. Without minimizing the trials of this life or their significance, David Murray challenges the dour, downcast, and joyless Christian to change their thoughts and feelings by the power of the Spirit and a little effort. This is an incredibly practical book, filled with the truth of Scripture, which helpfully and happily encourages and exhorts readers to renew their minds in the pursuit of Christ."

—JASON HELOPOULOS, ASSISTANT PASTOR, UNIVERSITY REFORMED CHURCH,
EAST LANSING, MICHIGAN; AUTHOR OF A NEGLECTED GRACE: FAMILY
WORSHIP IN THE CHRISTIAN HOME AND THE NEW PASTOR'S HANDBOOK:
HELP AND ENCOURAGEMENT FOR THE FIRST YEARS OF MINISTRY

"*The Happy Christian* truly challenged me to model a life characterized by happiness. People want to be happy. But we're losing hope that it's actually possible. We're content to experience brief moments of mirth instead of cultivating a lifestyle of abiding joy. David Murray reminds us that even in the face of sobering facts, happiness is possible when we put our faith in the paradoxically positive power of the cross."

—JEMAR TISBY, COFOUNDER, REFORMED AFRICAN AMERICAN NETWORK

"It is a pleasure to recommend David Murray's latest book, *The Happy Christian*. The subtitle, *Ten Ways to Be a Joyful Believer in a Gloomy World*, will surely resonate with believers and, hopefully, attract unbelievers. Dr. Murray imaginatively uses the disciplines of science and psychology to support his conviction that the Bible both calls Christians to a happy life and directs them how to live a happy life. Murray has a way of freshly stating the truths of God's Word, confronting us with the unsettling realities of the believing life but drawing us anew into the rich inheritance that we have in Christ. *The Happy Christian* is a must read."

—REV. IAN HAMILTON, AUTHOR OF *THE FAITH-SHAPED LIFE*

"We all want to be happy, but so many of us are not. That is why books on happiness are so popular. But these books are rarely as theologically solid as Dr. Murray's book *The Happy Christian*. This fact alone makes all the difference in the world, since the only happiness worth having is a happiness that will never end."

—DR. MARK JONES, SENIOR MINISTER AT FAITH
VANCOUVER PRESBYTERIAN CHURCH (PCA)

THE
HAPPY
CHRISTIAN

TEN WAYS TO BE A JOYFUL
BELIEVER IN A GLOOMY WORLD

DAVID MURRAY

NELSON
BOOKS

An Imprint of Thomas Nelson

Published in Nashville, Tennessee, by Nelson Books, an imprint of Thomas Nelson. Nelson Books and Thomas Nelson are registered trademarks of HarperCollins Christian Publishing, Inc.

Thomas Nelson titles may be purchased in bulk for educational, business, fund-raising, or sales promotional use. For information, please e-mail SpecialMarkets@ThomasNelson.com.

Library of Congress Cataloging-in-Publication Data

Murray, David P.
  The happy Christian : ten ways to be a joyful believer in a gloomy world / David Murray.
      pages cm
  Includes bibliographical references and index.
  ISBN 978-0-7180-2201-3 (pbk.)
  1. Happiness--Religious aspects--Christianity. I. Title.
  BV4647.J68M88 2015
  248.4--dc23

                                                          2014023683

Printed in the United States of America
15 16 17 18 19 RRD 6 5 4 3 2 1

*Dedicated to Joel Beeke, a special
friend, a wonderful mentor, and one
of the happiest Christians I know*

CONTENTS

CONTENTS

INTRODUCTION

THE HAPPIEST PEOPLE IN THE WORLD

RATE YOUR FAITH WITH a positive or a negative.

Now rate your life: positive or negative?

They're connected, aren't they? A positive faith produces a positive life; a negative faith, a negative life. That shouldn't surprise us. King Solomon wrote, "As a person thinks in his heart, so is he."[1]

We are what we think and believe.

What we think and believe about God, about ourselves, about others, about our problems, and about our world dictates and determines the quality of our whole lives: our happiness, our relationships, our creativity, our productivity, and even our physical health.

That's why I've written this book. I want you to have a positive faith and life. Or if you do already, I want you to have an even more positive faith because the more positive your faith is, the more positive your life will be. As Nehemiah said more than twenty-five hundred years ago, "The joy of the LORD is your strength."[2]

"Joy of the LORD?" "Strength?" "Positive faith?" "Positive life?" "Happy Christian?"

You're a bit cynical, aren't you? Perhaps it doesn't sound like anything you've experienced lately. It could be that you have too many negatives in your life to be positive. Or maybe you think "positive faith" or "happy Christian" sounds like a contradiction in terms. That's certainly how the media wants us to think about faith—as a liability, not an asset.

As a recovering skeptic, I understand your cynicism. Although you may have a deep and painful horizontal line engraved right across your soul, subtracting joy from every area of life, I want to show you how to add one vertical line to that negative symbol, transforming it into a positive sign and renewing your whole life in a positive direction.

The positive symbol I'm referring to stands at the center of Christianity. It's the cross of Jesus Christ, a symbol that graphically demonstrates how God can transform the most unimaginable negative into an almost inconceivable positive.

SPIRITUAL MATH

Christianity doesn't deny the difficult and painful reality of sin and suffering that runs through our lives, but with one vertical line from heaven to earth, with the incarnation, crucifixion, and resurrection of Jesus, Christianity promises to change the equation of our lives into a positive result. That's what God is all about. That's what the Christian faith is all about. And that's what this book is all about.

I've written *The Happy Christian* to help you live a powerfully optimistic and meaningful life in an increasingly pessimistic culture. I hope to persuade you that through daily faith in Jesus Christ, there is a way to overcome the deadly plague of negativity that's infecting our whole culture and rapidly spreading through the church.

I long to heal adults who have gotten so used to their own

negativity that they have no idea now what healthy joy looks like. I want to grab young people before this demoralizing virus contaminates them and to inoculate them with biblical principles and practices that will enable them to stand up and stand out in their despairing generation. I yearn to attract unbelievers to a faith that has been too often misrepresented by its friends, never mind its enemies. I aim to encourage Christians to be countercultural missionaries in our negative culture by demonstrating the positive power of the gospel in their lives. I aspire to see churches transformed into beacons of bright hope in a world of dark despair. I'm eager to show that where sin and suffering abound, grace can abound much more.[3] I dream about Christians being the happiest people in the world.

And this is not just about subtracting the negatives but also about adding the positives. My target is not just to get you from minus ten to zero, but from zero to plus ten; not just to end your depression, but also for you to soar with joy; not just to calm your anxiety, but also for you to know the peace that passes all understanding. I want to get you back to the norm, the average, the baseline, but also to raise your baseline, to rise above the average.

You may not be depressed, but couldn't you be happier? Even, as one secular book title put it recently, *10% Happier*?

The first book I wrote was *Christians Get Depressed Too*. I thought of calling this one, *Christians Can Be Happy Too!*

NEGATIVITY OVERLOAD

Hard to imagine, isn't it? We live in an increasingly negative culture in which it's easy to be dragged down with all the discouraging and depressing events that flood our hearts and overwhelm our minds. The recession, foreclosures, unemployment, and family breakdown dominate our media. The cost of college, health care, and senior care is soaring as job openings, house values, savings, and pension funds are shrinking. The church is increasingly marginalized as politicians, judges, journalists, and educators combine to ridicule fundamental doctrines, to challenge basic Christian morality, and to undermine ancient divine institutions such as marriage and the family. The Internet and TV bring every tragedy from all corners of the world onto our desktops and into our living rooms every day, feeding us a gloomy and bitter diet of disease, disaster, destruction, and death. As Christians find themselves increasingly on the losing side of the culture wars, sermons and prayers sound more like discontented defeatism than inspirational calls to worship and serve.

Opinion polls find the majority of Americans pessimistic about the country, with most saying that the country is on the wrong track. Even when reliable objective statistics reveal that many things have gotten better—racial tension, the standard of living, children's health, education, and teen crime rates—we think and feel they are getting worse.[4] Part of the reason for that is a negativity bias, our tendency to react more quickly and passionately to bad events than good ones. We also remember the bad events longer as we tend to ruminate on them five times more than on positive ones.[5]

In "Bad Is Stronger Than Good," an article published in the *Review of General Psychology*, Roy Baumeister and three other professors of psychology wrote, "Bad emotions, bad parents, and bad feedback have more impact than good ones. . . . Bad impressions and bad stereotypes are quicker to form and more resistant to disconfirmation than good ones."[6]

In some ways, it's amazing that we're not all completely depressed! Some have succumbed and are sunk in the depths, but most of us are still trundling along, unaware that we're on a slow and shallow decline into pessimism, despair, and hopelessness. Even our young people are less optimistic than previous generations, yielding their energies to life-sucking cynicism and suspicion.

Ipsos Mori research in more than twenty countries found that "most young adults in Europe, North America, Japan and Australia fear that their nations' best days are behind them. . . . In a stark warning, the head of the world's foremost economic research institute, the Organisation for Economic Co-operation and Development (OECD), described such pessimism among western youth as 'politically explosive.'"[7]

It looks frighteningly terminal, doesn't it?

The Cause Is the Cure

How do we reverse this? Our culture seems to be in an unstoppable death spiral, and Christians' moods and mind-sets are being dragged down with it. But they don't have to be. We may not be able to change our culture, but we can change the way we think about it. We cannot change certain events in life, but we can change the way we respond to them. In that sense, the cure is closely connected to the cause.

Remember: *we are what we think.* If our minds constantly feed on all this negativity, our moods will inevitably darken, taking everything else—our words, actions, health, relationships, and so forth—down with them into the abyss.

The opposite is also true. By filling our minds, words, and lives with positive forces and influences, we can live in a way and at a level we probably can't even conceive of at the moment. The results will be just as startling as we will experience improved physical, mental, emotional, spiritual, and relational health. We will see our lives metamorphose into something beautiful, and we will also learn how to help others soar higher and become happier. That is the vision of this book.

POSITIVE PSYCHOLOGY

Even secular psychologists have discovered the value of a more positive outlook on life. Until the late 1990s, for every one psychological study about happiness and thriving, there were seventeen studies on depression and other disorders. With this abnormally high negative-to-positive research ratio, most psychologists spent their time helping people with problems get back to an average human experience. Their aim was to help people who were operating at subnormal levels to get back to normal: sober up alcoholics, remove anxiety, reduce sadness, cool down anger, and so on. Little attention was given to making people happy and optimistic, to lifting them above the average, and to encouraging human flourishing and well-being.

In 1998, Martin Seligman, then president of the American Psychological Association, rebelled against this imbalanced negativity and led a shift to studying the positive side of the curve, the above average, the abnormally happy, and so on. Thus the new discipline of "positive psychology" was born with a new emphasis on what works rather than what's broken.[8]

Instead of traditional psychology's focus on "Why are people unhappy?" and "How can we help fix their problems?" positive psychology asks, "What makes people happy?" and "How can we help them flourish and excel?"[9] Jessica Colman summed up the aims: "Positive psychology attempts to balance the field of psychology and make it more complete by shifting the focus from repairing the worst things in life to enhancing the positive aspects. This can improve quality of life and prevent the pathologies that arise when life is empty and meaningless. . . . It studies the 'good life' by focusing on positive individual traits, positive subjective experiences, and positive institutions."[10]

If that's secular psychology's positive agenda, surely the

Christian faith has far more to be positive about; and to be happy in a sustainable, life-giving sort of way and not just for the length of a song—"Don't worry, be happy."

Yes, we must continue to get involved in the mess and rubble of people's lives. Of course we must continue to repent of and confess our own sin. But what about forging an additional positive path? What about adding the banjo to the violin? Jesus leads us through the dark valleys *and* beside green pastures and still waters. He wipes away our tears *and* teaches us how to rejoice. He fixes spiritual problems *and* promotes spiritual flourishing. He targets sins for demolition *and* graces and gifts for strengthening and exercising. He pulls the backslider out of the filthy ditch *and* shows the godly new vistas of spiritual beauty.

As the apostle Paul put it: We are "sorrowful, *yet always rejoicing*; as poor, *yet making many rich*; as having nothing, *and yet possessing all things*."[11] We're quite good at the sorrow, poverty, and nothing bit. But what about rejoicing, enriching, and possessing everything?

Positive Benefits

Positive psychologists are not shy about trumpeting the benefits and results of their discipline:

- Optimistic salespeople outsell their pessimistic counterparts by 33 percent.[12]
- Students primed to feel happy before taking math achievement tests far outperform their neutral peers.[13]
- Student freshmen's happiness levels predict their income nineteen years later.[14]
- Judged by their journal entries, happy nuns live an average of ten years longer than unhappy nuns.[15]
- Unhappy employees take fifteen more sick days a year.[16]

- Positive emotions produce dopamine and serotonin, which increase concentration, analysis, creativity, problem solving, and memory.[17]
- Positive negotiators conclude more and better deals than their negative or neutral colleagues.[18]

One meta-analysis of happiness research that brought together the results of more than two hundred scientific studies on more than 275,000 people found that happiness is the greatest predictor of success in our work, our home, our hobbies, and our relationships.[19] Surely personal experience also confirms that happier people tend to do better in their marriages and careers, as well as being more helpful, generous, and energetic.

These benefits and advantages shouldn't surprise us. As we've seen, psychologists didn't invent the power of a positive focus in life; they simply discovered what God had already revealed to Nehemiah thousands of years ago! "The joy of the LORD is your strength!"[20]

But Christians don't have only the advantage of historic precedent and divine warrant; we also have so much more to be positive about. Taste the sweetness in this small sample of blessings:

- We love and are loved by the one true and living God.
- God is our perfect Father.
- We know Jesus as our Lord and Savior.
- The Holy Spirit is sanctifying and empowering us.
- Our sins are forgiven.
- We are justified and adopted into God's worldwide and heaven-wide family.
- We have all the promises of God.
- Everything is working together for our good.
- God is our guard and guide.
- God lives in our hearts.

- Jesus has prepared a place for us in heaven and will welcome us there.

What mind-, heart-, soul-, and body-strengthening joy God gives us in the gospel! Christian happiness is so large, so multilayered, so multidimensional, that it's virtually impossible to define in one sentence. But let me try: *Christian happiness is a God-centered, God-glorifying, and God-given sense of God's love that is produced by a right relationship to God in Christ and that produces loving service to God and others.*

Where do I get that from?

Moses' deathbed!

As he is dying, Moses rouses himself one last time to enthusiastically pronounce multiple blessings (happinesses) on Israel's tribes.[21] He then takes a big view of the whole nation and joyfully exclaims, "Happy are you, O Israel! / Who is like you, a people saved by the LORD."[22] He happily calls them the happiest people in the world!

It was a *God-centered happiness*. It wasn't a happiness based on things or achievements (neither Israel nor Moses had any of these). It was a happiness based on truth, truth about God. Moses spent the previous three verses declaring multiple facts about God and all He was and did for Israel before climaxing with "Happy are you, O Israel!"

It was also a *God-glorifying happiness*. Moses doesn't just narrate facts about God like a dull and boring lecturer. No, he's exulting in God and exalting God as he speaks. He begins this final chorus of praise by saying, "There is no one like . . . God." God makes him happy, but worshiping God makes him even happier. God-centered happiness makes him glorify God happily.

Finally it was a *God-given happiness*. To the onlooker, Moses and Israel were in the saddest and most miserable circumstances.

Moses had experienced many disappointments and frustrations over his life, especially during the last forty years in the wilderness, and particularly in being banned from finally entering the promised land because he lost his temper once. Israel's forty-year history up to that point was a trail of thousands of carcasses in the same wilderness, and they were still outside the promised land!

Yet Moses pronounced God's people not just happy but the happiest people in the world! Incomparably happy. Happier than the most powerful and prosperous nations.

What can possibly explain it?

It wasn't something manufactured or manipulated; it was given by God. Given the circumstances, negativity and pessimism would have been much easier. But by grace, God enabled Moses to rise above every discouragement and sadness (without denying them) and to find his happiness in God. Like Paul, who faced similar harrowing circumstances, he was "sorrowful, yet always rejoicing."[23]

And if Moses and Israel had such happiness, how much more should the New Testament church and every New Testament Christian? If we claim to know much more about God (and we do) and claim to have experienced so much of His great salvation (and we have), how much happier we should be!

So why aren't we the happiest people in the world? And how can we change?

POSITIVE FAITH

I will identify the major causes of negativity and unhappiness in our lives and outline ten biblical and practical ways to tilt the balance of our attitude, outlook, words, and actions in a way that will lift our spirits, compel attention for the Christian faith, and make the church an energizing force in a life-sapping culture.

As I'll demonstrate, I'm not repackaging the "health, wealth, and prosperity gospel." Neither am I relaunching Norman Vincent Peale's *The Power of Positive Thinking*. I'm advocating a return to the overall positive balance of biblical truth and the elevating experience of real Christianity.

I'm not suggesting for a moment that we ignore or downplay sin and suffering. No, we have to face these powerful forces honestly and feel them deeply. But I also believe the Bible provides practical strategies for transforming even these huge negatives into ultimately positive experiences.

A New Normal

As you read on, I think you'll be surprised at how often you recognize the deep and damaging negative thought patterns and practices that presently characterize you. They are so common in our society and have been so long in our lives that they have quietly and subtly become the norm. This should not be the norm, however, and this is not the default we should simply accept.

There is a better way of living. There are biblical ways to get there. There can be a new normal. We can expect the help of God Himself in the process. We can inspire others along the way, and, one positive life at a time, we can transform our families, our churches, our communities, and even our nation.

A National Vision

Yes, this is about much more than personal transformation. Every pebble of positive faith ripples out to wash over our families, friends, churches, communities, and world.

And doesn't our world need it?

Consider, for example, America, a country that has historically been much more of a can-do than a can't-do society. It tends to celebrate success more than envy it, and its people are usually more willing to praise and encourage than to criticize and pull down. No surprise then that it has produced more positive people in its history than most other nations. Remember, "As a person thinks in his heart, so is he."[24]

But this invaluably positive American asset is in clear and tangible decline. The events of 9/11 left a deep scar on the American psyche, as have the disappointing and inconclusive wars in Afghanistan and Iraq. The political climate has been poisoned by excessive partisanship, especially among media cheerleaders on both sides. Political campaigns have divided people into special interest groups that set one American against another. The recession and painfully slow recovery have pushed the American dream over the horizon for many, with only 26 percent of Americans believing that the nation is heading in the right direction.[25] Student debt is soaring, as is student unemployment, with many young people unable to get off the starting blocks of life.

In a special 2014 survey commissioned for *The Atlantic* and the Aspen Institute, "nearly two-thirds of Americans—65 percent—question whether America will be on the right track in 10 years. They are also split on whether the country will be a 'land of opportunity' (33 percent say yes, 42 percent say no, and 24 percent say they don't know). In their view, the American Dream itself seems to be fading."[26]

The American church has been buffeted, too, with decreasing attendance and influence. A siege mentality is growing, with less confidence about bringing the Christian faith into the public sphere and to the nations of the world. Even Rick Warren, the usually upbeat evangelical leader, is "disheartened by what he sees as a malaise afoot in the land. . . . I feel America is in the emotional doldrums." He observed, "I think America is more divided today—and it's sad—than at any time since the Civil War."[27]

Although the negative symbol is deepening and widening in

American souls and in American society, while the positive sign is shrinking and reducing in power and influence, I believe the Christian faith can halt and reverse that trend here and all around the world. And the key is individual Christians and the Christian church repositioning the positive symbol of the Christian faith, the cross of Jesus Christ, at the center of their faith again.

The Most Positive Book in the World

Although I'll be referring to scientific research at times, this book is based on the Bible because I believe there is no more realistically positive book in the world than the Christian holy Scriptures. The church has not always been successful in communicating the Bible's uplifting and inspiring message. Overinfluenced by our culture, we have drifted into such a default normality of negativity that anyone calling for a more biblical balance is often viewed with grave suspicion. "He wants us to be happy? Burn the heretic!"

So, let me challenge you with very basic questions: If someone who had never encountered Christianity before wandered into your church or your home, what would be the greatest impression made upon him? If he had to sum up in one word the mood of the worship, prayers, and sermons of your church or the conversation at your family meal table, what would that word be? What if he was asked to describe your church or faith with either a negative or a positive symbol? Unsettling, isn't it? Does the gospel really mean "good news"?

SCIENCE AND THE BIBLE

It's not just the impact on others we should be concerned about; it's the impact of negativity on us as well. As I highlight throughout the book, science confirms and illustrates the Bible's teaching on the link between negativity and intellectual sluggishness, emotional fragility, physical frailty, economic decline, social decay, and spiritual backsliding.

What science cannot do is prescribe lasting solutions; the Bible alone can do that. If we look for answers on the horizontal plane, on the human level, we will only further entrench negativity into our hearts. But if we can start traveling in a vertical direction, looking up to God for His wisdom, we will reconnect with His positive truth and sense the energy of a growing optimism flowing into our lives no matter how much negativity surrounds us.

Come with me as I outline ways to disconnect from cultural negativity and reconnect with the positive truth of the Bible in order to recalibrate our lives and to live and serve more happily in this gloomy world. We're not only going to find and accentuate the positives that are already in your life. We're also going to address several negatives head-on, some of the things you think are utter disasters for you, for the church, or for your nation, and with the help of God's Word, turn even these into positives.

Enroll in Positive Math Class

I hope this metaphor won't turn you off, but I'm asking you to take a math class with me, a math class that will teach ten simple formulas, which all add up to the grand total of a *positive* faith and life.

Calculating each one of these ten formulas will tilt the balance of your life in an increasingly positive direction. When all ten are added together by daily spiritual exercise and practice, you will sense an unmistakable change in your mind, in your heart, in your feelings, in your attitude, in your health, in your relationships, in your soul, and indeed in your worldview. And even if this book does not make you a *happy* Christian, I hope it will make you a *happier* Christian.

We'll close our math class by looking forward to the day when all classes and calculations will be over, when all the negatives will be banished, and when all believers will experience the fullness of life in the new heaven and new earth full of new creatures in Christ.

In the meantime, let's get out those calculators and start adding.

Chapter One

HAPPY FACTS

FACTS > FEELINGS = POSITIVE+

FEELINGS HAVE BIG MUSCLES. They are often the most powerful force in our lives. They can bully our minds, our consciences, and our wills. They can even knock out the facts and bring truth to its knees.

This is perhaps okay when the feelings are good, when we experience joy, peace, and happiness. But more often anxiety, fear, sadness, and guilt rear their ugly heads and start shoving us around. That vicious tag team can quickly bruise and bloody us, confusing our minds and blurring our vision. Nothing looks good when we've gone a few rounds with them. We just want to slink out of the ring of life and crawl back into bed again.

How then can we get our emotions under control? How can we knock down guilt and wrestle fear to the ground? How can we summon allies like joy and peace to our side, especially when we often feel so alone in the fight of our lives? How can we be happy when there is so much to be sad about?

Many, many factors make up our moods—the weather, our bank balance, sports results, our genes, our health, our body chemistry, and our sleep—but no factor is more influential than our thoughts, especially our thinking patterns and habits.

THE 40 PERCENT SOLUTION

That probably surprises you, doesn't it? Because most people think that the way to happiness is more money, more friends, more success, more health, more fame, more beauty, more muscles, and on and on.

Scientists who study happiness (often called positive psychologists) have discovered that improvements in life circumstances or situations account for only about 10 percent of our happiness.[1] In other words, for all the effort people are putting into becoming more wealthy, healthy, popular, or muscular, the emotional return on the investment is minuscule. These positive events create some happiness, but it's usually minimal and brief.

These scientists also discovered that each of us has a baseline happiness that is difficult to change. Just as we all have a baseline weight that we tend to gravitate toward regardless of our efforts at dieting or muscle building, our parents have bequeathed us a happiness set point in our genes that we tend to return to no matter how many setbacks or triumphs we experience. Research has indicated that our genes explain about 50 percent of our happiness or lack of it.[2]

Now if you can count, you're beginning to get worried. If happiness is 10 percent life circumstances plus 50 percent genes, that leaves only 40 percent to work with. The good news is, that is still a relatively large number. No, it's not 90 percent, but neither is it 5 percent. There's still quite a lot of potential, a lot that's in our power to change, in this 40 percent. And what makes up that 40 percent? These same scientists tell us it's our daily choices about what we think about and do.[3]

And that's good news. Because of all these mood-altering factors, our thoughts are probably the easiest to change. There's nothing we can do about the weather, apart from moving to California.

Our bank balance never seems to change, no matter how much is poured into it. Relying on sports results to lift our spirits is like relying on a bungee cord. Our genetic inheritance is fixed until the resurrection. We *can* do quite a bit to improve our health until we get to about fifty, when it all starts to fall apart. Meds can sometimes balance our body chemistry and moods but often imbalance other areas. We could certainly increase and improve our sleep if spouses would stop snoring (not mine, of course), the baby would stop crying, and the teenagers would stop crashing around the house at midnight.

But our thoughts—what we think and how we think—are potentially powerful allies in the fight for optimistic faith in a pessimistic culture. Our thoughts can be changed, even if our circumstances can't. Gretchen Rubin articulated this in her best-selling book *The Happiness Project*: "I didn't want to reject my life. I wanted to change my life without changing my life, by finding more happiness in my own kitchen. I knew I wouldn't discover happiness in a faraway place or in unusual circumstances."[4] She didn't want to spend a fortune, travel the world, or wait for years: "I needed to find a way to do it here and now. I needed to change the lens through which I viewed everything familiar."[5]

In this chapter, we'll change the lens. We'll discover how unhealthy some of our thinking patterns are and how they determine and often damage our moods. We'll find out how we have fallen into some flawed thinking habits and default thinking patterns, many of which began early in life and have continued to develop and strengthen since then. We will also begin to see the connections between these thoughts and our moods, our feelings.

But this is not all about diagnosis; I also want to provide a prescription, a cure, a method of changing and retraining our thoughts, lifting them out of their old ruts, and raising them to a higher and healthier plane. And in the process, we will knock guilt down,

3

bloody anxiety's nose, put fear under our feet, and chase sadness out of the ring. Allies such as peace, joy, assurance, and confidence will then come running to our side, protecting and shielding us from future malicious assaults.

MAJOR SHIFT

This probably sounds a bit odd to you. We are very used to the idea of making diagnoses, fixing problems, or putting right what's wrong; we're not so familiar with the idea of prescribing positive action, growing graces, or expanding happiness. But until we major much more on getting above the baseline, on rising above the average, we will always remain vulnerable and uncomfortably close to falling into the abyss again. Basic faith will get us out of the negatives and back to the baseline average. But if we want to flourish and thrive, we have to aim higher; we have to build a *positive* faith.

Simple Formula

As I wrote in the introduction: "As a person thinks in his heart, so is he."[6] We are what we think. What we think is the major factor in determining how we feel. Two people can look at the same situation and walk away with two very different moods because they think differently about it.

A father looks at his son's artistic abilities and moans that he lacks the discipline to be a doctor. His mother, on the other hand, is excited when she thinks about how her son will beautify the world and bring pleasure to many through his paintings and poems.

Same facts; different feelings. Because the people have different thoughts about the facts.

Our hopes of living positive lives depend largely on getting our thoughts about the facts right. Most unhappy people are unhappy not because of their situation but because they let their feelings rule their thoughts, or they think about things in the wrong way.

The first step in making this right is identifying some of the ways our thoughts and feelings have gone wrong. Let me share some examples from my life. You'll probably recognize yourself in some of these.

DAMAGING THOUGHT PATTERNS

Black-or-White Thinking

I have the tendency to think in extreme, black-or-white categories. Shades of gray do not exist; it's all or nothing. For example, maybe my sermon goes so badly one Sunday that I conclude, "I was never called to the ministry." Or the fleeting thought passes through my mind: *God does not exist. I can't be a Christian if I ever think that, can I?* Whether preaching or praying, the extreme conclusion begins to drag down my mood.

Generalizing

Sometimes, when I experience something horrible, I'm convinced that the same thing will happen to me again and again. I remember the first time I asked a young lady for a date, only to be rebuffed. My conclusion? "Well, there's no point in ever asking anyone else, is there? This is always going to happen to me, and I better just get used to the single life." Another time I tried to witness to someone, but when the person mocked me, I moped around for days groaning, "I'll never win a soul for Christ, so I might as well shut up."

Filtering

I also have an amazing ability to pick out the negative in every situation and think about it to the exclusion of everything else. I filter out anything positive and find everything is negative. We're especially good at this when our kids come home with 90 percent on an exam. First question? "What happened to the other 10 percent?" Or we hear a great sermon, but all we can think about is the pastor's stupid grammatical mistake that spoiled the whole thing. Such tunnel vision is not good for the mood or the soul.

Transforming

Ever managed to transform a positive experience into a negative? Yes, I'm pretty good at that too. Someone compliments me. But instead of expressing humble thanks to her and to God, *What's she after?* is my suspicious thought. I read my Bible and find a verse that speaks assurance to my heart. But instead of thanking God, I think, *It's probably the Devil trying to deceive me.*

Mind Reading

Although I do not believe in psychics, I can read your mind. Yes, I know all your innermost thoughts about me. When you passed me in the mall without stopping to speak, I immediately knew it was because you hated me. I heard later that you broke your glasses and were on the way to the optician, but I know better.

Fortune-telling

I not only read minds; I also tell fortunes. At times I feel in my bones that things are going to turn out really badly, and sure enough it always happens. Another person I know with that skill convinced himself that his job interview would be a catastrophe. When the CEO saw him and said, "Cheer up, we're not the firing squad!" he knew his prophecy was about to be fulfilled. Funny how what we feel often determines what actually happens.

Telescoping

I've found this amazing telescope that helps me find and focus on the sins of the distant past in a way that leads to present feelings of guilt, condemnation, and fear. Then when it comes to my present blessings and benefits, I turn the telescope the other way around, shrinking the good things until they are nearly invisible. No one can trump me when it comes to magnifying guilt and minimizing grace.

Perfecting

"I should . . . I ought . . . I should . . . I ought." On and on it goes. An ever-lengthening list of obligations, duties, and targets. So much self-imposed pressure toward goals of unattainable standards, with all the frustration and resentment that accompanies the failure to reach them. Striving for the perfect day, the perfect home, the perfect yard, the perfect sermon, and the perfectly completed to-do list. Never realized. Never satisfied. Never content.

Personalizing

Thankfully, this is not one of my many skills, but younger people often fall into the trap of incorrectly viewing themselves as the cause of a bad event. I know one teenage girl who lost so many close relatives to death in a short space of time that she blamed herself for it all and lapsed into severe depression.

You don't need to be Sigmund Freud to realize that all these poor thought patterns will inevitably produce unhelpful emotions and behavior. If we always think about problems and negatives, imagine the future is hopeless, believe everyone hates us, or assume we have achieved *nothing* because we didn't achieve *everything*, or if we blame ourselves for things we had nothing to do with, we are on a dangerous downward spiral.

Such thought habits increase sadness, negativity, pessimism, and helplessness; they also undermine concentration, friendships, problem-solving ability, and motivation.

Good News! You Have a Plastic Brain!

The good news for those of us who tend to fall into one or more or all of these harmful thought habits is that we can retrain our brains to think more positively and feel more cheerful.

Until the 1970s, most scientists believed that brain structure and emotional makeup were primarily hereditary/genetic and more or less set in stone, especially after the teenage years. More recent research has demonstrated that we can actually change our brain structures and connections, improving our overall mood in the process.

So how do we change our brains? Is there a pill, an operation, or a one-off intervention? No, we retrain our brains by multiple little daily decisions. That's good news and bad news.

It's good news because it means we don't need to do anything dramatic, expensive, or invasive. We can do it here and now.

The bad news is that it involves effort, disciplined and determined effort, to increase the number of positive experiences in our everyday lives. These multiple little daily positives give us a quick squirt of happy emotions and improved performance, and as they become a habit, they raise our baseline happiness. Scientists call this neuroplasticity—yes, the brain is plastic, and that's actually a good thing—to convey how adaptable, flexible, and elastic our brains are.

X-Games and Mind Games

Let me take you into the forest to explain. My kids love to cycle through the paths in the woods that back up to our yard. But every year, new spring growth covers the pathways. For a few weeks, the kids slow down as they ride through, pushing away the leaves and branches that hang in the wrong place. They run over the fresh undergrowth rather gingerly, not wanting to wipe out. But as the days and weeks pass, the branches and undergrowth submit to the repeated assaults and clear the way for our would-be X-Gamers so they can fly through the forest with the greatest of ease.

Something similar happens in our brains. We create electrical and chemical pathways with our thoughts. As we think our way down these pathways, we strengthen the brain connections. As somebody put it, "Cells that fire together, wire together." The more we travel these mental paths, the faster and easier these paths become so that eventually our thoughts and resultant actions feel automatic.

Just think about how you learned to type at your computer. With practice it became easier as the pathways were more frequently used and the connections grew stronger and faster. So much so that you can now type almost without thinking. Your thoughts and actions have reshaped your brain pathways. Through repetition, a good habit has become ingrained and cemented in your brain structures and processes.

Renewing Our Minds

This plastic brain possibility opens up tremendous opportunities for personal change, growth, and development. Pessimists can become optimists. "No-men" (and women) can become "yes-men" (and women). Frightening obstacles can become inviting challenges. Difficulties can become possibilities. No, we cannot change reality, but we can change the way we view reality, regardless of age or stage in life.

These scientific discoveries are both confirmed and explained in Scripture. Through the apostle Paul, God calls us to "be transformed by the renewing of [our] mind[s]."[7] Thus, science and Scripture agree; we can retrain our brains, we can renew our minds, and thereby we can be transformed. Science and Scripture disagree, to some extent, about what needs to be transformed and how this takes place, and we'll consider these differences throughout this book.

For now, though, let's work through a few examples of brain retraining, mind renewing, and plastic remolding. I want to introduce you to a simple six-step method that will help you address bad thinking habits and change them for the better.

TO-DO EXAMPLE

Let's start with the bane of my life—my to-do list. I'm sitting at my desk at the end of a busy day, and I'm staring at my list in disbelief.

STEP 1: What are the facts? I started out the day with thirty items on the list, worked hard and completed fifteen tasks, but I added twenty more to the list.

STEP 2: What are my thoughts about the facts? I'm thinking, *Oh no, I've got more to do now than when I started out this morning. I've gone backward rather than forward. If it keeps going like this, I'm going to be completely stressed out, and I'll never manage a day off with my family this week.*

STEP 3: What are my feelings? Guilt, stress, anxiety, tension, fear, sadness, or whatever.

STEP 4: Can I change the facts? No, even if I set fire to the list, the tasks remain to be done.

STEP 5: Can I change my thoughts about the facts? Not without help, but my wife is an expert at this. She sees my furrowed brow and stiff shoulders, comes alongside me with

coffee and a cookie, and asks, "What's wrong, darling?" I
show her my to-do list, and she begins to laugh. "What are
you laughing at?"
"You don't think you accomplished anything today, do you?"
"No, look, I started out with a list this long, and despite all
I've done today, it has grown even longer."
"Okay, honey, now look at the twenty ticks on the page that
were not there this morning. And look at the tasks you've
added. Half of these can be done by your assistant, and
many of the others are just two-minute phone calls and
e-mails. You should be glad you've got so many meaningful
things to do in your life."
Do you see what she's doing? She's changing my thoughts
about the facts. She's helping me look at them differently,
to emphasize some and fade others, to interpret them more
positively, more in line with reality.
STEP 6: What am I feeling now? The furrow is being replaced
with a smile, the shoulders are beginning to relax, and a
sense of satisfaction about my day begins to grow.
The facts are the same. My thoughts about the facts are
different. And my feelings change for the better as a result.
That day off looks doable now, as does an early night with
my wife!

Although you can talk yourself through these steps or talk them
through with a friend, many people find it helpful, at least initially,
to write down their responses to each step, to recapture their feelings by putting words to them. Brain scans show that putting words
to feelings almost immediately diminishes the power of negative
emotions, improving well-being and enhancing decision-making
skills. Verbalizing the stress and helplessness you are feeling is the
first step toward regaining control.

TRAFFIC EXAMPLE

Next time you're sitting in a traffic jam and you start steaming, try to understand where these feelings are coming from by asking yourself these questions:

STEP 1: What are the facts? The facts are that I am in a two-mile backup, and the radio tells me it will take one hour to clear due to a breakdown in the fast lane several miles ahead.

STEP 2: What am I thinking about these facts? I'm thinking about the idiot who broke down in the fast lane. I'm thinking about all that I could have done with this hour. I'm thinking about how my friends will be wondering why I'm late for the committee meeting.

STEP 3: What am I feeling? I'm angry at the guy who broke down, I'm frustrated about the lost time, and I'm worried about what my friends will think about me for being late.

STEP 4: Can I change the facts? No, there is no way out of the traffic jam.

STEP 5: Can I change my thoughts about the facts? Yes, I can believe that this is God's plan for this hour of my life. I can be grateful for time to stop and think and pray in the midst of a busy day. I can practice my breathing relaxation techniques. I can listen to a sermon on the radio. I can pray for my friends. I haven't done that for a long time.

STEP 6: What am I feeling now? Slowly I feel peace, tranquility, calm, and trust in God coursing through my heart and body.

In each example, I've asked six questions in two groups of three. The first three—about facts, thoughts, and feelings—help us identify our thoughts and recognize how they affect our emotions and behavior. The second three—also about facts, thoughts, and feelings—help us challenge our thoughts, change them, and so change our feelings and actions. That's fairly easy to remember, isn't it? In summary:

- How did I get into this mood? Facts, thoughts, and feelings.
- How do I get out of this mood? Facts, thoughts, and feelings.

PSALM EXAMPLE

This is not some psychotherapy mumbo jumbo. This is actually the way the Bible trains us to think ourselves out of bad moods and painful feelings. Consider, for example, Asaph's experience in Psalm 77.

STEP 1: What are the facts? Asaph's life situation is not defined in detail in Psalm 77. Asaph calls it "the day of my trouble" (v. 2), a deliberately general description that fits many life situations.

STEP 2: What does he think about these facts? When he considers the troubles in his life, Asaph concludes that God has rejected him, doesn't love him, has broken His promises, and has even changed in His character (vv. 7–9). As a result, he thinks that the past was great (v. 5), but the future is bleak and gloomy (v. 7).

STEP 3: What is he feeling? He is inconsolably distressed by his trouble (v. 2) and overwhelmingly perplexed when he even thinks of God (v. 3). He feels abandoned by God and pessimistic about enjoying God's love and favor again (vv. 7–9).

13

Step 4: Can he change the facts? There's no evidence that
Asaph could change the facts or that his situation changed.

Step 5: Can he change his thoughts about the facts? At the
end of verse 9, he pauses, and he takes time to be quiet,
to still his soul and calm down. When he does that, new
thoughts begin to form, transforming his perspective and
outlook.

In verses 10–12, he deliberately forces his mind to think new
thoughts, to explore new areas for meditation. He says, "I'm not
going to think like this anymore. I'm going to change my thinking
habits and patterns." He firmly resolves:

I will remember the years of the right hand of the Most High.
I will remember the works of the Lord.
Surely I will remember Your wonders of old.
I will also meditate on all Your work,
And [I will] talk of Your deeds. (vv. 10–12)

Notice that he refocuses his thinking upon God's powerful acts
of providence through the centuries (vv. 13–20). Specifically, he
notes how God sometimes leads His people through deep waters
(v. 19) and sometimes through the wilderness (v. 20), but ultimately
He leads them to the promised land (v. 20). For the believer, this
is not just about thinking better; it's also about believing better. It
involves thought patterns in the head, but it also involves faith patterns in the heart.

Step 6: What is he feeling now? Judging by Asaph's words
in verses 13–20, there's a very different tone in his voice.
He no longer questions God's existence, character, and
providence but praises Him:

Who is so great a God as our God?
You are the God who does wonders;
You have declared Your strength among the peoples.
You have with Your arm redeemed Your people. (vv. 13–15)

Instead of doubt, there is confidence; instead of pessimism, there is optimism; instead of vulnerability, there is security; instead of distress, there is comfort.

Asaph's facts have not changed, but his feelings have because, with the help of God's Word and works, he has changed his thoughts about the facts. We can see similar patterns of spiritual and emotional therapy in Psalms 42 and 43; Job 19; and Habakkuk 3.

The key is to identify which specific thoughts drive particular emotions. If I think about loss, I'll be sad. If I think about sin, I'll feel guilty. If I think I'm too thin or too fat, I'll feel embarrassed. But if I think about God's gifts, I'll be thankful; if I think about God's beauty, I'll be inspired; if I think about God's sovereignty, I'll feel peaceful.

BIBLICAL ABCDE

Although most probably aren't aware of it and very few would admit to it, psychologists copy this biblical therapy while giving it a different name: the ABCDE method. Here's how positive psychologist Jessica Colman explained it in *Optimal Functioning*:

> Contrary to common perception, the events in an individual's life do not cause his or her feelings and behavioral reactions. A person's thoughts and beliefs about life events drive his or her feelings and behaviors. The first step in becoming resilient begins with self-awareness. Individuals are instructed to

become aware of their mental interpretations of negative events, or their "inner monologue" when things go wrong or they experience negative emotions. Once they are aware of the thoughts that cause their emotions and reactions, they can take measures to cultivate thoughts that lead to healthy outcomes.[8]

Sounds familiar, doesn't it? Let's see if the ABCDE method parallels the biblical pattern:

A = Adversity: The problem or pain in your life (the objective who, what, when, and where of the issue).
B = Beliefs: Negative thoughts about this problem or pain.
C = Consequences: The feelings and behavior that result from B.
D = Disputation and distraction: Challenging thoughts or beliefs that harm us with other explanations for the problem.[9]

Colman continued, "When a person is experiencing destructive or pessimistic thoughts, the first option they have is to distract themselves and attempt to place their thoughts and attention on more productive things. The second option is to dispute the negative thoughts, which is more effective because it makes the thoughts less likely to occur in the future."[10] You dispute a thought by imagining someone has said it to you and then, like an attorney, gathering as much evidence as you can to argue against it, in order to provide an alternative explanation to the one that is pulling you down.

E = Energization: If the disputation process is successful, people generally feel less pessimistic and more energized.[11]

Again, psychologists discover what God and His people already knew thousands of years ago!

Why not go back over the faulty thinking patterns we identified earlier in this chapter (generalizing, perfecting, and so on) and apply Psalm 77 therapy or the ABCDE technique to change these thoughts and consequently your faith and feelings for the better?

Also, going forward, cultivate sensitivity to these damaging thought habits returning and dragging you down. Develop an ability to challenge and change your thoughts, beliefs, and emotions by using these steps. As you do, remember the following four fundamental principles.

FOUR FUNDAMENTALS

Prioritize the Facts

When a detective comes across a murder scene, the wailing family members may be screaming out the name of the person they think did the terrible deed, but the wise detective will not be swayed by the hysteria. He'll encourage the understandably emotional family to leave the scene of the crime. He'll put the alleged perpetrator's name at the back of his mind while he begins to methodically gather as much hard data and evidence as he can.

Similarly, we must dial down our feelings in order to properly prioritize the facts in our minds. Once we've quieted our feelings, we can identify the objective facts.

Gather the Facts

A skilled detective carefully gathers all the relevant data and catalogs and organizes it. He wants to be sure of accuracy and comprehensiveness.

Similarly, when I counsel people who are depressed, I certainly ask how they are *feeling* and express sympathy for their emotional suffering, but most of all I want to gather facts, detailed and comprehensive information about their lives.

Usually when we do that together, we discover that at least part of the problem is that the depressed people are telling themselves a lie, a half-truth, or only half the truth. It's usually not deliberately deceitful. Some people can be so fixated on something that they blow it out of all proportion, or else they unintentionally exaggerate and distort reality.

Interpret the Facts

Once a detective has gathered all his evidence and witness statements, he begins to interpret the facts, to create a narrative as to how each piece fits the story. Two detectives may look at exactly the same evidence and come up with different stories due to interpreting the facts differently.

The same thing can happen in our everyday lives. For example, two women lose their jobs. One thinks that it's a disaster and that she'll never work again in that industry. The other regards it as an opportunity to learn new skills and maybe start her own business. Each has looked at the same evidence and come up with different reactions because each has interpreted the facts differently; each has told herself a different story.

The same contrasting emotions result from contrasting views of God. Under the headline, "Belief in Angry God Associated with Poor Mental Health,"[12] Ross Pomeroy explained how the way a believer conceives of God affects his or her mental health. Researchers at Marymount Manhattan College "found that belief in a punitive God was significantly associated with an increase in social anxiety, paranoia, obsession, and compulsion. Conversely, belief in a benevolent God was associated with reductions in those four symptoms. Belief in an indifferent God was not linked to any symptoms." The report concluded: "We propose that belief in a benevolent God inhibits threat assessments about the dangerousness of the world, thereby decreasing psychiatric symptoms" whereas "belief in a punitive God . . . facilitates threat assessments that the world is dangerous and even that God poses a threat of harm, thereby increasing psychiatric symptomology."[13]

Do you see how facts, faith, and feelings are so intertwined?

Use the Facts

After a detective has put together a crime narrative, he begins intensive questioning of witnesses and suspects. He takes the evidence and uses it to challenge and test people's stories until they break or give in.

That's what we must do as well when we get into negative and false thinking patterns. We need to deliberately and systematically organize the evidence to challenge our thoughts and feelings until they break and give in under the weight of the evidence.

Shawn Achor, Harvard professor and author of *The Happiness Advantage*, said in a recent TED talk that most assume that "our external world is predictive of our happiness levels, when in reality, if I know everything about your external world, I can only predict 10 percent of your long-term happiness. Ninety percent of your long-term happiness is predicted not by your external world, but the way your brain processes the world."[14]

Isn't This Just Positive Thinking?

Although this biblical strategy for changing our thoughts and feelings should result in more positive thoughts and feelings, this is not the same as what is known as "the power of positive thinking" as popularized through Norman Vincent Peale's best-selling book of the same name. Although Peale's book has some biblical verses sprinkled throughout, and although it has helped many people for a time, much of what he taught people had no basis or grounding in truth, especially in biblical truth, resulting in a lack of long-term results.

For example, he recounted how salespeople who started repeating, "I can do all things through Christ who strengthens me," increased their sales dramatically. What was not clear, however, was whether many of these people had any sense of who Christ was or did, which is really the key point in that verse.

Knowing who Christ is, what He did on the cross, and what He still does for us to this day strengthens the believer for every task. For Peale's salespeople, the verse became more like a mantra, a self-assuring, almost self-hypnotizing sense that a higher power was on their side. Their sales might have increased just as much if they had repeated, "I can do all things through the flying pink elephant who strengthens me," as long as they believed there was a flying pink elephant that was powerful and on their side.

Winning Gold and Losing God

British triple jumper, Olympic gold medal winner, and world record holder Jonathan Edwards professed to be a Christian throughout his athletic career and publicly credited all his success to God. "I can do all things through Christ who strengthens me" was often on his lips in pre- and post-competition interviews. Christians throughout the United Kingdom rejoiced to hear him testify to the power of Christ in his life.

But when he retired from competition in 2003, his faith began to collapse. By 2007, he had renounced Christianity and embraced agnosticism, seemingly without regret. The *Times* announced his apostasy with the headline: "'I've Never Been Happier,' Says the Man Who Won Gold but Lost God."[15]

Sports Psychology

In an interview posted on the Richard Dawkins Foundation website, Edwards admitted that the biblical verses he used to quote when competing were really just sports psychology dressed in religious clothes, confidence-boosting measures to give him a sense of higher purpose and divine assistance. He said, "I was always dismissive of sports psychology when I was competing, but I now realise that my belief in God was sports psychology in all but name. . . . Believing in something beyond the self can have a hugely beneficial psychological impact, even if the belief is fallacious."[16]

It was certainly positive thinking, but it was detached from the truth and had no basis in reality. Such positive thinking, as popularized by Peale and as practiced by Jonathan Edwards, ignores reality, makes up its own reality, or even denies it.

The kind of thinking I'm advocating is not so much positive thinking but *realistic* thinking, thinking that faces the facts (even the most unpleasant and unwanted facts), deals with the facts, uses the facts, and reframes the facts to move thoughts and feelings into a more appropriate perspective, resulting in a more positive mood. It's all about reasoning and persuading on the basis of evidence and truth. And its foundation is not faith in self, but faith in God.

Although faith in God is mentioned frequently in Peale's writings, what's most prominent is faith in yourself, as evidenced by the book's opening words:

BELIEVE IN YOURSELF! Have faith in your abilities! Without a humble but reasonable confidence in your own powers you cannot be successful or happy. But with sound self-confidence you can succeed. A sense of inferiority and inadequacy interferes with the attainment of your hopes, but self-confidence leads to self-realization and successful achievement. Because of the importance of this mental attitude, this book will help you believe in yourself and release your inner powers.[17]

Given that lack of self-confidence is one of the great problems besetting people today, it's not surprising that Peale began his book this way. In a survey of six hundred psychology students, 75 percent of them said the lack of confidence was their most difficult personal problem.[18] Peale was greatly mistaken, however, in seeing the cure as greater self-confidence and releasing "your inner powers." The right answer is greater God-confidence, releasing divine power into our lives. Not "believe in yourself" but "believe in God." That's what this book is all about. And it begins with Psalm 77 therapy, the mental and spiritual exercise of challenging and changing our thoughts and feelings with the help of the Holy Spirit.

Moral Obligation

Like physical exercise, this kind of mental and spiritual exercise is not optional but mandatory if we want to be emotionally healthy and glorify God. Many of us who wouldn't dream of viewing God's *Word* in a false or distorted way, think nothing of viewing God's *world* in a false or distorted way. As we view ourselves, our situations, and our relationships with others, we tend to dwell on and magnify the negatives and exclude the positives. This distorted view of reality inevitably depresses our moods. As Christians who love truth, we are obliged to challenge all falsehood and distortions of reality, especially when we find them in ourselves.

The only way to do this is to practice. Although we disagree as to methodology, I agree with Peale that "in attaining emotional control the daily practice of healing techniques is of first importance. Emotional control cannot be gained in any magical or easy way. You cannot develop it by merely reading a book, although that is often helpful. The only sure method is by working at it regularly, persistently, scientifically, and by developing creative faith."[19]

Psalm 77 provides the biblical structure and the pattern for that daily practice. Now let's take that into our daily lives by examining how to fill our minds with good news rather than bad news.

Chapter Two

HAPPY MEDIA

GOOD NEWS > BAD NEWS = POSITIVE+

SCIENTISTS ESTIMATE THAT FOR every hundred pieces of information that enter our brains, ninety-nine end up in the spam folder.[1] Noticing only one thing out of every hundred is a good thing. As many suffering autistic people will tell you, if you don't have a good mental spam filter, you can be overwhelmed with useless and harmful data.[2]

The problem is, many of us have spam filters that are fantastic at letting in only the negative things and filtering out the positive. That's partly because our educational, political, and business culture rewards negativity experts, those who can pick out a single negative in a sea of positives.

We ask our children, "What's wrong with this picture?" We set class assignments: "Critique this passage" or "Find the flaws in this article." We mark mistakes with red ink but don't waste blue ink on the correct answers. We scan our gardens for weeds. We admire debaters and politicians who can poke holes in their opponents' arguments. We promote lawyers who can detect a loophole from a hundred miles away. We love journalistic exposés. We are drawn to watchblogs and discernment ministries. We honor theologians who can destroy a heretic with one devastating put-down.

All this programs our personal spam filters to scan for negatives, problems, difficulties, lies, evil, and so on. With such a grim input of one-sided data, is it any wonder that we experience so much stress, demotivation, and relational breakdown?

Harvard psychology professor and best-selling author of *The Happiness Advantage*, Shawn Achor, saw this problem vividly when the global tax-accounting firm KPMG commissioned him to help its tax auditors and managers become happier. How had these successful professionals become so miserable? They spent their days looking for mistakes and errors, and that "talent" spilled over into every other part of their lives, including their closest relationships.[3]

We don't need to be accountants to have such spam filters! But the good news is that we can retrain our brains and renew our minds. Or to put it another way, we can reprogram our spam filters. We can educate ourselves to Scan for Positive and Affirming Messages, especially in our media choices.

In an age of multiplying and diversifying media sources, we don't need to accept being force-fed the junk food of what is evil, ugly, and distressing. Instead we can, and should, feed our minds a media diet that is biased toward what is good and beautiful. As the apostle Paul put it: "Brethren, whatever things are true, whatever things are noble, whatever things are just, whatever things are pure, whatever things are lovely, whatever things are of good report, if there is any virtue and if there is anything praiseworthy—meditate on these things."[4]

In this "epistle of joy," Paul was not arguing for unrealistic isolation from the bad news that inevitably fills a fallen world. No, this is not a warrant for monasteries and convents; but it is a warrant, and even a demand, that we choose *a deliberate imbalance* in favor of what is inspirational and wholesome instead of the mainstream media's imbalance on the side of what is dispiriting and gross.

GARBAGE IN, GARBAGE OUT

Such a media diet will change the way we think and the way we feel, speak, and act. That's hardly surprising. Just as the quality of the food we put in our mouths affects our thinking, feeling, and doing, so the kinds of words, sounds, and images we put in our ears and eyes will have the same effect. Garbage in, garbage out, as they say. Or as John Milton wrote in *Paradise Lost*, "The mind is its own place, and in itself / Can make a heav'n of hell, a hell of heav'n."[5]

Like many of us, the Philippian believers were habitual worriers,[6] their minds always racing from one unresolved anxiety to the next. But Paul holds out the prospect of an unimaginable and unsurpassable divine peace to garrison our hearts and minds, a peace that patrols the entrances to our emotions and thoughts. And the way to enjoy that peace patrol is to change our brain diet, what our minds feed upon.[7]

In other words, if we let what is false, offensive, dishonest, filthy, ugly, and loathsome into our minds, we might as well sign up for a course on how to be hyperanxious. These interlopers drive peace from the castle, lower the drawbridge, and invite the armies of worry and instability into the mental citadel.

GOOD IN, GOOD OUT

On the other hand, if we starve ourselves of mental junk and replace it with what is true, admirable, right, pure, beautiful, and attractive, peace will stand as a sentinel all around our feelings and thoughts, creating an impregnable fortress of calm and tranquility. The "peace of God" and the "God of peace will be with you."[8]

But this takes huge mental effort. "Meditate on these things," commanded Paul. That's not some kind of laid-back, freewheeling, blue-sky thinking. It means, concentrate and focus on these sub-jects; form rigorous thinking habits along these lines.

Lord Palmerstone, a nineteenth-century British politician, rec-ognized the incredible power of thoughts when he said, "Opinions are stronger than armies. Opinions, if they are founded in truth and justice, will, in the end, prevail against the bayonets of infantry, against the fire of artillery."[9]

How then can we marshal our thoughts into a powerful peace-making and peacekeeping force? Paul listed six areas of a healthy thought life that cover many subjects. Let's look at them in turn, especially as they apply to our media diet and then as applied to our ministry diet. And remember, we are consumers and creators in these areas. We are not only receivers of media and ministry; we are also transmitters. With the advent of the digital revolution, we're all now part of the media and ministry. We are influenced, and we are influencers. Multiple responsibilities!

MEDIA DIET

The sad news is that bad news sells better than good news, and sin sells better than purity. "If it bleeds, it leads" is the mantra of so much of our media. In *Upside: Surprising Good News about the State of Our World*, Dr. Bradley Wright explains how journal-ists are incentivized to tell us about the worst events and trends in the world because that's what attracts most ears and eyes. We want to know about all the dangers out there so that we can take evasive action.[10]

Wright proceeds to highlight how this also motivates the media to find bad news even in the good news: "If life expectancy decreases, people are dying younger. If it increases, it strains the social security system. . . . An unpreventable disease harms people;

a preventable disease means disparities in access to medical treatment. . . . High birthrates cause overcrowding; low birthrates cause school closings and lowered future tax revenues."[11]

Many activist and advocacy groups have a vested interest in selecting and emphasizing the negative. If the world is not getting worse, who's going to volunteer or donate to make it better?

In Philippians 4:8, the apostle Paul helps us swim against this powerful tide by teaching us six strokes. Unless we learn them and use them, we will be easily swept away by the currents of negativity into the whirlpools of fear, anxiety, hate, and depression.

True, Not False: "Whatever Things Are True"

Avoid listening to lies, misrepresentation, imbalance, and distortion, on both the left and the right of the political spectrum. Beware of journalists and broadcasters who spend most of their time exposing the lies of "the other team." An overemphasis on falsehood breeds only destructive cynicism, suspicion, mistrust, and hostility.

Gather facts rather than opinions, and use the facts to influence your outlook and mood. For example, think about some of these positives:

- Middle-class Americans live better than 99.4 percent of everyone who has ever lived.
- Americans are healthier and living longer.
- Literacy rates, family income, air and water quality are all up.
- Crime, the cost of living, and deforestation are all down.[12]

But what about the rest of the world? It's a basket case, isn't it? Not at all. The 2007 United Nation's Human Development Index found that 109 of 115 countries had improved in life expectancy, income, and education since 1990.[13]

Doesn't sound like yesterday's headlines, does it? It's not easy, but let's make a greater effort to seek out the most truthful, balanced, and fair reporting. Let's feast on truth wherever it appears and whoever is speaking it. And on a social level, let's surround ourselves with truth tellers rather than muck spreaders.

Noble, Not Base: "Whatever Things Are Noble"

The media tends to publicize the vile and sordid side of life. Reporters and resources are focused on the cesspools of our society. Instead of reporting and publicizing functioning families and thriving schools, they tend to use their pages and pixels to spotlight failure, brokenness, and disaster.

Check last year's *New York Times* bestsellers list. Some of the most popular books were childhood memoirs that describe the most horrific abuse and cruelty. *Fifty Shades of Grey*, which celebrates sadistic sex, occupied the bestsellers list for months and months, drawing massive media attention and debasing old and young minds alike.

"Don't do this to yourself!" appealed Paul. Trash the tawdry, and nourish the noble in your life. Seek out and consume books, magazines, websites, TV programs, movies, and art that elevate the heroic, that inspire awe, and that generate worship.

In *Positivity*, Barbara Fredrickson presents a palette of positivity, the feelings that paint the most vibrant and radiant lives. They include love, joy, gratitude, serenity, interest, hope, amusement, inspiration, and awe. Imagine the beautifying influence upon us and our world if we and our media painted with these rich colors.[14]

Right, Not Wrong: "Whatever Things Are Just"

When Paul said we should think about what is "just," he meant what conforms to God's law. Does that sound like most sitcoms, soap operas, and news features? Does the media celebrate right acts? Quite the reverse; the media focuses on sinful acts. People striving to live a righteous life do not make news headlines. If they are ever pictured in TV or on film, they are usually caricatured as out of touch, pitiable, contemptible, or irrelevant.

Paul urged us to seek out and celebrate right behavior, courageous actions, hardworking parents, loving fathers, devoted mothers, respectful children, happy families, gentle caregivers, honest employees, fair bosses, and so on.

This applies in business, too, and has a direct impact on productivity and profitability. A team of psychologists visited sixty companies and transcribed every word in their business meetings. They then analyzed each sentence for positive or negative words and worked out the ratio of positive to negative statements. Their conclusion? "There is a sharp dividing line. . . . Companies with better than a 3:1 ratio for positive to negative statements are flourishing. Below that ratio, companies are not doing well economically. . . . But don't go overboard with positivity. Life is a ship with sails and rudder. Above 13:1, without a negative rudder, the positive sails flap aimlessly, and you lose your credibility."[15]

The increasingly popular organizational change method of appreciative inquiry usually startles employees by asking first, "What's working well here? What's the best thing about this business?" With such a positive base, energy is then created to advance the changes that are required.

Purity, Not Filth: "Whatever Things Are Pure"

Most of us have a negativity bias, a tendency to think on bad or sad experiences, producing anxiety, anger, and other unpleasant feelings. This is true even when we have plenty of good and happy experiences to think about.

Dr. Rick Hanson, neuropsychologist and author of the book *Hardwiring Happiness: The New Brain Science of Contentment*,

Calm, and Confidence, said, "Our brains are naturally wired to focus on the negative, which can make us feel stressed and unhappy even though there are a lot of positive things in our lives."[16] His solution is not to avoid thinking about negative experiences but to train our brains to love lingering on positive experiences. As "neurons that fire together wire together," he said we can grow a more positive mind-set by taking extra time to think on the positives and letting them really sink in.

Even Christians find it hard to escape the tendency to turn from the light and to be attracted to the darkness. It's partly because there is often more darkness around than light. That simply demands even greater effort to think and talk about faithful marriages, godly young people, generous philanthropists, and honest politicians.

Beautiful, Not Ugly: "Whatever Things Are Lovely"

"Whatever things are lovely" is literally whatever moves us toward love. It's pointing us toward what is attractive and winsome, words and actions that compel admiration and affection. Perhaps the best modern word would be *beautiful*, hardly a word that comes to mind when we surf the Internet, is it?

In a day when many of us live among steel and concrete boxes of varying sizes and shapes, it's often very difficult to locate beauty in our immediate surroundings. At best our eyes feast on the mundane and the monotonous, at worst on decay and brokenness. Our noses are blocked with dust and grime, our ears are assailed with traffic and jackhammers, and our taste buds are dulled with mass-produced junk food.

We need to get out of the city, see the stunning mountains, savor the fragrance of the forest, taste fresh and healthy produce, and listen to the exquisite bird songs. And if that's too difficult, then get a BBC documentary like *Planet Earth* or *Deep Sea*. Travel our beautiful world, and plunge into our magnificent oceans from the comfort of your favorite armchair. Find ways to increase your intake of beauty through your various senses.

In the film *Celebrate What's Right with the World*, photographer Dewitt Jones explains the positive ethic of *National Geographic* and shows how his photos are continually trying to answer the questions What's right here? and What can I celebrate? By God's common grace, another unwitting promoter of Philippians 4:8.

Praise, Not Complaint: "Whatever Things Are of Good Report"

We're going to explore this further in a later chapter, but basically Paul was saying, "Focus on what is constructive rather than destructive." Feast on whatever makes people exclaim, "Well done!" rather than what makes them say, "That's terrible."

As you drive with your family, do you suggest topics that will show people in a good light or a bad light? Do you tell stories that will make your hearers praise God and others or those that will make people doubt God and condemn others? Do you shield your children from the destructively critical spirit of talk radio and substitute it with stimulating and inspiring conversation? Do you thank God for the national reduction in crime, the worldwide rise in literacy, and so on?

There is much good in everyday life that should be acknowledged and appreciated, regardless of whether it is done by a Christian. Whether it's a good product, a helpful service, a wise insight, or a superb article, praise and celebrate it. Don't look for what you can critique; look for what you can admire and invite others to enjoy it with you. As an experiment, why not try to go twenty-four hours without speaking negatively about anything or anyone? Instead, fill these hours with hopeful and optimistic words. To do this every day would be imbalanced and unrealistic, but to do it for a few days might help to right your listing ship and set it on a more balanced course.

As Paul put it in his summary of these six criteria: "If there is any virtue and if there is anything praiseworthy—meditate on these things" (v. 8). Norman Vincent Peale stated this negatively, but on this point he and Paul agreed:

> People manufacture their own unhappiness, . . . let us proceed to the formula for putting an end to this misery-producing process. Suffice it to say that we manufacture our unhappiness by thinking unhappy thoughts, by the attitudes which we habitually take, such as the negative feeling that everything is going to turn out badly, or that other people are getting what they do not deserve and we are failing to get what we do deserve. Our unhappiness is further distilled by saturating the consciousness with feelings of resentment, ill will, and hate. The unhappiness-producing process always makes important use of the ingredients of fear and worry. . . . We merely want to make the point at the present time and stress it forcefully that a very large proportion of the unhappiness of the average individual is self-manufactured.[17]

When Gretchen Rubin surveyed the results of her year-long happiness project, she was surprised to find that her biggest happiness boosts had not come so much from the good things she added to her life but from eliminating her bad thoughts and feelings.[18]

Time to Avert Our Gaze

I am writing this seven days after another school massacre in America, and the news is still dominated by the horrific event. If this horror had happened a hundred years ago, most of us would probably still not have heard of it. A limited narrative of facts would eventually have trickled across the country and maybe even reached a few other parts of the world. Perhaps there might have been a brief paragraph in the *London Times* and a few other significant international newspapers.

What a difference a hundred years make. Within seconds we know not only what happened in general but also all the horrific specifics. Within minutes we have eyewitness accounts. Within hours we have photos and video. By the end of the day we have hundreds, maybe thousands, of reporters swarming over the town. Press conferences are carried live; interviews with bereaved families and spared families fill the nonstop news cycle; the perpetrator's evil mind and twisted past are dredged; amateur psychologists opine on the ravings and rantings of evil. Old and new media are drowning us in a deluge of frightful information and fearful images.

After a day or so of this, I decided to pull the plug and avert my gaze.

It is neither necessary nor wise for most of us to know all this horrifying information. What good purpose does it serve to hear or read exactly how the murderer went about his vile business, what was heard or seen in the classrooms and offices, how victims tried to defend themselves and others, and more? It is deeply damaging to our short- and long-term mental, emotional, and spiritual health to expose ourselves to such bloodcurdling details.

I am not saying that we should know nothing about what happened or that we shouldn't sympathize deeply with the families and the community. I am saying that in such scenarios most of us need to know just enough to pray intelligently for the needs of the survivors, their families, and the community. But most of us get to know way, way more than that, darkening our waking hours and disturbing our sleeping hours. I don't think most of us realize the deep and damaging trauma we are inflicting upon ourselves.

Even secular sources are recognizing the harmful effects of

most news media. In "News Is Bad for You—and Giving It Up Will Make You Happier" the *Guardian*'s Rolf Dobelli argues that news "leads to fear and aggression, and hinders your creativity and ability to think deeply." He says it misleads, is toxic to your body, increases cognitive errors, inhibits thinking, wastes time, makes you passive, and kills creativity.[19]

Some Christians might need to know more of the detail about major disasters and tragedies, especially those whom God has especially called to interpret and explain these monstrous actions to the public and the church. But most of us don't need to glue ourselves to the TV and to Internet news. Instead, we should actively shield our families and ourselves from much of it.

"But won't that mean ignoring problems in the real world?" Quite the reverse, said Shawn Achor, "Psychologists have found that people who watch less TV are actually more accurate judges of life's risks and rewards than those who subject themselves to the tales of crime, tragedy, and death that appear night after night on the ten o'clock news. That's because these people are less likely to see sensationalized or one-sided sources of information, and thus see reality more clearly."[20]

I've gotten to the point where I read only a couple of headlines and perhaps the first paragraph of most reports about mass killings, tsunamis, terrorism, and other catastrophic events. I operate on a "need to know" basis, and I don't need to know everything. To me, that's putting Philippians 4:8 into practice.

And practice it we must. This was not just a theory for Paul; he could appeal to the people's memory of him: "The things which you learned and received and heard and saw in me, these do, and the God of peace will be with you."[21] He said, if you think like I think and do what I do, you will replace fear, anxiety, depression, and worry with divine peace.

MINISTRY DIET

But it's not just the diet that the world feeds us that we have to be concerned about; we need to guard our spiritual stomachs as well. These six criteria must also be applied to the ministry we sit under and the spiritual resources we read, listen to, and watch.

If we are in any ministry role—preachers, teachers, Sunday school leaders, or even parents—we must also ask if the diet we are feeding Christ's sheep meets Paul's checklist. What should we be feeding on or feeding to others? Using Paul's criteria, I suggest rebalancing along the following lines:

More Salvation than Sin

The gospel makes no sense and has no power for people who are not taught the doctrine of sin and experience conviction of sin. Although too many want to downplay sin, minimize God's law, and soften God's anger, the gospel message must begin with "all have sinned and fall short of the glory of God."[22]

But we don't want to linger there any longer than we have to. Some preachers, teachers, and parents love to dwell in the smoke and fire of Mount Sinai more than the love and grace of Mount Calvary. They want us not only to see and smell the prodigal's pigsty but also to wallow in its gruesome details. Sin is bad enough without sensationalistic overconcentration on some of the most evil atrocities.

Without losing the essential backdrop of our desperate human need, let's keep the spotlight on the multidimensional salvation that Christ has purchased. There are so many wonderful ways to describe it, picture it, and experience it. "God did not send His Son into the world to condemn the world, but that the world through Him might be saved."[23]

More Truth than Falsehood

Just as banks train tellers to spot counterfeit money by over-exposing them to real money, and doctors are trained to detect heart and lung disease by listening to thousands of healthy chests, so Christians would be more edified and better prepared to spot falsehood by focusing the majority of their reading and teaching on *the truth* rather than trying to know and counteract the innumerable errors, heresies, false religions, and cults that fill our world.

Yes, we need to know what's wrong about other people's worldviews and theologies, but we need far more to know what's right in our own. Let's fill our minds with biblical truth, with the doctrines of grace, with scriptural verses. Let's give more time to communicating the truth than to exposing error. Let's set forth the beautiful ethical directions of God's moral law, much more than condemning infractions of it. Let's exalt biblical marriage far more than highlighting the latest perversion of it.

More Wooing than Warning

Although every preacher must both woo and warn, the most regular note should be of wooing more than warning, more of the carrot than the stick, more of the beauty of holiness than the ugliness of sin, more of drawing Christ than highlighting the danger of the Devil, more of the attraction of heaven than the fear of hell.

Let's present Christ to our congregations or to our children and colleagues in all His glory. Let's show them how much Jesus is willing and able to save and how much He desires and delights to save. He does not save because He has to but because He wants to and enjoys to.

It's often said that Jesus preached on hell more than *anyone* else. That's true. But He did not preach on hell more than *anything* else. Yes, He warned a lot, but He wooed and won even more.

More Victory than Struggle

Trial, suffering, backsliding, defeat, and *temptation* are biblical words, but so are *victory, growth, maturity, progress, usefulness, fruit, service, opportunity, advance,* and *encouragement.* Paul wanted to know "the fellowship of [Christ's] sufferings," but he also wanted to know "the power of His resurrection."[24] He knew the continuing power of indwelling sin,[25] but he also knew the breaking of sin's dominion and the power of life in the Spirit.[26] Do our sermons, blog posts, prayers, and songs reflect this biblical emphasis?

Yes, we want to gently sympathize with strugglers, with the discouraged, with the defeated. But we don't want to make a virtue of these experiences, as if they are preferable to growth, assurance, joy, and other positives. We don't want to break the bruised reed or quench the smoking flax, but we don't want people to remain bruised and smoking either. We want to come alongside, splint their brokenness, fan their embers, and encourage them upward and forward.

Yes, we want to identify with and sympathize with persecuted Christians suffering in horrendous conditions around the world, but we must also inform ourselves and others of the number of people coming to faith in different countries and the wonderful impact of the gospel around the world.

More Celebration than Lamentation

It's easy for Christians to be sucked down into the vortex of moaning and groaning about the direction of our culture and society. I've been to prayer meetings that are just a litany of complaints about various government policies. Yes, there is "a time to mourn," but there is also "a time to laugh."[27] When we consider how many blessings we have compared to so many, we must sometimes sound like spoiled children, whining, whining, and whining for more.

The science writer Matt Ridley described being in an airport

39

bookshop current affairs section: "All [the books] argued to a greater or lesser extent that a) the world is a terrible place and b) it's getting worse. . . . I didn't see a single optimistic book."[28] Surely Christians can offer a compelling contrast to this worldly pessimism. As Pastor John Ortberg put it: "Two thousand years ago, a book whose core was *euaggelion*—good news—began to be widely read. We of all people should be able to recognize and celebrate and express gratitude wherever we find it. For all good news is God's good news, and to ignore it, hide it, minimize it, or distort it is neither mentally healthy nor spiritually sound."[29]

Of course, there is much to lament, but as Christians, we should usually hear the note of celebration above the note of lamentation. We have so much to be thankful for in the present and even more in the future. Remember the apostles even managed to celebrate that they were counted "worthy" to suffer persecution for Christ's sake![30] They took literally the Lord's command to "rejoice and be exceedingly glad"[31] even in the midst of great suffering.

More Life than Death

Why do most Christian books for children and young people major on the sacrifice and suffering of the missionaries and the martyrs, with few telling the fantastically inspiring stories of many ordinary Christians' lives?

Just as an undue focus on martyrdoms tends to deter unbelievers and terrify Christians, or at least make them feel as if nothing short of Christian martyrdom is worth noticing, we must add at least an equal proportion of positive portrayals of the Christian life, with examples of ordinary Christians doing great things in their everyday lives. Let's have more life narratives than death narratives.

Barbara Fredrickson found that people's positive to negative ratios are subject to a tipping point, and that's usually about the 3:1 mark. Notice that it's not 3:0. Negatives are an inevitable part of human life and even of human flourishing. Let's not deny reality and try to live in Fantasyland. Fredrickson's research, however, revealed that "for every heart-wrenching negative emotional experience," you should try to "experience at least three heartfelt positive emotional experiences that uplift you. This is the ratio that I've found to be the tipping point, predicting whether people languish or flourish."[32]

More Strengths than Weaknesses

The vast majority of Christian preaching and discipleship is taken up with highlighting weaknesses and trying to fix them: You're not giving enough. You're not witnessing enough. You're not praying enough. You're not visiting the sick enough. There's definitely a place for that. We need to be humbled and brought to confession.

But how about a much greater emphasis on Christian strengths and skills? How about cultivating and developing what's working well? One study of strengths-based education found that concentrating on improving one's strengths produces much greater success than working on improving one's weaknesses.[33]

Christians would differ in some ways from psychologists in what constitutes a strength or weakness. For example, Christians would view meekness and humility as virtues, whereas psychologists would tend to encourage self-confidence and self-assertiveness. Also, as God calls us to complete transformation, we don't want to say, "Ignore your weaknesses; just develop your strengths."

Having said all that, as Jesus' parable of the talents suggests, God gives particular people particular gifts and opportunities that we should especially focus on developing and strengthening.[34] And let's help others do this, too, by helping them identify and exercise their special gifts and strengths and by praising their growth and usefulness.

ACTION ITEMS

No one is going to change media and ministry diets and habits overnight, but let me suggest two warm-up exercises to get you started.

Three Blessings

Ask everyone at the family dinner table (or business conference table or elders' table) to list three good things that happened that day. The biblical basis for doing this should be obvious by now, but scientists have also found that spending even just five minutes a day at this trains the brain to develop the habit of scanning for and locating good things to think about. And since we can think on only one thing at a time, that also squeezes out mood depressors.

Our family now looks forward to doing this quite regularly. As we savor the food and God's goodness in our daily lives, it's certainly elevating our overall moods, even of our teenagers! Those eating alone can accomplish the same effect by writing down the positive events in a journal.

In a study of more than five hundred participants, those who worked on their strengths and completed the Three Blessings exercise lowered depression and increased happiness three months and six months later.[35] If unbelievers can accomplish this, how much more should Christians who taste God's mercy and grace in every crumb and drop.

Meditation

One way to learn how to develop a Philippians 4:8 mind-set is to rediscover the ancient art of meditation. If you need encouragement, consider these facts:[36]

- Meditation increases mindfulness, a sense of purpose, creativity, immune function, love, joy, contentment, relational satisfaction, and the frequency of virtuous acts.
- Meditation decreases mortality, stress, pain intensity, inflammation, blood pressure, sense of loneliness, negative emotions, and the length and severity of colds.

Or try these biblical motivations for meditation:

- It stops sin and starts good.[37]
- It makes you ready to witness.[38]
- It revives spiritual life and increases communion with God.[39]
- It makes you happier.[40]

Now that I've motivated you, what about a method? Here are ten suggestions. As you read them, note a couple of important differences between Christian meditation and most other forms of meditation. Whereas secular approaches to meditation involve emptying the mind or focusing on self, Christian meditation involves filling the mind with biblical truth and focusing on God. Also, secular meditation usually insists on thinking only about the present moment, forbidding any remembering of the past or looking to the future. Christian meditation, on the other hand, delights in remembering God's great redemptive acts in the past and joyfully anticipates the heavenly future of believers in paradise.

With these distinctions in mind, here are tips to help you begin Christian meditation:

> LIMIT: Set apart just five to ten minutes to begin with, and start with one short verse of Scripture or even part of a verse.

VARY: Some days choose a theological verse, others a practical or devotional text. Or meditate on one of God's blessings in your life.

WRITE: Write the text on a small index card, and put it in a place you will come across regularly, such as your purse or shirt pocket.

MEMORIZE: Memorize the text in two- to three-word blocks, and set specific times in the day—such as your coffee break or mealtime—to recall the verse.

FOCUS: Pick out the key words and look them up in a dictionary. Substitute some words with parallel meanings or even opposite meanings. Finding similar words or contrasting words can often help us to understand the original words in the verse.

QUESTION: Interrogate the verse (who, what, where, when, why, how?).

EXPLAIN: How would you explain the verse to a child or someone with no Christian background?

PRAY: Use the verse in prayer, worship, confession, thanks, or petition.

REVIEW: File the cards and every Sunday read them and test your memory of them.

DO: Make it not just an intellectual exercise, but let it lead to practice, such as believing, repenting, hoping, or loving.

And here's one further spur of motivation from Professor Jonathan Haidt: "Suppose you read about a pill you could take once a day to reduce anxiety and increase your contentment. Would you take it? Suppose further that the pill had a great variety of side effects, all of them good: increased self-esteem, empathy, and trust; it even improves memory. Suppose, finally, that the pill is all-natural and costs nothing. Now would you take it? The pill exists. It is called meditation."[41]

And what to meditate upon? How about starting with the Gospel of Done!

Chapter Three

HAPPY SALVATION

DONE > DO = POSITIVE+

I'VE TRIED COUNTLESS KINDS of to-do lists. I've experimented with colorful cards, complicated mind maps, sophisticated software, and innumerable apps. And none of them ever gets me closer to "Done!" I keep hoping that somehow the right technique, the right method, or the right program will move my inbox to zero, my desk trays to empty, and my latest to-do list to all checked off.

All in vain. E-mails keep arriving, reports keep dropping, and things to do keep multiplying. An insatiable cacophony of "Do! Do! Do!" taunts me as I reluctantly come to the depressing conclusion that I will never be finished, that I'll never be done.

Then I turn to Christianity and, to my unutterable and indescribable delight, I encounter the rare and refreshing words: "It is finished!"[1] Are there any happier words in the universe?

It is done. All done. Nothing in my spiritual inbox. Nothing in my trays. No lists to tackle. It is finished!

Jesus lived the life I could not live and died the death I dare not die. He took my duties and performed them perfectly; He took my failures and paid the penalty. That's the foundation, the starting point, the beginning of all true Christianity. Done! Done! Done!

And yet it's so difficult to believe, isn't it? Can it really be totally finished? Nothing left to do? What a hugely positive and happy difference it would make to the whole of our lives if we could really, really believe that. How much steadier and richer our joy if we could put and keep our faith in "finished."

Why is it so difficult to believe the Gospel of Done? And what could help us believe it better? These are the two questions I want to address in this chapter, first by looking at the handicaps to believing it and then at the helps. We're going to build a deeper, wider, and longer foundation for lasting happiness.

HANDICAPS TO BELIEVING THE GOSPEL OF DONE

Some horse races are handicapped, meaning that some faster horses must carry extra lead weight in their saddles to slow them down and give the other horses an equal chance of winning. Some of us are carrying spiritual lead weights in our souls that handicap our faith, slow us down, and prevent us from enjoying the fullness of victory through Christ Jesus. Let's try to find some of these lead weights and throw them out of our saddles.

The Lead Weight of an Accusing Conscience

We all have an inner voice that says, at varying decibel levels: "Do! Do! Do!" We're born with a prodding, needling conscience—a gnawing, innate sense of God's demands upon us—and in our own way we try to meet these demands and quiet the inner prosecutor.

We do what we can, when we can, as we can, and hope we have enough in the can. And yet the can is still rattlingly empty, isn't it?

We hear, "Do!" We do. We hope to hear, "Done!" Instead, we hear, "Not done . . . do more." The relentless, merciless, grueling, harrowing voice of God's law burrows deep into our souls.

We yell, "Quiet!" "Give me peace!" "Go away!" "Will you never be satisfied?" But the dos keep coming, adding, multiplying, and expanding. Inveterate resolution-maker Samuel Johnson wrote in his daily journal: "I have now spent fifty-five years in resolving; having from the earliest time almost that I can remember, been forming schemes of a better life. I have done nothing; the need of doing therefore is pressing, since the time of doing is short. O God, grant me to resolve aright, and to keep my resolutions."[2]

Resolution. Guilt. Shame. Remorse. Frustration. Resolution. Guilt. On and on it goes.

Until we hear a startling cry that's echoed in millions of hearts through the centuries: "It is finished!" It's done, all done, with nothing left to do. Take Christ's conclusive cross-cry to your conscience and silence this depressing, demoralizing, and discouraging inner cacophony.

The Lead Weight of a Demanding Church

It's also difficult to believe "It is finished" because of the church.

Most sermons major on "Do this; do that. Don't do this; don't do that." And if "Duty, duty, duty" is the preacher's demanding message, "Disobedience, disobedience, disobedience" is the hearer's condemning conviction.

Check the most common preaching topics in most churches: Christian parenting, Christian giving, Christian marriage, Christian vocation, Christian citizenship, Christian communication, and so on. Do, do, do! Sermon upon sermon, each demanding more money, more time, more commitment, more zeal, and more doing. Do, do, do! Fail, fail, fail! Down, down, down we go.

Sure, we need to hear about our Christian duties, but not at the expense of Christ's Done, and only after His Done has performed its soothing work in our souls.

Christ's decisive cry of completion should be repeated enough to ensure that His Done is always heard above the preacher's do.

The Lead Weight of Our Work-for-Wages Culture

It's difficult to believe "It is finished" because it contradicts the most basic rule of life in this world: Work = Reward. From our earliest days to our latest days, this law governs everything.

Do = Dollars. You work; you get rewarded. You don't work; you don't get paid.

That societal norm can make it so difficult to believe the core idea at the heart of the gospel: Christ works, but I get the reward. I don't work, but I get paid! That turns our culture upside down, back to front, and inside out. It's hard to get our minds around it, and it's even harder to get it into our heads and hearts.

When faith is so handicapped by the logic and weight of our personal experience, we must pray that God will not only remove this weight but also increase the blessed pressure and presence of grace in our lives until Calvary's countercultural cry is convincing enough to break our culture's unbreakable rule.

The Lead Weight of Unbelief

What are the ten most disbelieved letters in the Bible?

You're thinking about something related to six-day creation, aren't you? Or a literal, historical Adam? Or something about the Trinity or the divinity of Christ? Or maybe the exclusivity of Christ as the only way to God?

But it's none of these things. It's ten letters found in Ephesians 2:9:

N . . . O . . . T . . . O . . . F . . . W . . . O . . . R . . . K . . . S

Always the hardest ten letters for unbelievers to believe. Often the hardest ten letters for believers to keep believing.

I've asked many seniors about their hope for heaven, and

despite listening to thousands of N . . . O . . . T . . . O . . . F . . . W . . .
O . . . R . . . K . . . S sermons their entire lives, many still answer,
"I've done my best. I've gone to church. I raised my children to go
to church. I pray and read my Bible, and so on." But I'm longing to
hear them say, "I'm done with my doing and working; I'm resting
on Christ's work and Christ's Done alone."

Ask your children, your regularly evangelized children, "What's
a Christian?" and you'll be stunned at how often they'll give child
versions of the seniors' answers.

And though most Christians will be able to give you the "salvation by grace apart from works" answer in a theology exam, their
personal daily spiritual experience too often defaults to various versions of "salvation by works."

It's as if W . . . O . . . R . . . K . . . S is tattooed on our hearts from
birth. Regular gospel preaching and believing are the only laser
that can remove this deadly tattoo. Or perhaps it would be better
to say that regular gospel preaching tattoos these five life-giving
letters N . . . O . . . T . . . O . . . F in front of the five killers: W . . .
O . . . R . . . K . . . S.

How our lives would be transformed if we could really believe
and keep believing these ten unbelievable letters!

The Lead Weight of Christian Failure

It is difficult to believe "It is finished" because we keep failing
even after believing it. I mean, God might let us into the Christian
faith through His divine Done, but we've got to stay in by our own
doing, don't we? It's only fair, isn't it?

If so, we're done in because our own doing is never going to do
enough, even after believing in Jesus. We get in by His Done. We
stay in by His Done. We finish by His Done. If not, we're done.

That's why we need to keep preaching, hearing, and believing
the gospel of grace. It empties our saddle the first time we believe,

but as we have a tendency to pick up these weights again, especially when we fail, we need to hear the saddle-lightening gospel of "It is finished" on every lap of the track.

Calvary's successful cry is required not only to get us into faith but also to keep us in faith, to keep us believing in Him rather than in ourselves and to keep us looking to His Done rather than to our doing.

HELPS TO BELIEVING THE GOSPEL OF DONE

Yes, there are numerous handicaps to our believing the Gospel of Done, handicaps that keep us in miserable fear and darkness and away from the joyful rest and victory of Christ's finished work. God has provided some helps, however, to get us to gospel peace and to keep us there.

Rebelieve the Gospel of Done

"It is finished!" is our only hope of real happiness. It is the nonnegotiable starting point for reducing negativity and building positively for the future. But it's also the place we must return to every day of our lives. We must believe the Gospel of Done again and again and again.

And therefore it must be preached again and again and again. Too often people assume, "Well, we/they all know that already." But do we? Does the world?

Why don't you take a survey of a sample of unbelievers and believers, and ask them: "What is a Christian? What is the Christian faith? How does someone become a Christian?"

You'll be stunned by the misunderstanding and ignorance. The vast majority of people think that you become a Christian via dos and don'ts, and you stay a Christian in a similar way. Little wonder that so few are attracted to our churches or that Christians experience so little joy and zest.

God's law and conviction of sin have an important place in our lives and ministries. They show us our desperate need of outside help. However, the greatest emphasis of our lives and churches must be the divine Done, not the divine Demand. God's deeds, God's acts, must be kept ever in the foreground.

Our works are always waiting in the wings, looking for any opportunity to run onstage and replace Done with multiple dos, don'ts, shoulds, oughts, and musts. Their ugly costumes, stumbled lines, and amateur acting change the whole mood of the show, hogging the spotlight, silencing the applause, emptying the theater, arousing the ire of the critics, and bringing down the curtain on any hope of a long and prosperous run.

The most successful Christian lives are those that manage to keep the spotlight on Jesus Christ, the incarnation of the divine Done. But how do I get in to enjoy this show?

Faith.

Faith in Jesus is the entrance fee. Faith carpets the foyer. Faith unfolds the seat. Faith's program notes list Jesus as the only actor in this one-man show. Faith's spotlight fixes on Him alone and refuses to allow anyone or anything else onstage. Faith's ears hear the show's final line, "It is finished!" and Faith says, "Amen!" Faith's hands applaud and praise Christ alone. The noisy and cantankerous old critic, Mr. Conscience, is nowhere to be found in this scene of unmixed peace and joy. It is done. It is finished. The end!

Reexperience that happiest of truths every day of your life. And keep asking for an encore!

Many secular methods for obtaining peace involve trying to

empty the mind of fear, hate, guilt, anxiety, and so on. But how? Many have tried this mental exercise and failed. Only one thing can empty the mind of fear, hate, insecurity, regret, and guilt—filling the mind and heart with Christ's "It is finished." That powerful blood-red truth will vacuum up these vile squatters and populate us with peace and calm.

Refocus Bible Reading

Here's another survey question for you: What is the Bible all about?

Most popular answer: "To help us live better lives."

In other words, it is all about *me*. I am the main subject of the Bible. I hate to disillusion you—no, actually I'm glad to—but the Bible is all about God. He is the subject, the object, and every other grammatical term in between. Our first question when reading this book about God is not, "How does this apply to me?" but "What does this reveal about God?"

I sometimes imagine that if only I can get the whole world, including God, to orbit around me as the center of the universe, I will be happy, but that's the way to end up in a black hole. By putting God's Word and works at the center of our religious experience, of our Bible reading, our preaching, our worship, and our churches, we begin to orbit around the heat and light of His divine Son.

It seems to defy common sense, doesn't it? Surely if I have a problem, I need to focus on myself to get that fixed. That may be the case with medical issues. But with spiritual issues, the remedy can be found only by looking away from self to God. That's why Bible reading that keeps asking, "What does this reveal about God?" will put us and keep us in the trajectory of spiritual health and strength. God's person and God's works will cure us of over-focusing on ourselves and our works.

Restudy Salvation

Angels desire to study salvation.[3] According to the apostle Peter, they stand on their tiptoes, as it were, trying to peer into the great wonder of God's saving sinners by grace alone, without any contribution from the sinners He saves. These celestial beings crane their necks to investigate this incredible phenomenon. If angels who don't need salvation have such a joy-filled interest in it, how much more should we, whose whole lives and eternity depend on it?

Few of us can remember much of what we learned in high school. Some of us can hardly remember what we learned yesterday. It is no big deal, however, if I can't remember the French for *snail* or the number of ions in sodium phosphate. My French and chemistry teachers would be amazed at how well I can survive without that knowledge. But I cannot survive or thrive if I forget the gospel.[4]

That's why we need to constantly study salvation. End-times prophecy, ways to combat cults, church history, biblical languages, ethics, practical Christian living, and so forth, have their places, but they must never displace salvation as our favorite topic of study.

It is a vast subject with numerous ways of looking at it: justification, redemption, victory, reconciliation, atonement, and adoption. Perhaps you don't recognize or understand some of these words. Yet if you're a Christian, you've experienced them! So why not take one of them every year, explore it through sermons, books, and articles, and experience angelic delight as you expand your mind and heart with the joy of your salvation.

And don't let the study of these salvation truths distract or divert you from Jesus. The great doctrines of the Bible are like majestic royal robes. But they must not be studied in the closet. Take them off the hangers and clothe Jesus with them. They fit Him perfectly and beautifully. It is Jesus who justifies, it is Jesus who redeems, it is Jesus who reconciles, and so on.

Keep your eyes on Jesus, read about Him, believe in Him, talk to Him, listen to Him, and praise Him. No one can look to Jesus and not begin to look like Jesus, think like Jesus, act like Jesus, and even feel joy like Jesus.

Repent Immediately

So we believe in Jesus and rejoice in His salvation. Then we sin. Again.

What now?

Obvious, isn't it? We need to do something good to make up for it and bring that to the table to ensure our forgiveness. Or maybe we should just set a reasonable period of time, a healthy and respectful delay, before confessing. Or perhaps we manufacture some tears and some really deep guilt pangs in order to prove how genuinely sorry we are. We need to do some deed, do some delay, or do some guilt, don't we?

Do we?

No!

We need Jesus' Done again. "If we confess our sins, He is faithful and just to forgive us our sins and to cleanse us from all unrighteousness."[5] Don't do anything. Don't do a deed; don't do a delay; don't do a despair. Do nothing but turn to Christ's Done. Confess your sin without delay. Don't wait even a minute. Don't carry one miserable sin for one miserable second. Immediate sin, immediate confession, immediate forgiveness, immediate joy, immediate rest and peace.

Rest in Peace

Speaking of rest and peace, let me tell you about one of the most powerful sermons I *never* heard. In my early twenties, I was on the Isle of Lewis, Scotland, courting my hoped-to-be wife, Shona. I'd been brought up in the large and loud city of Glasgow, but Shona was raised in Ness, a little village at the most distant tip of one of the most distant islands in Scotland.

The island was one of the few places left in the world where everything closed on Sunday apart from churches. No shops, no buses, no planes, no gas stations, and no sports. Nothing!

Sound like a nightmare?

More like a dream, close to paradise actually.

I was sitting outside Shona's family home after the Sunday morning service one summer's day and realized that I'd never heard peace like that ever before. A deep and wide stillness lay over everything. That was what Sabbath rest was meant to be like, a community-wide shutdown of all unnecessary activity.

The parked planes, the docked ferries, the locked shops, the empty sports fields—all preached a visible and visceral message: it is finished.

Just as God designed the seventh day of the week to remind Israel of a finished creation, He instituted the first day of the week, Sunday, to remind Christians of a finished salvation.

Sadly, most modern Christians have no idea what such a community-wide Sabbath feels like and have no idea what they are missing. It rests the body and the mind and the soul. The external stillness of a Lewis Lord's Day was like a scaffolding for faith, supporting and confirming the faith that rests in total peace and complete stillness on Christ alone. It was also a visible and audible sermon to those who did not go to church, a weekly reminder of their Creator, of His demands as well as His supply.

Some years later, when I was called to pastor a congregation on the island, I often stood outside on a Sunday to buttress my faith with the tranquility and to remind myself of the conscience-pacifying, soul-refreshing, heart-resting, joy-stimulating message of a finished salvation that I was privileged to preach.

Sadly, by the time I left the island in 2007, the "modernizers" had succeeded in getting Sunday planes and ferries to run, one gas station had opened, and the roads were noticeably busier. It is still quieter than most places, but I can't help thinking that the Devil was delighted to have eliminated one of the last visible demonstrations of a finished salvation from the face of the earth.

I'll never forget the gospel power of that first silent sermon, and I often return to the memory of those rare Sabbath hours. In the meantime, in a much noisier community, I'm challenged, as we all are, to re-create that God-ordained stillness and silence in my home and family one day in every seven.

In a day of constant activity and busyness, I know it seems nonsensical to think that doing nothing can increase our joy and happiness. But why not try it for a while? Use the scaffolding of a weekly Sabbath not only to refresh your body and mind after all the week's doing but also to reinforce Christ's Done in your needy soul.

Begin and End the Day with Done!

Beep, beep, beep, beep, thump!

The day's agenda floods your mind and twists your stomach. So much to do. Too much to do.

Whisper, "It is finished!"

Repeat, "It is finished!"

Say louder, "It is finished!"

Whatever you will complete or not today, rest in the only work that will never need to be done again. Rest in the fact that Jesus has done the most impossible job in the world, done it perfectly, and made it available. Take it. Enjoy it. Build your life on it. Let it change your whole view of your life and work. Use His work to put your work into perspective. Believe His work is counted as yours. Despite all that you fear and dread about the next ten hours—a critical boss, a vicious competitor, a looming deadline, a complaining customer, an impossible sales target, unrelenting children, monotonous drudge—you have Christ's perfect work credited to your account. Yes, it is counted as yours, as if you did it. Are you humble enough to receive it?

And as you reset the alarm clock at the end of each day of incomplete lists and unfinished business, rest again in Christ's "It is finished." The most important work has been done and covers all our laziness, all our foolishness, all our time wasting, all our bad decisions, all our temper tantrums, all our losses, all our inabilities, all our everything.

Christ offers us His perfect CV and says, "Take this, and put your name on it. It is yours. Let this satisfy you. Let this fulfill you. Let this 'happify' you. Let this calm your mornings and soothe your evenings! It is finished!"

PERFECT PEACE

You will keep him in perfect peace,
Whose mind is stayed on You,
Because he trusts in You.[6]

So sang the Israelite believers to their Savior, and so may we to the same peace-purchasing Savior.

Perfect Peace in Our Consciences

Our consciences tell us that we have done wrong and we deserve to be punished by God. Sometimes the tone is condemning, sometimes mocking, sometimes lamenting, but always painful. There's only one silencer, and that's faith in Jesus' Done. When conscience accuses us of not doing this or not doing that, sometimes reaching back into our distant past for evidence, we pick up Jesus' Done! and shove it down its throat. Conscience may choke on it a little, but faith pushes it deeper and deeper until silence and peace reign again.

Perfect Peace in Service

When we've been saved, we want to serve our Savior. We have high hopes of living in a way that pleases Him. But the reality of our ongoing imperfection dashes these hopes as we slowly realize that we will never sing the perfect song, pray the perfect prayer, preach the perfect sermon, or speak the perfect testimony. But instead of giving up in defeated despair, we return to Christ's Done. We don't need to worship, serve, or witness perfectly. Jesus has done that for us, and His death has covered all our not doing.

And that's the best foundation and fuel for doing! We serve our Savior not to replace or add to His Done but *because of* His Done. Knowing that His Done covers all our not doing and failed doing liberates us to serve Him out of gratitude. His Done is our foundation for service. His Done is our fuel for service. His Done is our forgiveness for imperfect service.

Some people think that if you teach or preach Christ's Done too much, people will end up doing nothing. They'll just coast along in life and care nothing about holiness or service. Therefore, we're told, we have to guilt people into holy living and good works. That may work to a limited extent. Those who are burdened with guilt, fear, and anxiety may do a lot in the short term, but in the long run the most godly and energetic Christians are those who have most completely embraced and enjoyed the guilt-cleansing, fear-expelling, and anxiety-calming power of Christ's Done.

Last summer I was playing soccer at our church camp. My team was losing 4–0 and also losing heart. When the lunch bell rang, somebody on the other side shouted, "Right, next goal's the winner!" Well, you should have seen the energy course through my team again. Given a clean sheet to start over, hope was renewed, tiredness disappeared, heads were up, and legs were pumping again. That's why we need daily cleansing of our consciences with Christ's blood. It gives us a fresh start, a clean sheet, reenergizing and remotivating us to serve again.

Perfect Peace in Accusation

There is no more misrepresented group in society than Christians. We are falsely accused and inaccurately portrayed by politicians, the media, and educators alike. Individual Christians are often singled out for malicious accusation in their families and workplaces, especially on the Internet.

This can be so discouraging. What are we to do? Fight back? Retaliate? Sue? No, we return again to Christ's Done. He has cleared our names and characters. Our reputation is safe with Him. We can look to Him who right now vindicates us in our consciences, right now vindicates us in heaven, and one day will vindicate us in front of the whole world.[7]

Sometimes the accusations can come from within, and we can feel so self-condemned on every front that we hardly know where to start. Personal guilt is so long, deep, and wide that "It is finished" doesn't seem big enough. That's when, instead of trying to cover everything with this blanket at once, we should focus "It is finished" on one small area of life at a time. It seems counterintuitive—surely I need to spread this truth as widely as possible—and yet as researchers have also found, starting with small steps is the best way to take a large step.

Shawn Achor calls this principle "The Zorro Circle" and relates the story of how Zorro (real name Alejandro) was not always the courageous, swashbuckling, chandelier-swinging hero of books and movies. After some failed and abortive attempts to fight villains and defend the powerless, he ended up a despairing and broken drunk. That's when the aging sword master Don Diego arrived, took him under his wing, and began to retrain him by drawing a small circle in the dirt and forcing him to fight within that circle alone. Once he mastered that, he was allowed to face bigger and bigger challenges until he became the all-conquering Zorro we know from the films, swinging from chandeliers and doing push-ups above burning candles.[8]

Sometimes we need to draw a Zorro Circle for our consciences. We can gradually silence them by learning to fight our guilt in stages, one small circle at a time. Take the sword of "It is finished" and fight in the little circle of your covetousness. When you've put a Z on its chest (or maybe I should say F for "Finished"), draw the circle of lust and fight it to silence. And so on, small circle after small circle, until you are swinging on the chandeliers of joy and peace. You can forgo the push-ups over burning candles!

Perfect Peace in Dying

A couple of years ago I ended up in the hospital with a strange combination of leg and chest pain. The doctors diagnosed a blood clot in my leg that had traveled to my lungs and splattered all over them in lots of mini blood clots (multiple pulmonary emboli), a frequently fatal condition.

After starting me on anticlotting agents and commanding me to stay as still as possible, the doctors left me alone to wait for my wife to arrive. Those were solemn moments. From the doctor's words, I realized that I was on the edge of eternity, a breath away from facing God.

And I had perfect peace.

I'm not naturally courageous—probably a bit of a hypochondriac at times—but I was totally at peace with the prospect of death. I certainly didn't get that peace from anything I'd done or not done. No, I lay back, thought of Jesus on the cross, and found that His finished work was totally sufficient. He totally satisfied my conscience and gave me tremendous confidence about my impending meeting with God. Perfect peace.

Thankfully, death decided not to visit my ward that night. But it will visit me one day, as it will all of us. How will it find us? In a perfect peace or a perfect storm?

What a positive difference Christ's Done makes to our lives. To our deaths. And to our eternities. Is there a happier word in the world?

Let's maintain that glorious focus on Christ's Done because, as we'll discover in the next chapter, there are many forces to distract and divert us.

Chapter Four

HAPPY CHURCH

CHRIST > CHRISTIANS = POSITIVE+

IF YOU ASK MOST people why they don't go to church or why they don't want to become Christians, one of the most common answers is, "Christians are a bunch of hypocrites!"

Those who have left the church often give the same answer. Both groups have encountered Christians, experienced their inconsistencies, and decided, "If that's Christianity, you can keep it."

Even those of us who remain in the church are often deeply disappointed and discouraged by the failings and double standards of some fellow Christians. As we'll see, some of them are Christians in name but not in reality. Even the best Christians, however, have blind spots and inconsistencies that baffle and upset us.

We might not see them at the beginning when we are first converted to Christ. In the first bloom of Christian love, we might even think that some Christians and preachers belong to angelic ranks. But before too long, we discover our initial impressions were initial illusions, and we might even wonder whether we've fallen in with the fallen angels!

Although we may be tempted to give up and withdraw from

our churches in angry disgust, usually we keep going along, either loudly criticizing or inwardly seething at the failings of others.

At the root of this disillusionment is the successful satanic strategy of turning our attention away from Christ and directing us instead toward Christians. The more the Devil can keep us thinking and talking about Christians, the less we will be thinking and talking about Jesus. And the more we think and talk about Christians instead of Jesus, the more dismayed and downcast we will become.

I've certainly fallen into this soul-sapping habit at various points in my life, and I'm sure most of us succumb to it at times to some degree or another. For our spiritual and emotional well-being, we desperately need strategies to shift our attention away from the double standards and no standards of some Christians and upward to the soul-elevating Christ. That's what I'm going to provide in this chapter, first with *Christ-centered* analysis of this problem, then with *Christ-centered* solutions, followed by *church-centered* solutions.

CHRIST-CENTERED ANALYSIS

By keeping Christ at the forefront of our analysis of this problem, we are beginning the process of majoring more on Christ than on Christians. So how do we view this problem from His perspective?

Jesus Hates Hypocrisy

Jesus loves His people, but He hates hypocrisy. He doesn't wink at it, tolerate it, or excuse it; He abhors it. In the Old Testament, He spoke through the prophets to expose the evil of hypocrisy in Israel.[1] No matter how many sacrifices they offered, their duplicity and dishonesty wearied and disgusted Him. In the New Testament,

Jesus targeted hypocrisy from the beginning to the end of His ministry.[2] He still detests it and denounces it wherever it is found. What a comfort to know that it arouses His anger. Nothing is more frustrating than when we take our painful complaints to someone, only to elicit a resounding yawn. Not so with Jesus. He hates hypocrisy even more than we do.

Jesus Experienced Hypocrisy

Jesus was a victim of hypocrisy. He saw inconsistency among His people, and He experienced it throughout His life and even in His death. He spent much of His ministry enduring it, confronting it, and condemning it. He knows what it is like; He understands the pain of it; He sympathizes with us as we lament over it.

And remember, Jesus saw hypocrisy far more clearly and deeply than we can. His X-ray eyes penetrated every pharisaical mask and disguise to detect every gross contradiction between lips and life. And even more painful for Him, He saw the double standards and inconsistencies in even the best of His disciples. His painful experience of hypocrisy was a large part of His sin-atoning sufferings. But they also gave Him an ongoing sympathy and empathy with us. However pained we are by phony faith, we can take our pain to someone who felt it even more deeply.

Jesus Predicted Hypocrisy

We shouldn't be surprised at the existence of hypocrisy in the church. Jesus told us directly and through His apostles that there would never be a pure church in this world. It will always be a mixture of wheat and weeds, true and false, right and wrong, to the end of time.[3] If we grasp this, it should ease some pain of past experiences and also manage our expectations so that we avoid deeper disappointment in the future.

Jesus Uses Hypocrisy

Why did Jesus choose to do it this way? Why did He not create a pure church full of pure people or at least of exclusively true Christians? Why allow weeds to be mixed with the wheat?

Because He can use it for our good. He uses trials such as these to test and prove our faith. If I hang on to Christ despite all the pain that His professing people inflict on me and others, my faith in Him must be genuine.

He also uses these hassles to motivate self-examination. If so many people are so blind to their faults, there's a good possibility that I'm blind to mine too. That makes me examine myself to see whether I really am in the faith and living up to it.[4] Such self-examination shouldn't discourage but encourage us. The very fact that I'm concerned I may be a weed, that I may be wearing a Christian mask, is a sign of spiritual life.

That I'm concerned other people might be weeds and I want them to become wheat is another sign of having a spiritual life and being on the right side of the divide.

Sometimes Jesus uses these experiences to magnify His grace. When we see that even the best Christians have so much hypocrisy left in them, we marvel at what a gracious Savior He must be, to love and die for such mixed-up people.

Jesus Will End Hypocrisy

Although the church has been mixed throughout the ages, the day is coming when Jesus will separate the wheat from the chaff and gather all the weeds out of His field to be burned.[5] He will end the pain and distress of this present mixed state of the church and establish a church made up of a perfect number of perfect people. It will be a beautiful bride without spot or wrinkle or any other ugly defect.[6] He will separate the ungodly from the godly and all ungodliness from the ungodly. A perfect world, a perfect church, and a perfect me! That will be the happiest day we've ever experienced.

CHRIST-CENTERED SOLUTIONS

Okay, that explains the problem and starts getting my focus back on Christ's plan and purpose for it, but how do I respond to it? How do I stop getting so down at the failings of Christian pastors and people? What does positive faith look like in this crucible? How do I start lifting up my mind and my heart? How can I be happy in the midst of so much to make me sad?

Try to See Christ in Even the Worst Christian

Although Christ is molding each of His people into His beautiful image, no one shows that image perfectly. Our immaturity and sin blight and deform His work. No matter how marred the image, however, there is still a trace of that image somewhere in every Christian. The most disfigured Christians have something somewhere in their lives where they excel us in portraying Christ's image. It is up to us to find that and admire it.

When you are in a group and people start pulling down another Christian, why not suggest areas of the person's life and character that do show the work of Christ in him or her? Yes, there are obvious remnants of the Devil's destructive work, but why spotlight that instead of Christ's reconstructing work?

I've known some pretty grim Christians through the years, but as I look back, I admit I overlooked areas of their lives where Christ was undoubtedly leaving His fingerprints. Today, as we survey our fellow believers, let's make the happy choice to major on Christ's positive work in them rather than on all the Devil's negatives.

Pray for Hypocrites

We've all done it. We end up in company where we start criticizing someone, and very soon we've torn him in shreds and left him in pieces. Sometimes we don't need the help of company to do our shredding; we can grind the person to powder in the cruel confines of our own sharp-toothed minds. Although there can be strange short-term satisfaction in these sadistic pleasures, we actually inflict deep long-term trauma on ourselves.

When tempted to start drilling and sawing away at others, why not pray for them? If we really do fear they are hypocrites, they need our prayers far more than our incisive analysis. And in the process, we'll discover something: It is very hard to hate someone for whom we pray. It is almost impossible to pull someone down when we prayerfully raise him or her up to heaven for God's blessing. Prayer never changes God. It sometimes changes the person we pray for. It always changes us.

And remember, as most of the wheat was once weeds, by God's grace the remaining weeds can also become wheat.

Spend Time with the Inconsistent

It is easy to criticize from a computer keyboard or from a church pew, when people are at some distance away from us, when we aren't really involved in their lives, and we don't really know them. It is much more difficult to scorch people when we've had a coffee with them or walked a mile with them. Then we realize that they are human after all, that they've had an awful childhood, that they are enduring a depressing marriage, that they've never had sound Bible teaching, or that there is some other stress in their lives that puts their words and actions in a different light. Or we might discover that we've completely misjudged them and the fault is more in our perception and discernment than in their conduct.

Contrary to popular opinion, familiarity does not always breed contempt; often it can breed affection. Some have called this the "familiarity principle" and others have called it the "mere exposure effect." Whatever we call it, we've all experienced it; we tend to develop a liking for what we are most familiar with and exposed to, whether words, pictures, foods, or people.

Spending time with people should also make it harder to commit a fundamental attribution error. Although we excuse our actions and refuse to trace our bad deeds to bad character, when others do something bad, we immediately conclude bad character from their action. Let's show people the same favor we show ourselves.

Be Patient

As a pastor, I've also sometimes been appalled at the way mature Christians expect young Christians to come out of the shell as fully grown men and women of God. And when they aren't, down comes the sledgehammer upon them. Some older Christians have conveniently forgotten they were young once, somehow imagining they skipped spiritual infancy and adolescence.

As a pastor, I've been stunned at the way some poor specimens of Christianity have suddenly blossomed into beautiful flowers of grace and even into majestic cedars of Lebanon.[7] People I had given up all hope for were transformed into holy, zealous, steady, and reliable Christians. Sometimes getting married or having children did it. Sometimes it was going through a trial or suffering. But sometimes it was simply the sovereign work of God. I think God loves to revive His work in those we have written off and given up on.

Jesus taught us not to expect everything to change overnight when a person enters the kingdom of God by faith. Instead, He said the work of God is like a little piece of leaven that slowly, gradually, and inevitably leavens the whole lump.[8] In the meantime, we need patience.

Speak Positively About Other Christians

One of the most lethal habits Christians can fall into is to talk negatively about other Christians in front of their children or in front of unbelievers. I've seen children spiritually devastated due to regular Sunday meals that served up a diet of roast pastor, barbecued elders, and boiled Christians. In some cases, tragically, it turned the children away from the church for life. In other cases, the negativity created perpetually discontented church members of their kids. They had gotten so habituated to hearing pastors and churches criticized in their childhood that they could not break the cycle when they became adults.

One of the greatest favors we can do for our children is to speak positively about our pastors and about other Christians. Even when there may have been some flaws in the preaching or their lives, find the good things, highlight them, express appreciation for them, and discuss them with your kids. Draw attention to Christians who are serving the Lord well, and use them as models for your children. And when, regrettably, you may have to discuss a certain Christian's sins, do your best to also mention evidences of God's good work in that person's life.

When Sonja Lyubomirsky and her team interviewed people who had been singled out by their friends and family as "exceptionally happy," they found that "the happiest people take pleasure in other people's successes and show concern in the face of others' failures." In contrast, they found that the typical unhappy person is "deflated rather than delighted about his peers' accomplishments and triumphs and . . . is relieved rather than sympathetic in the face of his peers' failures and undoings." In general, they concluded, "the happier the person, the less attention she pays to how others around her are doing,"[9] which brings us to . . .

Springboard from Christians to Christ

When you are tempted to start mulling over someone's imperfection, instead think about the opposite perfection in Jesus. If you are pained by someone's harsh or lying tongue, consider how Jesus' words were "full of grace and truth."[10] If a friend is condemning the minister's self-promotion, turn his attention to the One who made Himself of no reputation and took the form of a servant.[11] If you are discussing the rampant materialism of some Christians, remember to also ponder the Christ who, though He was rich, made Himself poor, that we "through His poverty might become rich."[12] There is no sin found in a Christian that cannot act as a springboard to Christ and His beautiful holiness.

See Your Own Faults in Them

It is amazing how we can be especially hard on people who have the same peculiar failings that we do. It is a kind of perverse technique for salving our consciences: if I can find someone who's even worse than I am at this sin, it somehow makes me feel a whole lot better! The hypercritical are often the most hypocritical.

When you detect that you are being especially critical of another Christian, seriously ask yourself if this is your besetting sin as well. Are you appalled by Lesley's pride? Maybe it's so much like your own. Are you horrified by Jim's gossip? Maybe you're also spending way too much time on the phone and on Facebook. Are you aghast at the Browns' spending habits? Maybe you've not been in the black for years either.

God may have sent these people into your life to act as a mirror to your sins. Don't attack the mirror; use it to see what's wrong in your life.

Measure Christ's Forgiveness

As the person who has been forgiven most loves most,[13] ask the Lord to show you how much you have been forgiven. The more you appreciate the depth, length, breadth, and height of God's forgiveness, the more you will love Him.

But we can do this by proxy as well. When we see how much other Christians still sin, we can get the spiritual ruler out to measure the immeasurable pardoning love of God toward them. And when we realize that we can never find enough rulers or measuring tapes to record accurate dimensions of this forgiving grace, we can love God for that as well. He who has been forgiven much loves much. He who sees how much others have been forgiven loves God for that too.

Nothing silences criticism so much as pondering how Christ has loved people like us. That He loved me and gave Himself for me is amazing. That He loved *them* and gave Himself for *them* is sometimes even more amazing.

Identify the Accuser

The hypercritical tend to think of themselves as hyperholy. Unknown to them, however, they may well be at that very moment unholy instruments in the hands of the evil one. The Devil has made a career out of maligning and denouncing Christians, so much so that he is called the Christian's "accuser."[14] He lays his charges directly and via intermediaries, some of whom are unsuspecting Christians who actually think they are doing the Lord's work. He comes with lies about Christians and he comes with truths about Christians, but whether his allegations are true or false, his aim is the same: pull down Christians so as to pull down our thoughts, our emotions, and our actions.

Why not ask yourself whether you may be an unwitting pawn in the Devil's clever hands, doing his dirty work while he cackles in the background? And if you are a victim of unfair accusations via the Devil's proxies, pity them, pray for them, and identify the evil puppeteer who is pulling their strings.

Keep Jesus Front and Center

Our minds are a vast universe demanding to be filled. Each of our senses continually vacuums information into our internal galaxies, sending various facts and feelings into mental orbit, darkening or lightening our lives as they go.

We can't stop the sensory vacuums, but we can decide what gets sucked inside. We can direct our nozzles to the dark hypocrisy of other believers, or we can vacuum up truths about Christ. The former creates black holes; the latter produces a nonstop sunrise.

Luke spoke about darkness and light: "The lamp of the body is the eye. Therefore, when your eye is good, your whole body also is full of light. But when your eye is bad, your body also is full of darkness. Therefore take heed that the light which is in you is not darkness. If then your whole body is full of light, having no part dark, the whole body will be full of light, as when the bright shining of a lamp gives you light."[15]

Suck in the bright light of Christ; let Him and His Word dwell in you richly. Let His pet names for His people sink into your heart: My body, My little ones, My jewels, the apple of My eye, My saints, My friends, and so on.

Above all, consider what Jesus will yet do for all His people. Yes, we can look back and demoralize ourselves by busying our minds with the sins of other Christians. If that's your choice, then know that it is a surefire way to evict your joy and enfeeble your zeal. "Why serve with her? Why do anything when no one else is doing anything? Why do anything good when there's so much bad going on to undermine it all?"

Or we can look forward in hope that Christ will continue His work of sanctification in His people here below. They will lose some of their rough edges and cracks. They will yet shine a bit more brightly. However, we can look even farther forward with a greater and far more certain confidence that Jesus will eventually present His perfected people to His Father with exceeding joy and great glory.[16]

How amazed we will be to see in heavenly glory how God has perfected the most imperfect of His people. What a transformation! What a metamorphosis! What glory to God and goodwill toward men! What a Savior!

CHURCH-CENTERED SOLUTIONS

You may wish this section wasn't here. But I can't conclude this chapter without coming full circle and encouraging you to commit yourself to the Christians in your local church, yes, even those faulty, failing Christians. After we've tilted the balance to focus much more on Christ than Christians, Christ then sends us back among Christians to fellowship, worship, and serve with other believers in His church.

"But I can keep the focus on Jesus so much better if I just listen to sermons on my iPod, fellowship via Facebook, and witness via Twitter."

Regardless of the perceived advantages of eChurch or iChurch, God commands us to physically join with physical Christians in physical churches.[17] Even secular sources recognize the central importance of community for personal growth and development as well as recovery from depression and stress.[18]

Especially during crises we need outside help from other Christians, even though the natural human instinct may be to withdraw. Shawn Achor noticed that when Wall Street was panicking and the Dow Jones was plunging in 2008, traders didn't regroup and encourage one another. Instead these hypersmart people withdrew, canceling team meetings and other social activities, compounding demoralization, and making rebuilding much harder.[19]

We've all done something like that, more times than we'd like to admit. Disappointed in the church and in Christians, we have followed our natural instinct to give in, give up, and get away.

Maybe Yahoo will convince you to reinvest in your local church. As part of her so-far-successful efforts to turn around and rebuild the company, new CEO Marissa Mayer has banned all telecommuting.

Why is a futuristic company like Yahoo rewinding the future?

The leaders realized that for all the benefits of telecommuting, there were three areas where more was being lost than gained:

LOSS OF INFORMAL COMMUNICATION: It is much harder for telecommuters to have informal and unplanned interaction that shares knowledge, challenges people to see things from another's perspective, gets them out of their mental ruts, and stimulates creativity and productivity. Less communication means less collaboration.

LOSS OF TRUST: Telecommuting makes it harder to foster trust and solidarity. Face time is still the best way to build relationships. Studies have found that even occasional face-to-face meetings of virtual teams significantly increased trust and boosted performance.

LOSS OF ENERGY: Yahoo's office was virtually empty on a Friday, demoralizing and sucking the life out of the rare few who turned up to the ghost town.[20]

Telecommuting to Church?

If this is true of Yahoo, how much more of telecommuting to church? You might be able to get better sermons online, or it might be so much more efficient to listen to your pastor's podcast. But if you regularly telecommute to church, you are losing more than you are gaining. You are losing valuable opportunities to learn from the chance meetings with other Christians in the foyer, in the corridors, and in the parking lot. You are undermining trust and unity among Christians. And you are sapping vital energy from the demoralized body of Christ.

Get out of bed, get in the car, and get to your local church. You'll learn surprising lessons from the most surprising people, you'll build valuable relationships, and you'll get and give morale-boosting energy. Yes, there are huge positive benefits to this kind of social contact:

- George Vaillant, the director of the Harvard Study of Adult Development, which has followed more than two hundred men since the late 1930s to find what makes for the happiest and most fulfilling lives, concluded, "The only thing that really matters in life are your relationships to other people."[21]
- The "Very Happy People" survey assessed the top 10 percent of very happy people and found that they "were highly social, and had stronger romantic and other social relationships than less happy groups."[22]
- An empirical study of well-being among sixteen hundred Harvard undergraduates discovered that the greatest predictor of happiness was not GPA, SAT scores, family income, gender, or age, but social support.[23]
- National surveys find that when someone claims to have five or more friends with whom she can discuss important

problems, she is 60 percent more likely to say that she is "very happy."[24]

But relationships don't just improve our psychological well-being; they improve our physical well-being too:

- "Those who attend religious services at least once a week have a 25 percent higher life expectancy than those who don't." Victor Zeines, author of *Living a Longer Life*, said that's "probably because church attendance increases social support, a proven life-extender."[25]
- "On average, married people have a 15 percent higher life expectancy and live 1.17 more years than their unwed counterparts. Happily married pairs enjoy 'companionship and support, which lowers stress levels,'" said longevity expert Sally Beare, author of *50 Secrets of the World's Longest Living People*.[26]
- Social support increases survival rates among heart attack victims.[27]
- Studies "consistently show increased risk of death among persons with a low quantity, and sometimes low quality, of social relationships. . . . Social isolation is a major risk factor for mortality."[28]
- Although bereavement increases stress hormones, spending time with others and especially confiding in them reduce these harmful chemicals and associated health risks.[29]
- Those who had "a large network of friends outlived those with the fewest friends by 22%."[30]
- Women with life-threatening cancer who attended support groups following cancer surgery lived an average of eighteen months longer than those who isolated themselves.[31]
- A survey of three long-living people groups found that the

top two things they had in common were "put family first" and "keep socially engaged."[32]

We could travel back in time and hear Greek philosopher Epicurus say, "Of all the things which wisdom acquires to produce the blessedness of the complete life, far the greatest is the possession of friendship."[33]

Or we can hear twenty-first-century positive psychologist Martin Seligman say, "As a professor, I don't like this, but the cerebral virtues—curiosity, love of learning—are less strongly tied to happiness than interpersonal virtues like kindness, gratitude and capacity for love."[34]

Researchers, psychologists, philosophers, and even businesses like Yahoo agree that we need one another. As Martin Seligman put it: "Very little that is positive is solitary. . . . Other people are the best antidote to the downs of life and the single most reliable up."[35]

For all the downsides of Christian relationships, there are many more upsides. And remember, the church of God has far more promised to it than physical and psychological benefits. There is a rich spiritual dimension to Christian relationships that unbelievers know nothing about. We also have the promise of the Father's smile, Christ's presence, and the Holy Spirit's indwelling.

Let's now look to the future with that triple encouragement.

Chapter Five

HAPPY FUTURE

FUTURE > PAST = POSITIVE+

ONE KEY TO PRESENT happiness is a right view of the past and the future. Yet many of us have a wrong approach to both. Yes, we look backward and we look forward, but we look at the wrong things in the past and future.

I want to help you look backward better, but above all I want to help you look forward better because the more we have to look forward to, the happier we will be.

That's why, in general, youth is a happier time than old age. We start out in life with so many varied paths and exciting possibilities in front of us; places to go, people to meet, pleasures to experience. It is so hope filled and hopeful. And so it should be. God's given us a great world to explore and enjoy.

As our past increases and our future shrinks, however, our minds tend to start looking backward rather than forward. In some ways that's natural and normal since there's more to look back on than to look forward to. It can be good for us too; the past can be a source of tremendous joy and thankfulness as we reflect on the mercies we have received and enjoyed from God's good hand. But that lingering backward look can also cause deep pain and even despair as we ponder bad decisions, bad choices, and bad relationships. And we don't need to be old to be tortured by our past, as the horrific teenage suicide rate demonstrates.

I want to help you survey the past in a way that will not subtract from your joy but will increase it. The emphasis of this chapter, however, is that while you can draw delight from your past, the Christian's gaze should be primarily forward not backward, majoring on the future not on the past, on the front foot looking to the horizon more than on the back foot looking over your shoulder, cultivating optimistic hope rather than wallowing in pessimistic reminiscences.

A HEALTHY USE OF THE PAST

Let's begin, though, by examining how important the past is to Christians and how we can benefit from a backward look. Then we'll learn how to avoid tripping up and falling as we look back over our shoulders.

Biblical History

Christianity is a religion founded on the facts of history, so the past is an essential component. Without God's mighty words and works in the past, we would have no present or future worth speaking of. Our God and Savior is the ruler of history who has spoken and acted to save His people from their sins. Biblical history is redemptive history, and without history there is no redemption. We, therefore, begin the Christian life with a retrospective look to God's redemptive acts in the Old and New Testaments, especially the climactic acts of His Son's life, death, and resurrection.

We trust the biblical record and its interpretation of history. We believe that God ordained it, organizes it, and is moving it toward a meaningful and certain purpose. The more we know, trust, and love redemptive history, the brighter our present and future will shine.

Church History

One of the greatest and yet most neglected areas of Christian study is the history of the Christian church since pentecost. Sure, there were long dark ages and discouraging setbacks throughout the centuries, but there have also been magnificent triumphs and advances.

Sadly, many church history books tend to focus on the persecutions and the martyrdoms, which have a certain glory and beauty of their own. But what about the faith-boosting records of God saving, reviving, expanding, moving, and blessing His church in past ages and in other places?

Instead of an exclusive focus on our local church in our own day and age, narrowing our perspective and limiting our view, let's take a much wider and longer view of God's kingdom by studying the significant eras and events of worldwide church history.

World History

But we shouldn't confine ourselves to biblical or church history. We also want to trace the hand of God in all the world in all ages. Although world history books rarely mention God, nothing in their pages is detached from God and His perfect plan. He is working all things, including world history, together for the good of His church.

For example, if you study the period before Christ's coming to Bethlehem, you'll be amazed at how God had arranged everything so perfectly for His arrival. The Jewish nation was broken and hopeless; the Greek philosophical movement had run out of steam and lay exhausted on the sidelines; however, the Roman political system had brought peace, stability, and unprecedented mobility for potential missionaries and evangelists. As Paul summed it up, "When the fullness of the time had come, God sent forth His Son."[1]

We can't always see the links between world history, church history, and redemptive history, but we can believe these links exist and look forward to the day when God will reveal all the unbreakable connections between them. All things—yes, all things—are working together for the good of His people.[2] All things in every century and all things in every country.

A sense of God's sovereign control over all events, big and small, is vital for positive faith. Even non-Christians recognize that there's no happiness without some sense of control, although they usually speak of personal control. In *The Happiness Project*, Gretchen Rubin wrote,

> The feeling of control is an essential element of happiness—a better predictor of happiness than, say, income. Having a feeling of autonomy, of being able to choose what happens in your life or how you spend your time, is crucial. Identifying and following my resolutions had made me feel far more in control of my time, my body, my actions, my surroundings, and even my thoughts. Getting control of my life was definitely an aspect of my happiness project, and a greater feeling of control gave me a major boost in happiness.[3]

If this is the happy effect of frail and fleeting human control, how much more happiness should positive faith in God's almighty and all-encompassing sovereign control produce!

Although Arianna Huffington called it "coincidence" rather than providence, she spoke of her delight in discovering the "magic power" of seeing things "come together." She said, "I've always had a deep love of the mysteries of coincidence and how they can give us tiny glimpses of the structure of the universe—or even a glimpse into the fact that there's a structure at all."[4] Huffington went on to speak of the benefits of rejecting the idea that "we live isolated and alienated in an indifferent universe"[5] and (remember to substitute divine providence for her "coincidence" in this quotation): "People who notice coincidences most tend to be more confident and at ease with life. Every coincidence they experience— even the minor ones—confirms their optimism."[6] If Huffington could draw such optimism from coincidences, shouldn't the Christian believer be able to draw much more from observing providence under God's sovereign control?

One thing to be careful about is not to read or watch too much world history without a balancing input from redemptive history. Last winter, I was reading *Unbroken*, the harrowing story of Louis Zamperini's experiences in various Japanese POW camps. At the same time, I was watching a DVD series on the Second World War in the Pacific. As I did so, I found I was sinking deeper into sadness with every page and episode until finally I decided it was all too much. I gave up on the DVD series, and I skipped to the happy ending of *Unbroken*. There are no prizes for making ourselves as sad as we can be.

There are good times in world history, times of civilization and progress, and we should prioritize the study of such periods rather than the worst times. But even the best times are meaningless times unless faith connects them to redemptive history.

Personal History

God commands us: "Look to the rock from which you were hewn, / And to the hole of the pit from which you were dug."[7] Sometimes we might be tempted to think, *I've been saved. Let's forget my past. The only way is upward and forward.*

As believers, however, we must remember the past from which the Lord saved us. If done rightly, it is not painfully humiliating but happily humbling. Instead of leaving us wallowing in guilt, it makes us so thankful to God for what He delivered us from. Now and again let's deliberately and consciously recall the slime and the grime of our past lifestyle and sing Psalm 40 once more:

> *He also brought me up out of a horrible pit,*
> *Out of the miry clay,*
> *And set my feet upon a rock,*
> *And established my steps.*
> *He has put a new song in my mouth—*
> *Praise to our God;*
> *Many will see it and fear,*
> *And will trust in the LORD.* (vv. 2–3)

This not only humbles us but also exalts the Lord who has rescued us from the mud and hewed us from the rock. What a deliverer He is!

Even our preconversion life can give us material to reflect upon as we remember how God looked after us when He was the last thing on our minds. I often think about the many times the Lord protected me and delivered me in my unconverted days. I can think of one occasion when He literally closed a door that I was desperate to push through to pursue sinful pleasures. Other times He got me home when I had no recollection of going home. To return to Psalm 40:

> *Many, O LORD my God, are Your wonderful works*
> *Which You have done;*
> *And Your thoughts toward us*
> *Cannot be recounted to You in order;*

If I would declare and speak of them,
They are more than can be numbered. (v. 5)

Christian History

Let's not stop at remembering our humbling past. Let's also remember our positive past, the many encouraging memories of God's goodness to us, especially since we've been converted. The Old Testament patriarchs and the Israelites regularly raised stone memorials to God's goodness. The prophet Samuel raised a stone and called it Ebenezer (literally, Stone of Help), saying, "Thus far the LORD has helped us."[8]

Again, unbelievers have a thing or two to teach us about the value of mementos to prompt positive memories, as Gretchen Rubin discovered:

Studies show that recalling happy times helps boost happiness in the present. When people reminisce, they focus on positive memories, with the result that recalling the past amplifies the positive and minimizes the negative. However, because people remember events better when they fit with their present mood, happy people remember happy events better, and depressed people remember sad events better. Depressed people have as many nice experiences as other people—they just don't recall them as well. With this knowledge in mind, I vowed to take steps to help everyone in the family to experience happy times more vividly.[9]

We, too, can squeeze maximum happiness out of each happy event or experience by looking forward to it, enjoying it in the moment, communicating our enjoyment of it to others, and deliberately remembering it in the future.

We can also get together with other Christians and reminisce about God's goodness to us through the years. Again, even secular researchers have found that sharing memories with other people produces multiple positive emotions like happiness, contentment, amusement, and higher morale.

Together we can taste and savor God's goodness and mercy that have followed us all the days of our lives, and with God's help, we can beat unbelievers at this happiness game.

A DAMAGING USE OF THE PAST

Having identified some positive uses of the past, let me now alert you to some dangerous backward looks and some strategies to limit or repair the damage.

Sins

The Devil can often highlight sins from our past to tempt us to despair of forgiveness or even to tempt us back into the same sins again. In such tempting times we need the promises and power of God. He has promised to forgive *all* our sins,[10] to separate them from us "as far as the east is from the west,"[11] and He has assured us of His delivering power from every temptation.[12] Remedy the pain of such a backward look with the joyful future hope of freedom from all sin and temptation and the enjoyment of perfect holiness.

Injustice

We live in an unjust world, so it won't be long until we experience the pain of injustice. We've seen truth fallen by the wayside while lies strut in pomp. We've seen purity in prison and wickedness set free. Psalm 73 becomes our complaint, but we must also make it our comfort. Yes, let's sing the first sixteen verses with pain and anguish, but let's go on to sing the remaining verses with forward-looking confident hope of vindication for the righteous and justice for the wicked.

Failure

We can become obsessed with our wrong decisions, our failed exams, our rejected ideas, our parenting blunders, our marital disasters, our spiritual backslidings, and our missed opportunities. But while we must confess our folly in such events, we must not dwell on them and beat ourselves up with them every day. Some people can be so obsessed with their past mistakes that they miss present gospel opportunities that are right under their noses. Our all-wise God forgives our folly, can make our folly part of His all-wise plan, and calls us to learn from our past mistakes so that we can improve our future and perhaps help others have a brighter future too.

And remember, success might have been even worse for us than failure! Victory can become a catastrophe when it becomes the basis for self-confidence, false confidence, or overconfidence. Examples abound in politics, sports, and business, and it's easy to spot in such media-saturated areas. If we look closely enough and think deeply enough, however, we can also find plenty of examples in churches and in the lives of individual Christians.

A church starts growing, attracting admiring glances and even media attention, but when the pastor begins to take the credit, boasting of numbers converted and counseled, while scorning smaller churches and smaller pastors, wise Christians begin to tremble. They see painful catastrophe approaching in the midst of the confident triumphalism.

Perhaps this explains why the church of Christ is often defeated, divided, and depleted. God is saving the church from the risk of catastrophic victory—a victory that would result in long-term harm rather than health.

According to the Kaufmann Foundation, around 50 percent of Fortune 500 companies began in a recession.[13] This partly explains why Clayton Christensen, a Harvard Business School professor, has claimed that the recent recession would "have an unmitigated positive impact on innovation. . . . The breakthrough innovations come when the tension is greatest and the resources are most limited. That's when people are actually a lot more open to rethinking the fundamental way they do business."[14] In other words, scarcity can be an opportunity, a boon rather than a bane.

That's true in the spiritual realm as well and provides the flip side to the risk of catastrophic victory. By God's grace, the church and the Christian can snatch victory from the jaws of every defeat. We would not have Psalm 51 without David's horrific backsliding. We would not have Paul's letters to the New Testament churches without their divisions and disasters. We would not have humbled Peter's sympathetic letters without his triple defeat at the hands of young servant girls.

I've seen churches lose half their members and prayer meetings come alive. I've seen pastors leave churches in the lurch, transforming "coasting" elders into leaders. I've seen Christians lose their income and prosper spiritually. I've seen Christians lose loved ones in tragic circumstances and grow in love to God. I've seen a murderer sentenced to life imprisonment find true freedom and eternal life in Christ.

Spiritual recession, scarcity, and loss provide us with opportunities for spiritual breakthroughs and for a fundamental rethinking of our spiritual lives. Ask God to turn your defeat into a victory, your bane into a boon, and your recession into prosperity.

Bereavement

As we get older, death's shadows multiply, darken, and lengthen: a beloved mother, then a lovely child, then a precious husband. How can we live without them? We look back to better days and cannot imagine anything good in our lonely, quiet future. Perhaps this is why men over forty-five have some of the highest suicide rates.[15]

But even here, in our darkest valleys, we have the hope of God's never-leaving presence with us, we have the hope of eternal life for our saved loved ones, and we have the hope of reuniting with our saved relatives in a much better place and condition. Look forward with triple hope rather than backward with terrible despair.

Nostalgia

Although nostalgia used to be viewed largely as a negative, recent research has found that there can also be good nostalgia when it is used to help us feel we have roots and continuity with the past. John Tierney wrote about this beneficial nostalgia in the *New York Times*:

> [Such] nostalgia has been shown to counteract loneliness, boredom and anxiety. It makes people more generous to strangers and more tolerant of outsiders. Couples feel closer and look happier when they're sharing nostalgic memories. On cold days, or in cold rooms, people use nostalgia to literally feel warmer. . . . [It makes] life seem more meaningful and death less frightening. When people speak wistfully of the past, they typically become more optimistic and inspired about the future.[16]

Like the psalmist in Psalm 42, we can all remember when we've used good memories of the past to get us through hard times and to encourage us when we're feeling down.

Bad nostalgia, on the other hand, romanticizes the past by ignoring or minimizing its problems and difficulties. That tendency explains why most people say their best decade was their teens or their twenties.[17]

The remedy for bad nostalgia is not only good nostalgia but also Christian hope. We stop looking backward with rose-tinted spectacles to some imaginary golden age by looking forward with faith-tinted spectacles to the reality of golden streets. Let's now pivot from the past to the future.

OUR HOPE-FILLED FUTURE

Although the past can bring much good into our lives and even potentially damaging backward looks can be turned around into positives, I want the major emphasis of this chapter and of our lives to be on the future, not the past. In the Christian life, forward looks should outweigh backward looks because no matter how wonderful the past has been, the best is yet to be.

And yet, somehow the known past seems more secure than the unknown future. In fact, the future is looking darker by the day. How will I provide for my retirement? What will the world be like for my children? Will the church survive the never-ending sexual revolution? Yes, areas of the future can terrify us and dishearten us.

Christians have a future hope, however, that should form a much larger part of our conscious thoughts than our present or our past. Our prevailing viewpoint is *forward, onward, advance.*

A Definition of Christian Hope

Let's begin our forward look with a definition of Christian hope: *Christian hope is a realistic expectation of and joyful longing for future good and glory based on the reliable Word of God.*

Realistic Expectation

Christian hope is based on reality. It is not like the lottery player who hopes for the great payoff, only to join the millions of disappointed players every week. It is not like the student who has failed to study for her finals but hopes for the best. It is not like the gardener who never weeds but still hopes for big, healthy vegetables.

None of these hopes have any foundation in reality. They are based on personal desires, ambitions, and luck. None of these hopeful people have any ground or confidence that their hope will be realized. At heart, they probably know that their hopes will be dashed; that's hardly a hope with inspirational or life-changing energy! But Christian hope has never been dashed on the rocks of reality. Every Christian hope has been fully realized.

Joyful Longing

We can have a realistic expectation of something that is based on reality, and yet it gives us no joy as we anticipate it. We may know that next week we are going to have a hernia operation, but we're hardly excited about it or longing for the first slice of the knife!

Christian hope, though, not only expects but also longs for. It anticipates, it looks forward with joy, and it even wishes it to come quicker. We expect certain things to happen, we are thrilled at the prospect, and we hasten the day. A Christian pessimist is an oxymoron, a contradiction in terms.

Future Good and Glory

Without denying that there may well be hard things and painful experiences in our future, Christian hope lasers in on the good that is in our future:

- God will guide our lives.
- God will never leave us or forsake us.
- God will work all things together for our good.

- God will produce gold from our dross.
- God will sustain and provide in our weakness and helplessness.
- God will get us ready for heavenly glory.
- God will utterly defeat death, sin, and Satan.
- God will provide a new body in a new heaven and a new earth.

No wonder the creation that presently groans in bondage looks forward to singing when it joins with the children of God in their glorious emancipation.[18] The heavens, the earth, the seas, and the fields will constitute a vast choir of praise to God. The blood-stained fields of Gettysburg, the poppy-growing fields of Afghanistan, and the polluted and poisoned acres of our overworked fields and overfished seas will unite in worship of our awesome God of hope-filled liberation.

The Reliable Word of God

This is not a hope floating in the midair of human speculations. This is not a hoping for the best. This is not a vain and ethereal hope. This is a solid and grounded hope because it is all based on God's sure word of promise. As the psalmist said, his hope of dawning in his darkness was based on God's Word.[19] How many Christians, like John Bunyan's pilgrim, have unlocked their depressing dungeons with God's word of promise?

> Now a little before it was day, good Christian, as one half amazed, brake out in this passionate speech: What a fool (quoth he) am I, thus to lie in a stinking Dungeon, when I may as well walk at liberty? I have a Key in my bosom, called Promise, that will (I am persuaded) open any Lock in Doubting-Castle. Then said Hopeful, That's good news; good Brother, pluck it out of thy

bosom, and try. Then Christian pulled it out of his bosom, and began to try at the Dungeon door, whose bolt (as he turned the Key), gave back, and the door flew open with ease, and Christian and Hopeful both came out.[20]

It is no coincidence that the Bible ends with Revelation, a book that looks toward Christ's and the Christian's final victory in heaven, on earth, and in the new heaven and the new earth. The Christian hope is explained, inflamed, and sustained by God's Word.

THE BENEFITS OF CHRISTIAN HOPE

Hope has lots of friends. It never lives alone. It comes with a happy company of other blessings and benefits. For example:

Hope Moves You Forward

The more you hope, the less you will reminisce. The more you long for the future, the less you will yearn for the past. Hope deletes regrets and underlines expectations. It diminishes drag and increases momentum.

Hope Energizes the Present

It is worth living today because tomorrow, the eternal tomorrow, is so much brighter. What's doomsday for most is coronation day for us. What most dread as *the end of time*, we desire as *the beginning of eternity*.

But our present-energizing hope is not just looking to the ultimate solutions in the eternal tomorrow. Our hope in God also calls us to look for temporary solutions in much nearer tomorrows. By that I mean that the Christian should have hope that God will help humanity solve many of this world's problems, just as He has in the past. Although the economist Julian Simon's survey of world history does not credit God's role, he does demonstrate that though society has serious short-term problems, we almost always find some kind of long-term solution. He wrote:

> Almost every economic and social change or trend points in the positive direction, as long as we view the matter over a reasonably long period of time. That is, all aspects of material human welfare are improving in the aggregate.[21]

Our problem is that we often see only the short-term problems but not the long-term solutions, which makes us more pessimistic than is warranted.

I can't for the life of me understand why so many preachers harangue their congregations with all the worst statistics while rarely mentioning any positive ones that show improvements in many areas. It is not only a prejudicial and damaging misrepresentation of God's work in God's world; it is also a huge demotivator and demoralizer. Cultivation of fear and anxiety may produce short-term attention and immediate responses, but over the long term, it disillusions and discourages.[22]

Hope Lightens Darkness

Hope does not deny or remove the reality of dark and painful providences. It shines a bright light into these valleys, however, and points to the sunrise at the end of them. But we don't need to wait until heaven for hope to pay off. There are emotional, spiritual, and even physical benefits in the here and now. Using new brain imagery techniques, scientists "are uncovering a host of biological mechanisms that can turn a thought, belief or desire into an agent of change in cells, tissues and organs. They are learning that much of human perception is based not on information flowing into the brain from the outside world but what the brain, based on previous experience, expects to happen next."[23] To put it simply, expecting an event can bring as much benefit as the event itself.

How much joy we are missing by not exercising hope!

Hope Increases Faith

Faith fuels hope, but hope also fuels faith. As Hebrews 11 makes clear, hope and faith are very closely tied together, the one enlivening the other. Without faith, we cannot soar in hope, but without hope, faith will limp home. The greatest believers are the greatest hopers and vice versa.

Hope Is Infectious

Just as we can drag others down by our recriminations and moping, so we can inspire and motivate through our inspirational hoping. It not only encourages other sagging Christians, but it also affects depressed unbelievers who cannot help but ask a reason for the hope they see in us.[24]

Hope Is Healing

When I counsel depressed people and their caregivers, one of the first things I do is try to give them hope. By definition, depression is a sense of hopelessness: things cannot and will not get better. That's why I want to give them the hope that in the vast majority of cases, they will get better, there is a way out, and there are things that they can do to help themselves in their felt helplessness. That hope itself is a huge step toward healing.

Dr. Hermann Nabi's research found that pessimism can undermine even our physical health. He found that a "low level of pessimism had a robust association with reduced incidence of stroke."[25] The Mayo Clinic website links high levels of negativity and pessimism with increases in mortality, depression, stress, and heart disease.[26]

Of course, pessimism is sometimes warranted and even healthy for us; we ignore warning signs at our peril. But many of us would get closer to health and balanced realism with less pessimism and greater optimism.

Hope Is Practical

Hope does not mean we just sit and wait for utopia to appear. Not at all! Hope motivates action. Research into optimism has found that "optimists set more goals (and more difficult goals) than pessimists, and put more effort into attaining those goals, stay more engaged in the face of difficulty, and rise above obstacles more easily."[27]

When we hope for better days for the church, we serve the church. When we hope for the conversion of our children, we are motivated to share the gospel with them. When we hope for God's blessing on His Word, we listen to it much more avidly. Hope produces action.

Hope Purifies

Whatever persecution we experience in this world, the day is coming when we will not be just *called* sons of God, we will be *like* the Son of God. This inspires and motivates us to persevere to the end and to persevere in holiness: "Everyone who has this hope in Him purifies himself, just as He is pure."[28]

Hope Broadens the Mind

Unlike negative emotions that tend to narrow people's outlook, potential, and possibilities, a positive emotion like hope broadens people's minds and especially the range of possible actions they can conceive of in any particular situation. Hope makes people more receptive to ideas and more creative about producing their own.[29] Scientists have found that students infused with a positive emotion such as hope literally see more; their peripheral vision is wider and sharper.[30]

Hope Stabilizes in the Storm

Researchers have discovered that optimists "cope better in high stress situations and are better able to maintain high levels of well-being during times of hardship."[31] Optimistic people seem to experience less pain and stress than their pessimistic peers and also tend to gain and grow more from trials.[32]

There are forty-five drawings of anchors in one of the Christian catacombs, the caves and tunnels where Christians hid during the Roman persecutions. Hope was their anchor during those terrible, dark storms.[33] Like the anchor, hope grabs what is out of sight. The cable of faith casts out the anchor of hope and lays hold of the steadfast rock of God's promises.

Hope Is Realistic

Norman Vincent Peale's idea of hope is founded on a denial of reality. In *The Power of Positive Thinking*, he wrote,

> Expect the best at all times. Never think of the worst. Drop it out of your thought, relegate it. Let there be no thought in your mind that the worst will happen. Avoid entertaining the concept of the worst, for whatever you take into your mind can grow there. Therefore take the best into your mind and only that. Nurture it, concentrate on it, emphasize it, visualize it, prayer-ize it, surround it with faith. Make it your obsession. Expect the best, and spiritually creative mind power aided by God power will produce the best.[34]

This is more like self-hypnotism than hope in God. Christian hope sees reality, faces it, feels it, accepts it, and yet rises above it on the wings of faith. The worst things do happen regardless of what we deny with our minds. Peale has no help for those who face real suffering and sorrow in their lives. But in his most extensive treatment of Christian hope, the apostle Paul describes the blessed duet of groaning in pain and soaring with hope.[35]

Hope Defends

Paul also depicts hope as a defensive helmet[36] that must not be taken off and laid aside until the battle is over. That image points us to the main area of vulnerability and danger—the mind or thoughts. That's the key area in building up hope, and it's to the mind we will turn in our conclusion. Hope defends our minds by helping us to hope, but biblical hope also protects by shielding us from unrealistic expectations. To put it bluntly, Christian hope is not the same as the American dream.

THE DEVELOPMENT OF CHRISTIAN HOPE

How do you develop and build Christian hope so that you are more oriented to the future than the past, so that you are moving forward in faith rather than loitering in the past and in unbelief?

First, *develop self-awareness*. You need to understand and measure to what extent you are looking backward as opposed to looking forward. Even in conversation with friends and family, consider how much conversation is over the shoulder rather than horizon scanning.

Second, when you realize how much you are looking backward, *wrestle your mind into a more forward-facing posture* as the psalmist does in Psalm 42. Challenge yourself, "Why am I dredging up the past? Why am I being so nostalgic? Trust in God, I shall yet praise Him." List the things you will yet do by God's grace rather than mourn over what you did or did not do.

Third, *fill your mind with God's promises*: promises to you, to the church, to the world. Use past fulfillments to assure you of future fulfillments.

Fourth, *practice baby-step hope*. Scientists distinguish little optimism and big optimism. Little optimism is specific and short term (e.g., my work will go well today). Big optimism is longer term and more general (I will enjoy eternal life with Jesus in heaven). Sonja Lyubomirsky explained, "Little optimism predisposes people to behave in constructive, healthy ways in specific situations (e.g., completing the next project at the office), whereas big optimism produces an overall feeling of vigor; it makes you feel resilient, strong, and energetic."[37]

Sometimes it is very difficult for us to take the huge leap of faith to the end of our lives and the hope of heaven. Big hope is too big! But we can exercise little hope, take smaller steps, exercise more local and short-term optimism in order to build the more heavenly eternal hope. Next time you're given a challenge, you face a difficulty, or you're asked to move out of your comfort zone, don't yield to despairing pessimism, such as, "I'll never manage that." Instead, focus on your God-given strengths and resources.

Stanford psychology professor Carol Dweck found that people who believe their abilities are fixed tend to stagnate and underperform, whereas those who believe they can improve their abilities usually perform well and continue to grow.[38]

If those without the Holy Spirit can grow and develop in this way, how much more should those of us with the additional help of the Holy Spirit to empower and enable us?

Fifth, *surround yourself with hopeful people*. As a pastor, I have visited many hopeless people, even Christians who have gotten waylaid into a mind-set of dark despair and bitterness about the past. I always try to visit one of my more optimistic members after that. I think of one older woman in particular who had more sufferings than most of us put together, and yet she always maintained a generous and happy spirit. She was one of the most heavenly minded women I ever met. I went to raise her spirits, and she invariably raised mine!

Sixth, *don't let your view of how the world will end drive your news diet.* Although some Christians believe the world is going to get better and better until there is a golden age for Christianity around the world, many Christians take a more pessimistic view of the end times, which in turn inclines them to pay more attention to pessimistic news items that confirm their beliefs.

Whatever our theology of the end times, let's make sure we balance our news diet in the meantime. If we don't, we can expect to suffer from spiritual and emotional anorexia.

Seventh, *share your hope by speaking of it to others.*[39] I'm sure you remember how excited you got as a child at Christmastime, and the more you talked about it, the more excited you became. Sometimes your parents had to stop the talk because you were getting so excited that you could hardly sleep. Imagine how much more expectant we would be if we talked about heaven more frequently and positively.

Finally, *motivate hope by grasping the huge benefits of hope.* Researcher Laura King asked a group of people to write their vision of their "best possible self." They were to visualize their best possible future in all their roles and relationships. Compared to other groups who wrote on other topics, this group was significantly happier in both the shorter and the longer term and even reported better physical health months later.[40]

Numerous studies have shown that hope improves decision making, motivation, academic outcomes, relationships, and goal setting.[41]

Again I ask, if that's what the Christ-less hope of unbelievers can do, how much more can the Christ-full hope of believers do?

Maybe you are surprised at how many times I've quoted unbelievers and called us to learn from them and excel them. Prepare to be further shocked, because I'm about to devote a whole chapter to the subject!

Chapter Six

HAPPY WORLD

EVERYWHERE GRACE > EVERYWHERE SIN
= POSITIVE+

WHAT DO YOU SEE when you look at your neighbor? Do you see his dodgy business dealings, his chaotic garage, his overgrown lawn, his marital tiffs, and his bad language?

Is that all you see? Is there nothing good you can think of?

What about the time he helped you start your car that icy morning? What about his devotion to his wife (despite their noisy arguments)? Or his kindness to your children? Or his heroic service in Operation Desert Storm?

Are these qualities not worth pondering and appreciating?

Now let's get in the SUV and go to your workplace. Right, what do you see there?

A barking boss, cheating colleagues, complaining customers, and unreliable computers?

Is that all you see? I know it is all you talk about when you come home every night. But are you seeing the whole picture? Is there no one with any skill, talent, or virtue? Does everyone treat everyone like dirt every day? Are there no kind words or actions in the staff room? Do the computers accomplish nothing? Do customers never express appreciation?

Seriously ask yourself, challenge yourself, are you seeing the whole picture? Or are you overlooking or ignoring a number of God-given benefits and blessings in your workplace?

DAMAGING AND DELIBERATE BLINDNESS

If I've just described you at home or at work, then you are closing your eyes, ears, and mind to the grace of God. This is not only a serious sin, but it is also incredibly damaging to you.

"Never!" you retort. "I deeply appreciate God's grace. I talk about it all the time. But these people and places are just sinful. They have no idea of God's grace. The people are lost and going to hell. The places are fallen, decaying, and destined for everlasting burning. I know God's grace when I see it, and it ain't anywhere to be found over the fence or in the factory."

I agree that such people and places are marred by sin and misery. Without salvation, they are doomed. And yet, I insist that you are choosing not to see the grace of God in these people and places. I'm not talking about God's *saving* grace, of course, but what is often called His *common* grace.

Saving grace is reserved for God's people alone and results in their salvation and sanctification. *Common* grace is experienced by everyone to one degree or another, and although this results in significant benefits and blessings in everyone's life, it neither saves nor sanctifies anyone.

Common grace includes all the gifts and blessings that God distributes to everyone (hence, common) and His restraining of evil in us and around us. All of that—the positive giving and the negative restraining—is grace because it is God dealing with His creatures in mercy, not justice. Professor John Murray put it this way: "Common grace is every favor of whatever kind or degree, falling short of salvation, which this undeserving and sin-cursed world enjoys at the hand of God."[1]

DENY OR DOWNPLAY SIN?

I don't want to deny or downplay sin and its terrible impact on our world and its people, on our neighbors and family. If all we see in these areas is sin and misery, however, we're closing our eyes to God's work of grace all over the world and all around us. Yes, God's common grace is really that common; it extends to all places and all people to some degree.

If we shut out common grace, we're also shutting down worship and joy, because the more we recognize God's common grace, the more we will worship God and the more joy we will have in our lives. Common grace produces common worship and common joy. It will change the way we look at everyone and every place. Instead of just looking for evidence of sin—usually not hard to find—we will also look for evidence of God's work and rejoice in it. We will be less suspicious and cynical, more open to beauty, and more enthusiastic to praise. We will appreciate God and His works.

It may sound more pious to focus only on the sin and lostness of people. But if we do that, if we exclude from view God's work in them, through them, and around them, we shutter our eyes to a beautiful part of God's daily work, and we miss an opportunity to worship Him for His gracious work.

That's the theme of Steve DeWitt's superb book, *Eyes Wide Open: Enjoying God in Everything.* His thesis is that as God created beauty, is the Beauty behind every beauty, and is the measure of what is truly beautiful, all created beauty should lead us to give thanks, honor, and worship to Him.[2]

With DeWitt, I want to pry open your eyes and your heart to

see and value God's common grace, but I want to start by renaming it. "Common" sounds so, well, common. It could be read and heard in a demeaning way, as if it is grace that's not worth much, cheap grace as it were. So let's call it "everywhere grace."

EVERYWHERE GRACE IS FOR ALL

Why doesn't the rain fall only on Christian farmers' fields? Why do the wicked enjoy vacations in Hawaii? God's everywhere grace: "He makes His sun rise on the evil and on the good, and sends rain on the just and on the unjust."[3]

Why do the evil have such full freezers, and why do the wicked have such happy times? God's everywhere grace that fills their hearts with food and gladness.[4]

God's everywhere grace is everywhere and experienced by everyone. Or to put it negatively, there is no one and no place on earth that is devoid of everywhere grace.[5]

That's not just true of the Grand Canyon, Niagara Falls, and the Scottish islands. Go to the most notorious high-security prison in Venezuela, go to North Korea's gulags, go to Al Qaeda training camps in Pakistan, and even there you'll find evidences of God's everywhere grace.

Find the most sadistic child abuser, the most disturbed serial killer, or the most monstrous terrorist, and you'll find everywhere grace somewhere in his life. You'll find traces of God's undeserved kindness. Even breath itself.

It is hard to see—the evil is so thick and dark that it almost envelops everything else—but awful though these places and people are, none of them are as bad as they possibly could be. As the apostle John said, the Lord "gives light" to every person who comes into the world.[6]

Even the most hardened criminals have some code of honor that draws the line somewhere in what they would or would not do. North Korean prison guards can still extend surprising mercy to their terrified captives. Al Qaeda operatives cook one another food and share funny stories around their campfires. These are only traces, the remaining vapors of God's everywhere grace, but if we can see it there and in these people, can we not more easily see it in our workplaces and in our bosses?

And even if for a time you cannot see God's everywhere grace in the people around you, what about the animals? Yes, God's everywhere grace extends to animals too. Why don't the animals tear one another to pieces until there's only one left? What can explain the affection of our dogs, the playfulness of our cats, and the cuteness of our hamsters? God's everywhere animal grace.

Of course, God's everywhere grace is not everywhere in the same proportions. God gives it according to His sovereign wisdom and power, and He chooses to give more of it to some people and places than to others. God may even give more of His everywhere grace to unbelievers than He does to believers who have experienced His special saving grace! That's why we sometimes find unbelievers who are kinder and nicer people than some Christians.

EVERYWHERE GRACE IS MOTIVATED BY LOVE

I decided not to rename this everywhere grace "love," because love does not necessarily include the idea of undeservedness. God's everywhere grace, however, is connected to His love. It flows from His heart of love toward His creatures and His creation.

Some Christians don't like the idea of God's common grace toward unbelievers because they say that *grace* is a word that applies only to Christians. They may allow us to speak of "God's restraining providence" that prevents the wicked from being as bad as they possibly could be. But they don't see anything positive in God's disposition or attitude to the unbeliever. They certainly don't want to speak of God having a love for anyone other than His own chosen people. They think that cheapens and weakens the idea of God's love. "How can God love those who are not Christians and may well never be Christians?"

When challenged to explain God's good gifts toward unbelievers, these Christians sometimes say that "God is fattening them for the slaughter" just like a farmer fattens turkeys for Thanksgiving by giving them good food. Hardly evidence of love!

Although the logic is impressive, the theology is wrong. Just because God has a special saving love for His people does not mean that He has no love of any kind or degree for unbelievers. I don't believe the Bible supports this idea of God coldly and callously feeding unbelievers simply to fatten them for slaughter. No, His acts of kindness and compassion toward them are motivated by a loving desire to do them good, demonstrate His goodness to them, and call them to Himself.[7]

When we are commanded to love our enemies by not only refraining from harming them but also by doing them good, we are to use God's loving relationship to His enemies as our pattern. In other words, we are to love them by blessing them, doing good to them, and praying for them. By doing this we will show that we are children of our Father and come closer to perfectly representing Him.[8] This biblical analogy is a far cry from God fattening people for slaughter.

That's not to say that God loves them with the same love He reserves for His people. But it is love nonetheless. Even though it is a lesser love, it is not a little love. God loves the unsaved more than we have ever loved anyone.

EVERYWHERE GRACE DOES NOT SAVE

Everywhere grace does much good to all who experience it. It enhances people's characters, lives, and surroundings. We can't imagine and don't want to think what we and our world would be like without it. All the happiness, joy, peace, contentment, and order in the world are the result of this almighty blessing. If it were not for God's everywhere grace filling our world day by day, our neighbors would turn into devils and our world into hell. The only reason we will not be robbed, raped, or murdered today is God's common, everywhere grace. How thankful we should be that even the worst leaders we've been given are not as bad as they could be.

And it's not just the externals—the outward person or the environment—that it impacts. It also influences the inner person, though without going so far as to save the soul. Everywhere grace imparts and stores up human virtues such as generosity, patience, and parental love. It exerts a moral influence, giving consciences a sense of right and wrong and stirring up guilt to restrain further sin. It works on the heart, although it does not renew or regenerate it. More grace is needed for that. Or rather a different kind of grace is needed—the special, sovereign, and saving love of God.

We mustn't separate these two kinds of grace entirely. No, they are intimately connected. The one should lead to the other. Everywhere grace is given to lead people to seek God's special saving grace. So much everywhere grace is given that it leaves us without excuse for not seeking special saving grace.[9]

Everywhere grace is intended to draw us and call us to the special grace that's located only in Christ. Paul challenged all recipients of everywhere grace: "Do you despise the riches of His goodness, forbearance, and longsuffering, not knowing that the goodness of God leads you to repentance?"[10]

Do you see that? One of the most powerful tools in our

evangelistic armory is the goodness of God. If we tell people only about their sin and refuse to point out God's mercy and grace in their lives, we are missing out on a vital evangelistic lever. By highlighting God's existing mercy, we encourage sinners to seek even more mercy.[11] And if they don't, they are without excuse.[12]

Everywhere grace does not save, but it does point us to the One who does.

EVERYWHERE GRACE PRODUCES WORSHIP

Worship need not be confined to our private devotions and our corporate worship. Yes, these are the times when we should expect to see the character of the Lord and bow before Him with joyful and reverent praise. We can see traces of the Lord's character in all of His creation, however, especially in the apex of His creation, humanity. As Steve DeWitt wrote, "Each human person individually bears more of a reflection of God than the rest of the universe combined."[13]

When we see *beauty*, even if it is on the easel of an unbelieving artist, in the writing of an unconverted novelist, or in the face of a supermodel, we trace it to the Beautiful One and worship Him.

When we see *power*, even when exercised by a non-Christian president, even when bursting out of the biceps of an atheist weight lifter, or even when seen in the legs of a leopard, we trace it to the Powerful One and worship Him.

When we see *wisdom*, even when it is displayed by an atheist journalist, a Muslim neighbor, or an unbelieving lecturer, we trace it to the Wise One and worship Him.

When we see *love*, even in imperfect relationships, in our unbelieving children, or in the soldier sacrificing his life for his friends, we trace it to the One who is love and worship Him.

When we see *loyalty*, even in a twenty-five-year employee, even in the patriotism of the French, or even in that of a dog to his master, we trace it to the covenant faithfulness and unbreakable loyalty of the Faithful and Loyal One and worship Him.

When we see *patience*, even in most of the drivers stuck in the same traffic lane, in the irreligious nurse, or in the hardware store employee as he deals with our stupid questions, we trace it to the One who is powerfully patient and worship Him.

When we see *humility* in the service of the street sweeper, the toilet cleaner, or the garbage gatherer, we remember the humble service of the One who came not to be served but to serve and give His life a ransom for many.

When we see *mercy, truthfulness, creativity, diligence*, or whatever other virtue, wherever we see it, we use it to rise up to its ultimate source and worship Him. These everywhere graces reveal so much about our everywhere God.

Steve DeWitt described nature as God's self-portrait: "God creates beauty so we can know what He is like."[14] God made every-thing—"every atom, every grain of sand, every bird, every water molecule," every person (including you)—as a reflection of His nature.[15]

The temptation is to take it for granted, to overlook it, to take no notice of it, or even to attribute it to the person rather than to God. But that's not what the psalmist did. He deliberately opened his eyes and sought out evidences of God's everywhere grace, and wherever he found it—in the fields, in the sky, in the seasons, in the animals, in people, and even in military victories—he turned that everywhere grace to God's everywhere glory in celebratory praises and humble worship.[16] Again, Steve DeWitt put it beautifully: "Since everything God created is theology (God-knowledge), all creation is a treasure hunt in which God has left clues—essentially pictures of Himself. . . . Like a bread-crumb trail, earthly beauty chaperones us on a path to 'see' the beauty of Christ, for His beauty to lead to wonder, and for wonder to lead us to a life of worship."[17]

EVERYWHERE GRACE IS FOR THE
GOOD OF THE CHURCH

What if God's everywhere grace is successfully resisted? What if those who receive it refuse to respond to it and seek God's saving grace? Has it failed? Was it pointless?

Not at all, although God's everywhere grace calls sinners to Himself and leaves them without excuse or defense if they fail to respond, the primary purpose of everywhere grace is the good of the church. God blesses everyone and everywhere for the sake of His people. All the gifts and graces we see in the world are to assist and advance the church in its work and witness. As we read in Genesis 39:5, "The LORD blessed the Egyptian's house for Joseph's sake."

God blesses the world for the benefit of the church and every Christian in it. His multiple varied blessings of industry, business, government, science, friendship, art, food, music, water, seasons, talents and gifts, conscience, courts, medication, air conditioning, and more are ultimately working together for the good of those who love Him.

That's why we shouldn't be ashamed to use non-Christians for goods and services. Sometimes Christians and churches may decide to buy a certain good or service from a company simply because it is a Christian company. The product or service may not be the best, but it has a Christian owner. That's faulty thinking, thinking that results from failing to understand God's everywhere grace. If God has enabled a non-Christian to make the best product or provide the most efficient service, we should gladly buy from him or her and regard it as God's grace to that person and to us.

Another area of confusion is when the church refuses to accept and use truth simply because it has been discovered by non-Christians. Take, for example, the area of counseling people with depression. There is much that we can do as Christians to minister to them. God has given us so much suitable truth in His Word to help the downcast. But He has also allowed non-Christians to discover truth in nature that can help such sufferers. To reject this help is to reject God's everywhere grace. As one of the Reformers said:

> If we regard the Spirit of God as the sole foundation of truth, we shall neither reject the truth itself, nor despise it wherever it shall appear, unless we wish to dishonor the Spirit of God. Shall we say that the philosophers were blind in their fine observation and artful description of nature? . . . No, we cannot read the writings of the ancients on these subjects without great admiration. But if the Lord has willed that we be helped in physics, dialectic, mathematics, and other like disciplines, by the work and ministry of the ungodly, let us use this assistance. For if we neglect God's gift freely offered in these arts, we ought to suffer just punishment for our sloths.[18]

Everywhere grace can help us fill out some of the details of the general principles that God gives us in His Word. Take eating, for example. The Bible has explicit instructions on eating and principles that we can deduce. But the Bible does not tell us all we need to know about eating. So we learn from nutritionists (even non-Christian, evolutionary nutritionists) about how to eat in ways that will improve our physical, mental, emotional, and, therefore, spiritual well-being. We read this knowledge through the lens of the Bible because the Bible is sufficient to keep us from falling into error as we read this world. Theologian Herman Bavinck said,

> The Christian, who sees everything in the light of the Word of God, is anything but narrow in his view. He is generous in heart and mind. He looks over the whole earth and reckons it all his own, because he is Christ's and Christ is God's (1 Cor. 3:21–23). He cannot let go his belief that the revelation of God in Christ, to which he owes his life and salvation, has a special character. This belief does not exclude him from the world, but rather puts him in position to trace out the revelation of God in nature and history, and puts the means at his disposal by which he can recognize the true and the good and the beautiful and separate them from the false and sinful alloys of men.[19]

Everywhere grace also prepares people to be messengers of grace. Just as God used the apostle Paul's pre-Christian education in Tarsus and Jerusalem to make him a better preacher of saving grace, so God prepares us for unique ministries and service by giving us unique pre-Christian backgrounds, experiences, and training.

EVERYWHERE GRACE USUALLY USES MEANS

God sometimes bestows everywhere grace by direct interventions to do good or restrain sin. God usually, however, uses means. For example, He uses creation to remind His creatures of His existence and some of His attributes.[20]

God uses providential events such as storms, tsunamis, and

earthquakes to remind us that there is a Judge and we shall have to deal with Him one day.

He also gives and sharpens human conscience so that even those who have never read the Bible know what is right and wrong and that they will be judged for their moral choices.[21]

The existence of the Bible, the church, the weekly Lord's Day, and the presence of Christians also restrains sin and cultivates outward morality and civility in the wider populace, though such changes stop short of salvation.

God ordains civil government to punish evil and encourage good and also raises up specific leaders at special times to fulfill His will, even though they may not know or acknowledge Him.[22] He gives life to them and gives them certain helpful and beneficial gifts, abilities, and characteristics that will be a blessing to the world and the church.

Another reason that people do good is the God-given internal motivation to help others, sometimes called "altruism." Think, for example, of all that Bill and Melinda Gates have done through the Gates Foundation: promoting vaccination programs in Africa, funding AIDS research, reducing polio and malaria, and sponsoring many other charitable projects. Of course, many much smaller acts of altruism are unpublicized every day as everyday people express everyday love to their neighbors.

Even the God-given instinct to create and explore is harnessed by God to bless His world. Although since his death, we have discovered some of the more unsavory aspects of Steve Jobs's character and business practices, his drive, ambition, and perfectionism motivated many of his employees to amazing heights of imagination and innovation. In doing so, he transformed personal computing, the music industry, cell phones, and digital animation.

Public opinion, education, security cameras, competition, democracy, Apple, and Microsoft are gifts of God and tools in His hands for establishing order, inculcating responsibility, pursuing excellence, helping charities, alleviating suffering, and encouraging diligence in daily duties.

EYES WIDER OPEN

We cannot deny the terrible damage that sin has wrought in our world and our lives. When we obsess over how bad things are, however, we tend to deny or ignore the everywhere grace of God in every part of the world and in every life, resulting in pessimism and even depression. There is no excuse for this, as Martin Seligman underlined:

> You have to be blinded by ideology not to see that almost everything is better in every wealthy nation than it was fifty years ago: we now have about three times more actual purchasing power in the United States. The average house has doubled in size from 1,200 square feet to 2,500 square feet. In 1950 there was one car for every two drivers; now there are more cars than licensed drivers. One out of five children went on to post–high school education; now one out of two children does. Clothes—and even people—seem to look more physically attractive. Progress has not been limited to the material: there is more music, more women's rights, less racism, more entertainment, and more books. If you had told my parents, living in a 1,200-square-foot house with me and Beth, my older sister, that all this would obtain in only fifty years, they would have said, "That will be paradise."[23]

And yet "the average American, Japanese, and Australian is no more satisfied with life than fifty years ago, and the average Brit and German is less satisfied."[24] I'm pretty confident that Christian satisfaction and happiness have plunged even more.

The opposite should be the case. The Christian should see far more beauty in the world than the non-Christian. Steve DeWitt argued that if we love [Christ], we will love "seeing Him in all the created wonders in this world."[25] He added, "Once our heart is alive to God's beauty in Christ, it is also alive to God's beauty everywhere else."[26] DeWitt urged us to stimulate our physical senses to improve our spiritual senses: "All our senses [should] become partners with the eyes of the heart in perceiving the glory of God through the physical world. . . . Everywhere I look, everything I feel, hear, smell, and taste transmits the beauty of God through the beauty of creation."[27]

Let's join Clyde Kilby, a friend of C. S. Lewis and J. R. R. Tolkien, who resolved:

- At least once every day I shall look steadily up at the sky and remember that I, a consciousness with a conscience, am on a planet traveling in space with wonderfully mysterious things above and about me.
- Instead of the accustomed idea of a mindless and endless evolutionary change to which we can neither add nor subtract, I shall suppose the universe guided by an Intelligence which, as Aristotle said of Greek drama, requires a beginning, a middle, and an end. I think this will save me from the cynicism expressed by Bertrand Russell before his death, when he said: "There is darkness without, and when I die there will be darkness within. There is no splendor, no vastness anywhere, only triviality for a moment, and then nothing."
- I shall open my eyes and ears. Once every day I shall simply stare at a tree, a flower, a cloud, or a person. I shall not then

be concerned at all to ask *what* they are but simply be glad that they are. I shall joyfully allow them the mystery of what Lewis calls their "divine, magical, terrifying and ecstatic" existence.[28]

I'm not asking you to close your eyes to human sin; that is everywhere, sad to say. I am asking you to open your eyes wider to God's grace that is beautifully everywhere. Steve DeWitt stated, "Beauty is beautiful, no matter who makes it."[29]

Without ignoring or belittling sin and its effects, let's use everywhere grace to rebalance our view of the world and enable us to locate and celebrate God's good gifts in it as never before, resulting in joy in our hearts and praise to our gracious God. And speaking of praise, let's now consider the multiple benefits of praising one another a bit more.

Chapter Seven

HAPPY PRAISE

PRAISE > CRITICISM = POSITIVE+

I'M A SCOT, AND Scots don't do praise. Of God sometimes, but never praise of one another.

Instead, we specialize in pulling people down, thinking the worst of others, and puncturing anyone who achieves anything. We can't let a compliment pass without balancing it with criticism, and woe betide people who make anything of their lives: "They're just full of themselves!"

Where did this come from? Well, there's no question that the cynical "build 'em up to pull 'em down" media is partly to blame. The evil envy of rabid and rampant socialism has also eaten away at much goodwill and gratitude toward achievement and achievers. But I'm afraid that a distorted theology of sin has also contributed to this soul-shriveling cynicism.

AMERICAN CONTRAST

I didn't see it so clearly when I was part of it, but with the distance of seven years in the USA between me and my homeland, it is painfully easy to recognize and grieve over. Perhaps it is especially the contrast of now living happily in America that's helped me identify this Scottish ailment and my contribution to it. If there's one thing most people think about Americans, it is that they are probably the most optimistic and cheerful people in the world.

True, this warm openness can sometimes lapse into gullibility: witness Jimmy Swaggart, Benny Hinn, Enron, Lehman Brothers, and so on! They wouldn't have gotten very far in Scotland, I can assure you. There's something so refreshing about the American desire to think the best, say the best, and do the best to others. The cheerful celebration of success and the willingness to offer encouragement and praise are such a contrast to so much of Scottish life, yes, even Scottish church life.

DISTORTED CALVINISM

But why did I partly blame a distorted theology of sin for this? Well, the biblical belief in the sinfulness of all men and women seems to have been sometimes misapplied to exclude any appreciation of humanity, even redeemed humanity. "Don't want to make him/her/them proud, do we!" Praise, encouragement, appreciation, and affirmation are somehow thought to be incompatible with a belief in the universal sinfulness of men and women. To praise is to apostatize; to encourage is to backslide; to recognize achievement is to risk the damnation of the achiever.

If someone is praised, get a criticism in quickly. If someone does well, remind him and everyone else of his previous failures. If someone gets a promotion, "Well, what goes up must come down (we hope)." There are happy Scottish exceptions, of course, but the corrosive effects of this negative spirit are wide and deep and still plague me too.

PRACTICING PRAISE

That's why I found Sam Crabtree's *Practicing Affirmation*[1] so challenging and yet so helpful. I'm amazed that this book has not had much wider acclaim. As John Piper wrote in the foreword, it is a "one-of-a-kind book." Do you know of any other book that deals with the subject of how to praise others and to do so as a habit of life? No, neither do I. Yet, as the book demonstrates, it is a topic with lots of scriptural support and explanation, together with huge consequences for our families, friendships, and fellowships. Although I think a Scot like me needs to practice affirmation far more than Americans, there's no question that American Christians increasingly need it too.

Worrying Trends

I say that because among other worrying recent trends in America, I'm afraid that the celebration of good is weakening, and a cynical critical spirit is spreading. I can't say for sure where this has come from, but the inundation of bad news at home and abroad, the hostile hate-filled political climate, unjust corporate rewards, and some politicians' regular planting and cultivating of class and economic envy are all playing their heart-chilling, soul-shrinking roles. The overemphasis on building self-esteem in secular counseling has also caused an overreaction in some Christians so that they are afraid of saying anything positive to anyone.

So, let me help you implement *Practicing Affirmation*, by giving you ten encouragements to become a better encourager.

TEN ENCOURAGEMENTS TO ENCOURAGE

Encouragers Imitate God

God praises people. Far-from-perfect people. Sinful people.

Amazing, isn't it? There may be bad things in their past, their present, or their future, and yet God praises them and inspired the biblical authors to record that praise.

> NOAH: "You are righteous before Me in this generation."[2]
> JOB: "There is none like him on the earth, a blameless and upright man, one who fears God and shuns evil."[3]
> ROMAN CENTURION: "I have not found such great faith, not even in Israel!"[4]
> NATHANAEL: "Behold, an Israelite indeed, in whom is no deceit!"[5]
> CANAANITE WOMAN: "O woman, great is your faith!"[6]

Part of being perfect as our Father in heaven is perfect[7] is imitating Him in verbally affirming others.

Jessica Colman identified four possible responses to someone who shares good news with us:[8]

> ACTIVE CONSTRUCTIVE: We share the happiness of the person telling the news and respond enthusiastically by asking for more details and by helping her savor the news. Example: "Fantastic! I'm so pleased to hear that. I'm looking forward to hearing more about that."
> PASSIVE CONSTRUCTIVE: The response is supportive but quiet and understated rather than excited and interested. Example: "That's quite nice."
> ACTIVE DESTRUCTIVE: The responder diminishes the person or the news with critical and pessimistic comments. Example: "That won't work. Have you considered the downsides?"
> PASSIVE DESTRUCTIVE: The response ignores the news completely and overlooks the person's feelings. Example:

"Well, whatever. . . . You'll never believe what happened to me today."

God is an active, constructive responder! And so should we be.

Encouragers Glorify God

One reason why we are so reluctant to praise someone else is that we're afraid of robbing God of glory. We somehow think that more praise for a man or woman means less praise for God. That's a mistake because God is glorified when we recognize and highlight the work He is doing in other people. In fact, as Sam Crabtree says, "We rob God of praise by not pointing out his reflection in the people he has knit together in his image."[9]

But there is a way of doing this to maximize the glory God gets from His good work in others. Notice the way the apostle Paul did it: "I thank my God through Jesus Christ for you all, that your faith is spoken of throughout the whole world."[10] The Romans are encouraged, and God gets the glory. Crabtree calls these "God-centered thank-you's."[11]

Pastor Erik Raymond recommended that pastors collect God-glorifying encouragements:

In order to help myself to be cognizant of God's continued work of grace in his church, I have created a label in my Gmail account entitled "Pastoral Encouragement." This label functions like a folder in many other inbox systems. It is a drawer, if you will, where I can keep these snapshots of gracious encouragement. Inside of this label there may be direct notes to me but there are also various observations or instances when people are thinking or acting biblically. This is good for my soul. I strongly encourage pastors to do similarly. This helps you to be reminded of God's continued work of grace, your weakness, the fact that you labor for souls, and it shows true evidence of grace in your congregation. This will likewise serve to drive you to Christ, the head of the church.[12]

Encouragers Don't Wait for Salvation

"But what about the unsaved? Surely if we praise them for anything, they may think they're not sinners and therefore have no need of salvation."

I understand the soul concern behind this question, especially in our nonjudgmental, hypertolerant secular education system, where students are very rarely reminded of their flaws and failings. Surely we don't want to add to this problem of deceiving people that all is well with their souls?

No, of course, we don't want to deceive anyone about the reality of spiritual need and danger. And yet, neither can we allow the world's extreme to push us off the biblical balance. Just because the world rarely criticizes doesn't mean that we rarely praise just to balance out the error. Our standard, our measure, is the Bible, which encourages us to trace God's work, even in the lives of unbelievers. Sam Crabtree explained, "In the same way that Yellowstone Park is a reflection of common grace, unregenerate persons reflect graces not intrinsic to themselves. To affirm the beauty of their character is to draw attention to the undeserved grace that God has bestowed upon them in the form of faint echoes of Jesus, even in the presence of as-of-yet unperfected flaws in those same individuals."[13]

Encouragers Don't Wait for Perfection

One day Barnabas walked into a messy church plant situation in Antioch, immediately pinpointed what was wrong, and started to fix it without delay. Is that in your Bible? It is not in mine. Instead I read, "When he came and had seen the grace of God, he was glad, and encouraged them all that with purpose of heart they should continue with the Lord."[14]

I don't believe Barnabas was simply a spin doctor, putting his finest gloss on what he really saw and thought. He was absolutely genuine. He didn't see imperfection. He saw progress; he saw growth; he saw increase. What an example to us, not only in our view of our church and other churches, but perhaps especially in dealing with our children. If we wait until they are perfect before we praise them, we will never praise them.

Next time your son saves money rather than spends it recklessly, why not say to him, "Well done, Joe. God helped you resist the temptation to splurge and gave you the self-discipline to save the money for something really worthwhile." This way, "while the child's growth in character is commended, God is identified as the source."[15] By noticing and praising such choices, we increase the chance of their happening again. Sam Crabtree was clear: "Affirmation is not about lowering standards. It is about commending incremental progress toward those standards as those standards reflect the character of Christ."[16]

But won't that build up a person's self-esteem? It might, but what's so bad about that? There is a biblical and truthful self-esteem. In a wonderful little book, *Overcoming Spiritual Depression*, Arie Elshout commented:

> It is wrong to pat ourselves on the back when something has been accomplished as a result of our initiative. It is equally wrong, however, to focus on what we have not accomplished. In 1 Corinthians 15:10 we have a clear example of humility accompanied with a healthy opinion of one's accomplishments: "But by the grace of God I am what I am: and his grace which was bestowed upon me was not in vain; but I labored more abundantly than they all: yet not I, but the grace of God which was

with me." Paul knew very well that he daily offended in many things (James 3:2; cf. Rom. 7; Phil. 3:12), and yet he did not go so far as to cast out all his accomplishments. I do not believe that this is God's will. In contrast to sinful forms of self-confidence and self-respect, there are also those that are good, necessary, and useful. Without a healthy sense of these, human beings cannot function well. We may pray for an appropriate sense of self-confidence and self-respect, clothed in true humility, and we must oppose everything that impedes a healthy development of these things (be it in ourselves or others) with the Word of God.[17]

Encouragers Open the Door to Change

Far from discouraging change, encouraging the less-than-perfect actually maximizes the chances of their continuing to progress. Just recall who helped you learn at school or make progress in sports. They were the teachers and coaches who praised and encouraged you, weren't they? Praise opens our ears and pushes us through the pain barrier. Studies have shown that "enhancing patients' expectations through positive information about the treatment or the illness, while providing support or reassurance, significantly influenced health outcomes."[18]

One way that bosses try to help their employees improve is to conduct a 360 where everyone in a person's circle is asked to list his failings. Often, the criticism is so overwhelming that paralysis rather than transformation is the result. Martin Seligman suggested an alternative 360 that he called "Appreciative Inquiry." He explained, "Merciless criticism often makes us dig in our heels in defense, or worse, makes us helpless. We don't change. We do change, however, when we discover what is best about ourselves and when we see specific ways to use our strengths more. I go into large organizations and get the whole workforce focused on what it is doing well. They detail the strengths of the corporation and tell stories about their coworkers at their very best."[19]

The University of Michigan has developed its own Positive 360.[20] Why don't you or your church do the same? It might change the most unchangeable.

Encouragers Help Evangelism

When most young people are asked today why they left the church or why they don't go to church, most of them identify judgmentalism. The church does not take its agenda from young people, and part of the church's mission is to announce the judgment of God on sin. What many of these young people identify, however, is that the church seems at times to be *only* about judgment, *only* about critique, *only* about condemnation.

Why do you think Barnabas was so eminently useful in the early church? His gift of encouragement was so helpful in evangelism. His good news spirit helped the good news get a hearing. Sam Crabtree warned, "Consider this: we risk damning others by not praising them. There are people around us in peril of hell unless we commend them. . . . Affirmation is a way to gain a hearing for the gospel. . . . Our listeners will be more inclined to hear us if they believe we're not angry at them, but grateful for them."[21]

We're not talking here about manipulative, televangelist-style flattery, but genuine, heartfelt appreciation. Which brings us to . . .

Encouragers Are Honest

Honest encouragers praise only the praiseworthy, not the blameworthy. Honest encouragers praise proportionately, not exaggeratedly; they give bronze praise to bronze achievements and gold to gold standards. Honest encouragers praise simply because the person is praiseworthy. They do not praise to get something out of the person or to prepare for giving something bad to her, such as criticism.

We'll return to offering criticism later in this chapter, but Sam Crabtree is especially hard on "the sandwich method," the correction strategy that puts every criticism between two slices of praise. Sam describes the manager who used the sandwich method so much that employees began to dread hearing any praise because they knew what he was about to fill the sandwich with. Although he boasted about his method, his employees eventually called it "the baloney sandwich!" Sam urged, "Let affirmations stand alone, separated from correction. . . . [C]orrection packaged with the affirmation will contaminate and weaken the affirmation, perhaps making it altogether fruitless. . . . Corrections tend to cancel affirmations, and the closer the proximity to correction, the more crippled the affirmation."[22] Sam argued against that close proximity of correction to affirmation. In its place he proposed a much longer-term context of loving affirmation as the necessary backdrop to any loving correction.

Encouragers Strengthen

The root meaning of the verb *to encourage* is "to strengthen."[23] That's what encouragement does. It builds emotional, mental, relational, and even vocational muscle, as Shawn Achor highlighted in *The Happiness Advantage*:

- Managers who recognize and encourage their employees see increased productivity.
- The U.S. Navy squadrons that won the most prizes for efficiency and preparedness were those with the most encouraging commanding officers.
- The ideal ratio for positive to negative interactions for a successful team is 6 to 1.[24]

Encouragement even improves people's physical health! In *Be Excellent at Anything*, Tony Schwartz cites research that shows how workers who felt unfairly criticized by a boss or felt they had a boss who didn't listen to their concerns had a 30 percent higher rate of coronary disease than those who felt treated fairly and with care![25]

In a study published in the *Journal of Research in Personality*, forty-five undergraduate students wrote about an intensely positive experience each day for three consecutive days. The second group wrote about a control topic. Three months later, the students who wrote about positive experiences had better mood levels, made fewer visits to the health center, and experienced fewer illnesses.[26]

On the relational side, Shawn Achor encouraged managers to write one encouraging e-mail to someone before they start work each day, not only to make the managers happier but also to strengthen that relationship and to motivate similar behavior in the recipient.[27] Or to put it more bluntly, "Geese honk encouragement and fly in formation. Skunks travel alone."

We see this relational strengthening in Barnabas, too, as he gave people the benefit of the doubt and drew them into ministry.[28] Encouraging people is one of the best ways for a pastor to build relationships in his church and strengthen the church overall.

Just think of how you could strengthen a family member or a fellow believer by helping her identify one of her strengths or gifts and encouraging her to exercise that gift.

We need to learn the language of positive emotions, which, like all new languages, may initially feel awkward, embarrassing, and uncomfortable. Author and business leader Tony Schwartz said, "Heartfelt appreciation is a muscle we've not spent much time building, or felt encouraged to build. Oddly, we're often more experienced at expressing negative emotions—reactively and defensively, and often without recognizing their corrosive impact on others until much later, if we do at all."[29]

As we've already seen, there are four different ways that people respond to good news from others, but only one response is a relationship strengthener. Active and constructive responders build better relationships and have less conflict and greater fun in their marriages. Studies indicate that positive emotional exchanges are "the foundation on which stable and satisfying relationships rest."[30]

As King Solomon observed, encouraging others will also strengthen the encourager: "The generous soul will be made rich, / And he who waters will also be watered himself."[31] Sam Crabtree called this "the boomerang effect,"[32] which also explains C. S. Lewis's observation: "I had not noticed how the humblest, and at the same time most balanced and capacious, minds, praised most, while the cranks, misfits and malcontents praised least."[33]

Encouragers Go Public

It is good to praise individuals privately. But from time to time we should do so publicly as well. Building an open and transparent pattern of public encouragement will, one hopes, "infect" others and spread the habit. That was the regular apostolic practice: "After the uproar ceased, Paul sent for the disciples, and after *encouraging* them, he said farewell and departed for Macedonia. When he had gone through those regions and had given them much *encouragement*, he came to Greece."[34]

One way to improve our encouraging skill set is to be more specific. Martin Seligman, who has been hired by the US military to improve the army's leadership skills, highlights this enhanced encouragement technique: "We teach the sergeants to praise the specific skills as opposed to a vague 'Way to go!' or 'Good job!' Praising the details demonstrates to their soldier (a) that the leader was really watching, (b) that the leader took the time to see exactly what the soldier did, and (c) that the praise is authentic, as opposed to a perfunctory 'Good job.'"[35]

Encouragers Are Disciplined

But what if I'm naturally more critical? What if I'm not a natural encourager like Barnabas? Well, it can be learned. Yes, like almost everything else, it is a skill that, with God's help, can be grown and developed by disciplined practice until it becomes natural. That was author and pastor Tim Challies's experience:

> One day it occurred to me that I was going to have to *discipline* myself to encourage others. And so I took the strange and seemingly-artificial step of calendaring time to encourage others. It sounds strange, I know, but I opened up my calendar and created a 5-minute appointment recurring every three days. The appointment simply said "Encourage!" And so, every third day, while I was hard at work, a little reminder would flash up on my screen. "Encourage!," it said. And I would. I would take the opportunity to quickly phone a friend or dash off an email to someone I felt was in need of encouragement. This felt very artificial. I felt like a fraud as I, with a heart of discouragement, attempted to be an encouragement to others. But as time went on, it began to become quite natural. I soon found that I no longer felt the same spirit of discouragement within me. Encouragement slowly became more natural. What had begun as a discipline that felt artificial, soon became a habit that felt natural.[36]

Contrary Voices

"But, but, but," I can hear other voices saying, "'those who are in the flesh cannot please God' (Rom. 8:8)." Is not even "the plowing of the wicked" sin (Prov. 21:4)? Does not the wrath of God rest on the unbeliever (John 3:36)? And what about "there is none who does good, / no, not one" (Rom. 3:12)?

If all that is true, what's the point in praising and affirming unbelievers? Is that not like admiring a car's shiny paint job as it heads over the cliff? "Jump, run, escape for your life" seem more appropriate.

So how do we balance on this biblical knife-edge? We don't want to fall off on the side of encouraging unbelievers in pharisaical self-righteousness. But neither do we want to treat all unbelievers as if they were Hannibal Lecter. Here's a quick guide to walking the knife:

- We should recognize God's work/image wherever it appears, even in the life of an unbeliever.
- We should trace all good to God and encourage unbelievers to see any good, any progress, any improvement as the gift of God.
- We should regularly remind unbelievers that although it is good to be/do good (at least it is better than being/doing evil), that's not good enough. They need to be born again; they need to repent and believe the gospel.
- The best good works, even the best believer's best works, are full of imperfection and weakness and need to be repented of.
- We should sometimes remind unbelievers that our commendations and affirmations are only from a human perspective. God's view may be very different, and at the end of the day His view is the only one that matters.

The Westminster Confession of Faith summarizes the Bible's teaching about this as follows: "Works done by unregenerate men, although for the matter of them they may be things which God commands; and of good use both to themselves and others: yet, because they proceed not from an heart purified by faith; nor are done in a right manner, according to the Word; nor to a right end, the glory of God, they are therefore sinful and cannot please God, or make a man meet to receive grace from God: and yet, their neglect of them is more sinful and displeasing unto God."[37]

In answer to the question "Should we praise unbelievers?" Yes, but make sure it is regularly set in a wider law/gospel context that stirs the unbeliever to seek the only One who is good: God.[38]

And if you needed any further encouragement to be an encourager, you'll discover that as you encourage others, you will be encouraged; as you strengthen others, you will be strengthened; as you make others happier you, too, will be happier.

CONSTRUCTIVE CRITICISM

And what about when we have to be the skunk? What about the place of correction and rebuke? It certainly has a place, especially in a world so full of sin. But what is its place? Done rightly it, too, can increase happiness for the critic and the criticized.

It Is Preceded by Praise

As already discussed, I don't believe in the sandwich principle that says you must put a slice of praise before and after every criticism. That tends to devalue the praise. I do believe, however, that for criticism to have any hope of accomplishing anything, it should be set in the wider context of praise. There should be praise in the bank before we start drawing down with any criticisms.

It Is Infrequent

Some people think that a little bit of praise sprinkled here and there permits them to launch frequent nuclear missiles at their unfortunate targets. "But I praised you last year!" Positive psychologists recommend a praise-criticism ratio of at least 3:1 and ideally closer to 5:1. But when relationships get to that healthy point, no one is counting!

It Is Limited

Effective criticism aims at one specific target and refuses to take potshots at anything else. "And while we're at it, let me tell you . . ." Please don't.

In the article "Bad Is Stronger Than Good," Robert Sutton argued that it is more important to limit and reduce the negative than boost the positive. He referenced Roy Baumeister's classic paper of the same name, which found: "Bad emotions, bad parents, and bad feedback have more impact than good ones, and bad information is processed more thoroughly than good. Bad impressions and bad stereotypes are quicker to form and more resistant to disconfirmation than good ones."[39]

Sutton then applied these findings to marriage: Scary, isn't it? Yet it was confirmed by several studies that, among relationships where the proportion of negative interactions exceeds this one-in-five rule, divorce rates go way up and marital satisfaction goes way down. The implication for all of us in long-term relationships is both instructive and daunting: If you have a bad interaction with your partner, following up with a positive one (or apparently two, three, or four) won't be enough to dig out of that hole. Average five or more and you might stay in his or her good graces.[40]

Sutton then turns to business and calls employers to remove bad apples, toxic colleagues, deadbeats (withholders of effort), downers, and de-energizers (those who always express pessimism, anxiety, insecurity, and irritation).

In some ways the church is to be a haven for bad apples, toxic colleagues, deadbeats, downers, and de-energizers (the disciples spring to mind). The challenge is to transform such (as Jesus so clearly did). And there is no greater power on earth to accomplish this than grace: "Where sin abounded, grace abounded much more."[41]

It Majors on Majors

If you're going to criticize every fault and failing of everyone around you, you're going to be very busy and lonely. We live in a sinful world. The best of us are full of flaws. We simply must learn to overlook minor faults in others—not talk about them to other people and, if possible, not even think about them. Save your critical energy for worthy targets. That way you'll help yourself and others.

It Is Supported by Evidence

Make sure that you're criticizing what God criticizes, that you're not basing everything on your preferences or prejudices. Also, can you prove it? Can you point to evidence to support your criticism? Are "I think . . ." and "I feel . . ." and "I suspect . . ." the best you've got? Then let it go.

Its Aim Is Building, Not Demolishing

All criticism involves some element of demolition. There is wrong conduct to be torn down or wrong beliefs to be razed. But the ultimate aim is to build something better, even beautiful, in its place. If our motive is to leave a person's life in smoldering ruins, we are doing the Devil's work. But if our aim is a better person, a stronger person, a more mature person, we are in the business of *constructive* criticism.

It Is Prayerfully Considered

It is so easy to spout an ill-considered or unconsidered criticism in response to an immediate event or conversation. That will rarely accomplish anything beneficial and usually will result in a shouting (or crying) match. No matter how tempting, it is almost always advisable to take at least twenty-four hours and to pray over it. That should help purify the motive, identify the best target, and dampen the emotions. Which brings us to . . .

It Is Dispassionate

This is probably my greatest weakness in this area. I find it hard to be calm and cool about things I'm disappointed or angry about. People can tell from my red face, my tense voice, and my shaky hands. Not surprisingly, their defenses go up, as does their temperature. Not a recipe for building anything good.

It Is from the Right Person

The Bible is very clear about the need to respect our elders. Usually that means we will rarely offer criticism to our superiors, or if we do, it will be with strict qualifications. I've sometimes been asked by a boss or an older Christian to say whether I notice anything in his character or conduct that is wrong. I find that almost impossible to do. And I think that's an acceptable instinct. Our superiors should usually look to their superiors for correction. And let's focus on those whom the Lord has committed to our responsibility.

It Is Humble

Being critical makes us feel intellectually and morally superior, and it also makes others think the same of us. For example, critical book reviewers are viewed as more expert than positive reviewers. Little wonder we enjoy criticizing so much!

Pride is the motivation behind a lot of criticism. And yet, pride makes criticism ineffective. I mean, have you ever changed as a result of an arrogant person pointing out your faults? No, neither have I. In fact, I've probably decided to do what I was doing wrong with even more determination. But when a person humbly comes alongside me, confesses his faults, admits his struggles, maybe even in that particular area, then my ears are open and so is my heart.

Personal humility, then, is the key to this whole praise/criticism conundrum. It makes people open to our criticism, and it makes us open to praising others. We may initially get less pleasure from praising than criticizing, but we will certainly give more pleasure.

ALLELUIA FROM HEAD TO FOOT

Let's reduce our negative criticisms of others and increase positive praises. Positive faith, positive health, and positive relationships will be the happy sum.

And if this is true of praising people, how much more true is this of praising God? Augustine said a Christian should be "an alleluia from head to foot."[42] Can't say I always agreed with this. When I was a young Christian, worship was a preliminary to the main event, the sermon. Singing was like soup or salad: you had to do it to get to the steak. The tantalizing dessert of Christian service followed, the sweet experience of going out into the world with the gospel on lip and in life. By that time the "boring" soup or "tedious" salad was long forgotten.

Twenty-plus years later, worship is often my favorite Christian experience, especially public worship. Although I'm no singer, I just love to sing with God's people and to lift up my eyes to heaven and believe that God sees and hears and enjoys my joyful noise. It is just so good for the soul, so comforting, so energizing, so inspiring.

Let's all be top-to-toe alleluias, body-and-soul alleluias, muscle-and-mind alleluias. Let's give God the praise and honor He deserves and discover what we are about to explore in the next chapter, that it is indeed more blessed to give than to receive.

Chapter Eight

HAPPY GIVING

GIVING > GETTING = POSITIVE+

JACK CHAMBLESS IS PROFESSOR of economics at Valencia College. Every year he starts his class by asking his students to write a ten-minute essay on what the American dream looks like to them and what they want the federal government to do to help them achieve that dream. He described last year's results:

> About 10% of the students said they wanted the government to leave them alone, not tax them too much, and let them regulate their own lives. But over 80% of the students said that the American Dream to them meant a house and a job and plenty of money for retirement, and vacations and things like this. But when it came to the part about the federal government, 8 out of 10 students said they wanted free health care, they wanted the government to pay for their tuition. They want the government to pay for the down payment on their house. They expect the government "to give them a job." Many of them said they wanted the government to tax wealthier individuals so that they would have an opportunity to have a better life.[1]

Professor Chambless's students belong to the Entitlement Generation, also known as the Gimme Generation. They think they can have and should have whatever they want, whenever they want, and from whomever they want it, while others pay for it. Or more simply, as one Occupy protester painted on her placard, "Where's my bailout?"

In an article entitled *The New Me Generation*, Jake Halpern described this Gimme Generation as "smart, brash, even arrogant, and endowed with a commanding sense of entitlement."[2] But is it making them any happier? Not according to the title of psychology professor Dr. Jean Twenge's book *Generation Me: Why Today's Young Americans Are More Confident, Assertive, Entitled—and More Miserable Than Ever Before.*

This entitlement mentality destroys initiative, independence, inventiveness, resourcefulness, motivation, the fear of consequences, and the link between cause and effect. It promotes indulgence, jealousy, conceit, laziness, and self-centeredness. It creates bad winners and bad losers.

It damages charity because the rich leave charity to the government and withdraw from contact with the poor; the poor just get handouts from an impersonal, faceless, soulless state rather than from real, caring people. It damages marriages by putting the focus on "What can I get from him or her?" rather than "What can I give?" It damages the relationships between bosses and their workers by making each try to get the most out of each other rather than each trying to give the most to the other.

In this chapter, I want to show you how reversing the Getting > Giving formula can positively transform giving to charity, giving of thanks, giving in marriage, giving of forgiveness, and giving in leadership. In other words, Giving > Getting = Positive+.

Let's begin by discussing one of the beatitudes in the Bible.

GIVING TO CHARITY

"It is more blessed to give than to receive."[3] The *giver* happier than the *getter*? Go-givers happier than go-getters? Surely some mistake? That goes against all our intuitions and instincts. Let me help you believe and act upon it by giving you ten reasons why it is more blessed to give money than to get it.

Giving Obeys God's Command

The Old Testament has way more commands about giving—who, when, and how much—than the New Testament. The New Testament writers seem to have assumed that as God had given far more to us in the New Testament—giving His Son to die for our sins—our increased giving should follow logically and easily. But just in case we might miss the link, there are also some clear New Testament commands.[4] All God's laws are given to enhance and elevate our lives, so obeying this command will not spoil or ruin our happiness but rather increase it.

Giving Submits to God's Lordship

Every act of obedience recognizes that there is a higher authority in our lives, that there is a Lord over us who is entitled to honor and respect. Due to our temperaments, personalities, or circumstances, we may find some commands relatively easy to obey. Our submission is really tested, though, in the areas where our nature and circumstances make obedience more difficult. For most of us, money is one of those areas. The wallet is often the last citadel to fall to God's rule, and even when it does fall, it gets rebuilt and resecured again all too quickly. But when enabled to submit our wallets to Christ's lordship, we give clear and powerful testimony that He is Lord of all.

Giving Exhibits God's Heart

God is *the* giver of every good and perfect gift.[5] He is the superlative giver. And although God's gifts are unprecedented, unrepeatable, and unbeatable, we are still called to copy God's giving, to be minipictures of His infinitely large heart. What a privilege and honor to be His image bearers in this way. The larger our hearts, the larger the picture we paint of God's character. What do people think of God when they think of the way we use our money?

Giving Illustrates God's Salvation

At the heart of the gospel is sacrificial self-giving. That's why when the apostle Paul wanted to encourage the Corinthians to give more, he pointed them to the person and work of Christ: "For you know the grace of our Lord Jesus Christ, that though He was rich, yet for your sakes He became poor, that you through His poverty might become rich."[6] Yes, you abound in faith, love, and so on, but "see that you abound in this grace of giving also."[7] When we give sacrificially, painfully, and lovingly, we draw a small-scale picture of the gospel message.

Giving Trusts God's Provision

The biggest deterrent to giving is fear, the fear that if I give away too much, I won't have enough for this or that. When we give sacrificially, above and beyond what is comfortable and easy, we express our faith and trust in God to provide for us and our families. This is an argument not for folly but for faith. Many Christians have discovered the joy of casting their crumbs of bread upon the waters and multiple loaves returning after many days.[8] It is such a delight to see God fulfill His promise of provision when we obey Him.

Giving Widens God's Smile

The Lord loves "a cheerful giver."[9] It delights Him to see His people gladly opening their hearts and hands to provide for the needs of His church and indeed of all His creatures. Through Paul, God repeatedly commended and praised those who gave of their funds and themselves to gospel work.[10] Nothing makes a Christian happier than knowing that she's made God happy, and happy giving means a happy God.

Even secular research indicates that people who give money to charity end up happier and wealthier than those who don't, implying that how much we give away is at least as important for our happiness as how much we earn.[11]

Giving Advances God's Kingdom

Most of us have contributed to Apple in one way or another. We have helped to grow the company from a garage operation to the worldwide empire it is today. And I'm happy about that because it is a company that has brought many blessings to the world, certainly to my little world.

But think of what blessing results when we fund the mission of Christ's church. We are paying salaries of ministers and missionaries; we are funding resources for outreach, evangelism, and discipleship. But above all we are investing in the spiritual and eternal welfare of people from every nation, tribe, kindred, and tongue. Our dollars are changing homes, relationships, countries, and even the eternal destiny of many souls. Although most of us can't trace the impact of every dollar we donate, God traces it, and I believe that in heaven He will reveal all the lives our money has touched through the years and even bring us together with those who have been blessed by our giving—and those who have blessed us by their giving.

Giving Promotes God's Sanctification of Us

Giving promotes not only God's work through us but also God's work in us, our sanctification. Giving money, especially when it pains us, is work that requires much self-denial and self-crucifixion. Every act of giving weakens and breaks our sinful and selfish nature, however, empowering God's work of grace in our hearts. Yes, dollars leave our pockets, but sin also leaves our hearts. And that's a great deal. Priceless actually.

Giving Testifies to God's Power

Although we are not to let our left hand know what our right hand does, it is pretty obvious that Christians give a lot to their churches and Christian charities. Even secular observers have noticed with amazement how generous Christians often are with their money. They may not say it, but they surely must think it: *This must be the real deal for people to give away so much of their money. They must really believe this stuff. The God they worship and serve must be incredibly powerful to make His people so generous.*

Giving Praises God's Character

Giving in a right spirit is an act of worship.[12] It is rendering God a tribute of praise. It is saying, "You gave me everything, and here is a small expression of my gratitude and praise for all Your good gifts. It is only a token, a sample of what I really feel, but You know the heart that lies behind it." David sang, "What shall I render to the Lord / For all His benefits toward me?"[13]

"But, but, but," you say, "it sounds as if God gets all the benefits from my giving. What blessing do I get from it?" Well, I hope you're not motivated to give by what you can get out of it. Nevertheless, it is not only God who is blessed by our giving; we are blessed too.

- *Giving away a tenth of our income improves personal finances*: "Researchers compared tithers to non-tithers using nine financial health indicators, and found that tithers were better off in every category."[14]
- *Spending money on someone else makes you happier*: Students who were randomly assigned to spend money on others experienced greater happiness than those assigned to spend money on themselves.[15]
- *Spending money on shared experiences produces more happiness than selfish purchases*: Money spent on doing things together produced more happiness than buying things.[16]
- *Giving increases health and well-being*: It gives a sense of meaning, increases physical activity, strengthens social bonds, improves immune function, and even slows down aging.[17]
- *Giving increases love for and from others*: Giving connects people and cultivates a sense of community.
- *Giving money or time to charity increases subjective well-being, as much as doubling household income:*[18] Volunteering reduces depression, increases longevity, raises mood, improves time-management skills, and enhances relationships.[19]

Why not try it and see how much more blessed it is to give than to receive?

GIVING THANKS

But there's more to giving than money. There's also giving thanks, another activity that produces blessings for the thanks-giver. Studies have shown that gratitude is a powerful force for creating positive changes in individuals, families, and organizations. According to Sonja Lyubomirsky, a research professor of psychology, "The expression of gratitude is a kind of metastrategy for achieving happiness."[20] Here are some of the more detailed findings, published in books such as *The Happiness Advantage, Flourish*, and *Optimal Functioning*:

- Grateful people have more energy, happiness, and friends and also enjoy better sleep and overall health.[21]
- Writing down what made people happy and what lowered stress levels and increased a sense of calm.[22]
- Counting acts of kindness done and received increases levels of positivity.[23]
- A study of resilience and emotions following the September 11 terrorist attacks on the United States found that gratitude helps people cope with painful and stressful life events.[24]
- Grateful people are more helpful people because they remember how thankful they feel when helped.
- Gratitude reduces negative comparisons with others.[25]
- When we express our gratitude to others, we strengthen our relationship with them.[26]
- Gratitude reduces negative emotions like anger, envy, greed, and anxiety.

Thanksgiving is much more than saying "Thank you" for a present or benefit we've received. The world's most prominent researcher and writer about gratitude, Robert Emmons, said it is "a felt sense of wonder, thankfulness, and appreciation for life."[27]

We can boost gratitude in our lives by intensifying the feeling of it for each positive event, by increasing the frequency of it throughout the day, by expanding the number of things we're grateful for, and by expressing gratitude to more people. But the most effective multiplier of gratitude, said Emmons, is humility: "At the cornerstone of gratitude is the notion of *undeserved merit*. The grateful person recognizes that he or she did nothing to deserve the gift or benefit; it was freely bestowed."[28]

Again, don't we Christians start with such an advantage here, given that our whole faith is based on grace, the sense of a completely undeserved salvation that has been freely given us by a gracious God?

Gratitude Journal

Many have found it helpful to maintain a weekly gratitude journal. In one study, some participants were asked to write down five things for which they were thankful once a week for ten weeks. Another group was asked to list five problems every week. The findings? Those in the grateful group were more optimistic, more content, and even physically healthier than the complainers.[29] Similar results have been found even among chronically ill patients.

One happy side effect is that when you realize how much God and others have done for you, you are humbled that they should love you and care for you so much.

Gratitude Visit

Gratitude has been found to be especially powerful when expressed directly to a person by phone, letter, or face-to-face.

Why not look back over your life and locate someone to whom you owe a special debt of gratitude—a parent, an uncle, an employer, or a sports coach. Write a letter and send it, read it over the phone, or, best of all, read it in person. Be specific about what the person did and how it helped you.

Gratitude researcher Martin Seligman instructed people from all walks of life to write and then hand deliver a letter of gratitude to someone who had been especially kind and caring to them but whom they had never properly thanked. Other participants were given alternative happiness exercises. Sonja Lyubomirsky commented about

Seligman's findings: "Those participants who did gratitude visits showed the largest boosts in the entire study—that is, straightaway they were much happier and much less depressed—and these boosts were maintained one week after the visit and even one month after."[30]

Maximizer or Satisficer?

We can also try to cultivate a "good enough" attitude to our purchases. Psychologists such as Barry Schwartz have noticed that one downside of the abundance of consumer choice through increased mobility and online shopping is that it is harder for people to find pleasure in their purchases. Increased choice leads to increased expectations, increased anxiety that we've missed a better deal, and increased regret when we see that what we bought is anything less than perfect. Schwartz called these agitated consumers "Maximizers." Going all out for the optimum decision, they spend many hours and expend much energy before they make their choices. The downside is that they also tend to be more remorseful, depressed, and anxious about their choices.[31] Maximizers maximize the deal but minimize satisfaction in it.

In contrast, "Satisficers" maximize satisfaction. They don't strive for the best possible deal but can accept "good enough." Although Satisficers usually get a poorer deal than Maximizers, they are usually much happier people and get more satisfaction in their purchases.

To become a better "satisficer," psychologist Barry Schwartz recommended the following:

- Setting deadlines for decisions.
- Limiting the number of shops you will research.
- Making decisions nonreversible.
- Focusing on the good elements of the decision.
- Accepting a degree of buyer's remorse.
- Limiting comparison with others.[32]

Although coming from a secular psychologist, these useful practical tips help us apply the general biblical principles "in whatever state I am, to be content,"[33] and "in everything give thanks."[34]

Savoring

Some positive psychologists also encourage the practice of savoring, the conscious and intentional practice of taking pleasure in the good things of life. Savoring begins by anticipating a good event or experience, by generating positive feelings about it before it happens. Then there is the present enjoyment, which can be enhanced by generating and prolonging joy, interest, and excitement in the moment. After the event, we reminisce; we produce and maintain positive feelings by focusing on the good things that happened in the event.

As far as I know, none of these positive psychology experts have Christian faith. And yet God is using them not only to confirm the Bible's teaching about giving (thanks) making us happier than receiving but also to work out the practical details of how to increase gratitude in our lives for everyone's benefit.

It is the kind of thing that makes us wonder how unbelievers sometimes seem to have more understanding of biblical principles than Christians! But the apostle Paul helps us make sense of this. He said that when unbelievers, who "do not have the law, by nature do the things in the law," they show "the work of the law written in their hearts."[35]

GIVING IN MARRIAGE

The main question most people ask in marriage relationships today is, "What can I get out of it?" Especially, "What sex can I get out of it?"

And when the investment of time, money, emotion, and sexual energy does not pay off as expected?

Separation.

And the search for a better return from someone else. Someone else who'll fit into my life better. Someone else who won't take so much of my time. Someone else who will fill me rather than drain me.

But if people are trying to *get* more than they *give*, no one's going to be happy, and marriages are doomed to premature and painful endings.

In contrast, the question the Bible calls us to ask is not, "What can I get?" but "What can I give?"

Strangely, when each party is focused more on giving than getting, the result is more getting for both parties. In marriage it really is "more blessed to give than to receive."

In Ephesians 5, the apostle Paul presented Jesus as the ultimate model of this self-giving love. Because He loved us, He sacrificially gave Himself for us. Because He loved us, He sacrificially submitted to His Father's will. What a union such self-giving created! And what a pattern for marriage!

Paul's basic argument in this passage is that the more we give of ourselves in the service of a spouse, the more union, intimacy, satisfaction, and fulfillment we will discover and enjoy in marriage. Let the "What can I give?" question drown out and drive out the "What can I get?" question in every situation:

When you argue: "What can I give up to resolve this?"
When you've hurt one another: "What apology can I give to heal this?"
When you're on vacation: "What can I give to make his vacation better?"

When you're in bed: "What can I give to enhance his or her enjoyment of physical intimacy?"

When you're budgeting: "What can I give up this month to give her more spending money?"

When you're talking: "How can I give her more of a listening ear?"

When you're leading: "How can I serve her better in my leadership?"

When you're submitting: "How can I give him more respect when I disagree with his decisions?"

When you're filling free time: "How can I give him the most pleasure today?"

When you're offended: "How can I give him the benefit of the doubt?"

When you're betrayed: "How can I give him grace?"

When you have no feelings of love: "How can I act in love?"

When you think she is not as attractive: "How can I love her as the Lord loved the church?"

When you see his ugly side: "How can I help him become more beautiful?"

When he's depressed: "How can I give him encouragement?"

When she's lost sleep: "How can I give her rest?"

Give, Give, Give

Give your mind, your heart, your eyes, your hands, your body, and your money. Give financially, emotionally, physically, intellectually, sexually, and spiritually. Give away yourself, your whole self. And if you believe the Bible rather than your instincts and your culture, you will be more blessed in that giving than in all the getting you can imagine.

The great aim of all this marital giving is that eventually each of us gives so much of self away, each has all of the other, and the two become one; we lose so much independence and become so interdependent that we become "one flesh" in every way.

This is incredibly hard to believe and even harder to practice. Our sinful nature is characterized by self-centeredness, self-righteousness, self-promotion, self-sufficiency, self-will, self-worship, self-love, and self-praise. We are selfaholics, and yet marriage calls us to be servaholics in order to be happyholics.

A German study that followed 1,761 people for fifteen years through their single years and into married life found that "people were no happier during the years after marriage than before marriage, and the average 'marriage boost' in happiness lasted for only two years."[36]

There were significant differences in some people's experiences of marriage. In *The How of Happiness*, Sonja Lyubomirsky highlighted Markus and Roland, two participants who married their wives while the study was ongoing. Markus's happiness "increased more than average when he got hitched, and eight years later he is *still* happier being married (just declining a tiny bit from his high point) than when he was single. Roland, on the other hand, ended up *less* happy during the first two years of marriage and has become even less happy in the five years since."[37]

What made the difference? Lyubomirsky explained:

Markus didn't want the effects of marriage to "wear off"; he didn't want to adapt to the rewards of marriage and take it for granted. So he decided to dedicate himself to be the best husband he could be and not take his wife and their relationship for granted. He consciously remembers to say, "I love you," to bring her flowers, to initiate plans, trips, and hobbies, to take an interest in his wife's challenges, successes, and feelings. In contrast, Roland was disappointed at the outset that matrimony did not live up to his idealistic expectations and since then has failed to observe the slow and steady deterioration of his relationship.[38]

Scientists have found that we tend to adapt to positive change in our lives. Whether it is marriage, a better job, a bigger house, or a sports victory, the initial boost of happiness and well-being fades and the "better life" becomes the new normal.

Markus and Roland teach us that although increases in happiness often fade as we get used to them, we can slow down that process by keeping our love alive and our happiness lively through deliberate and determined acts.

John Gottman, author of *The Seven Principles for Making Marriage Work*, psychologically dissected hundreds of married couples and after completing his observations was able to predict which marriages would work and which wouldn't with 91 percent accuracy. He said that the biggest secret of successful marriages is that the partners talk at least five hours more per week than others.[39]

Gottman and others have numerous practical suggestions for improving marriage, all of them involving giving more than getting. However, the elephant in the room remains: How do we accomplish this? How do takers become givers and sustain this in the long term? How do selfaholics become servaholics? What power can turn us inside out?

We need the great Self-denier working in our hearts. I'm talking about Jesus Christ, of course, the Servant who can turn the worst selfaholics into the best servaholics.[40]

Study Christ's life and ask yourself how you, too, can serve rather than be served. Above all, study His death. Studying His life will shrink your "I" a little, but when you stand before His cross, your "I" will begin to crack and crumble, even at its very foundations. Just as Paul directed the Philippian selfaholics of his day, we, too, are called to grasp that Christ's servaholism atones for our selfaholism.[41] And as we grasp that supreme act of self-denial on our behalf, we will not only serve, but we will serve out of selfless motives. We will stop thinking about what we are giving up, we'll see what He gave up, and we'll begin to ask, "What can I give up?"

GIVING FORGIVENESS

Perhaps one of the most painful experiences in life is being deliberately harmed by someone else. Car crashes, even fatal ones, are accidents; no one sets out to deliberately injure or kill with a car. Cancer is also an impersonal attacker, an internal cellular malfunction.

But when someone willfully abuses us—verbally, physically, financially, emotionally—that feels altogether different. That pushes our pain levels off the scale and can feel worse than the most serious physical injuries or diseases. It wasn't an accident; it wasn't a mistake; it wasn't a malfunction. Someone purposely decided to wrong and damage us. There's a personal choice, a human will, behind the pain.

That's searing agony.

Was that not the worst part of Christ's sufferings? Not so much the nails or the thorns, but the malice of the soldiers, the denial of Peter, the desertion of the disciples, the betrayal of Judas, and, above all, the felt abandonment by the Father.

Avoid or Attack

Our most common responses to being abused are either attack or avoid, retaliate or distance, both of which result in even greater damage to us and others, including anger, bitterness, resentment, and even depression. Carrie Fisher said, "Resentment is like drinking a poison and waiting for the other person to die."[42]

But there is an alternative to taking vengeance or taking cover, and that's giving forgiveness.

Full Forgiveness

The fullest and best kind of forgiveness is when our attacker or abuser confesses his sin, asks for forgiveness, and we are enabled to do so from the heart, just as God for Christ's sake did for us. This kind of reconciliation is one of the greatest joys for any Christian to experience. It is so liberating, so refreshing, so exquisite.

What if there is no confession, no repentance, no request for forgiveness?

Are we doomed to carry around this burden for the rest of our lives? Or do we forgive anyway, regardless of whether the person wants forgiveness?

That seems to be the most common approach today. I've lost count of the number of times some tragedy has occurred—a mass shooting, a terrorist attack, a drunk-driving fatality—and the victims or their relatives, usually Christians, start forgiving the offenders within hours or days of the crime.

I understand the motive and the desire to present an attractive witness about Christian forgiveness to the world. But it is not a faithful witness to God. It does not reflect how God forgives, which is to be our pattern and model. Here's why: *God does not forgive those who do not want forgiveness.*

Here's how God forgives:

1. God is willing, ready, and eager to forgive everyone. That's His beautiful nature, His compassionate character, and His constant desire.
2. God offers forgiveness to everyone. God offers to release those who have offended Him from their deserved punishment and alienation from Him. There's a big difference

between offering it and giving it. Offering it is unconditional; giving it is conditional.

3. God does not forgive everyone regardless of the response to His offer. Although He offers forgiveness to all, not all respond. Some don't even think they've done anything needing forgiveness.

4. God's forgiveness is conditional on repentance (Luke 13:3; 17:3; Acts 2:38). God's forgiveness is conditional on the offender's wanting forgiveness and wanting to turn from his or her offending ways.

5. Forgiveness through repentance produces reconciliation on both sides. Offering forgiveness reduces the temperature of the conflict, but only the giving of forgiveness, in response to repentance, ends it.

Having seen how God forgives, let's remind ourselves of the basic biblical principle: *our forgiveness is to be patterned on God's forgiveness* (Eph. 4:32; Matt. 6:12, 14–15).

Therefore . . .

1. We must be willing, ready, and eager to forgive everyone. This is not easy and usually requires gospel work to be done in our hearts as we realize how much God has forgiven us.

2. We must offer forgiveness to everyone. This step and the previous step together are lesser forgiveness, sometimes called "positional" forgiveness. We are in a position where we are ready to forgive, and we offer it freely. If this is what people are talking about when they say, "I forgive the person who raped and murdered my daughter," that's fine. It is more than fine; it is amazing grace and can be given only by God. It is not forgiveness in the fullest biblical sense, however, and must not be confused with it.

3. We must not forgive everyone regardless of the response to our offer. Forgiving someone before he or she repents is ungodlike, it avoids dealing with serious issues, and while it might offer temporary and superficial relief, it does not produce long-term satisfaction to the conscience or reconciliation.

4. We must forgive upon the condition of repentance. According to Matthew 18:15–17, if a person sins, we must reprove him. If he does not respond with repentance, we must take it to another level. If he repents at any stage, we must forgive him.

5. Forgiveness through repentance produces reconciliation on both sides. Full forgiveness, sometimes called "transactional" forgiveness, happens when all five steps occur, resulting in deep and lasting reconciliation. This is the kind of forgiveness that most glorifies God, most benefits the offender, and most satisfies the offended.

I don't want to minimize the releasing power of steps 1 and 2. Some people say, "I can never forgive until Jim repents." If that is so, they are going to carry around a huge and growing load of resentment as they pile up unresolved conflicts in their lives. But if by God's grace they are enabled to take these first two steps, to work through positional forgiveness, they will experience wonderful load-lightening relief.

Here's a sample prayer if you're in this situation:

Lord, Jim has done me great wrong, but won't confess it or ask for forgiveness.

I can't therefore forgive him without misrepresenting You or damaging his spiritual welfare.

However, I'm not going to carry this pain around to burden

and burn my mind and heart for years. I'm handing this over to You because You said, "Vengeance is mine, I will repay."

Lord, You know I don't want Your vengeance executed on Jim, but with this prayer I'm promising no more vengeance on my part. I hand that right over to You.

I promise not to dwell on this incident. Instead I transfer it to You and trust You to put it right in Your own time and way. You know I am ready to forgive Jim fully, freely, and forever, should it ever be asked for.

Please help Jim to understand Your view of sin and forgiveness through this painful time. Amen.

Although this is not the full forgiveness that we crave to give, it is better than the alternatives and better for us too. Psychologists often lack the theological basis for offering true forgiveness to their clients, yet they recognize that forgiveness helps bitter people become better people. Sonja Lyubomirsky argued that whereas "preoccupation, hostility, and resentment that we harbor serve only to hurt us, both emotionally and physically," empirical research confirms that people who forgive are "happier, healthier, more agreeable, and more serene. They are better able to empathize with others and to be spiritual or religious. People who forgive hurts in relationships are more capable of reestablishing closeness."[43]

Amazingly, Lyubomirsky's first strategy for practicing forgiveness is to appreciate being forgiven! It is a pity that it has taken scientists a couple of thousand years to discover that what Jesus was teaching all those years ago is true. Of course, "scientific" forgiveness is only on the horizontal plane. Lyubomirsky asks us to recall an instance of when we did wrong to someone and were forgiven. If such relatively minor offenses against such relatively minor people can help us to forgive, how much more being forgiven by a holy

God for offenses not just against His law but against His love. As Jesus said, he who has been forgiven much, the same loves much.[44]

GIVING IN LEADERSHIP

Stop!

I know, you just saw "leadership" in the title of this section and thought, *Not me, skip to the next chapter.* But everyone is a leader, including you.

We all have influence in at least one other person's life. We all have people who look up to us as models and examples. If you are a mother, you are leading your children. If you are a Sunday school teacher, you are influencing your students. If you are eighteen years old, the seventeen-year-olds are looking to you. If you've been at your job for a month, today's new recruit is watching your every step and misstep. If you have a younger brother or sister, you are a supermodel to them! Scary, isn't it? Whether we are aware of it or not, we are leading all the time and continuously influencing others for good and for evil.

It doesn't take much to find many examples of evil impact, usually caused by leaders using their position for their own good rather than the good of those they lead. Wherever we look—families, churches, companies, governments, sports—we find leaders who are motivated by what they can get out of those they lead rather than by what they can give to those they lead. And the cursed result of trying to get more than is given is abuse of power, unhappy families, divided churches, resentful employees, discontented citizens, and losing sports teams.

What would the opposite look like? What would "giving" or "servant" leadership look like? And what would be the blessings of such positive leadership?

Positive Leaders Serve with Cheerfulness

When people think of you, what image or picture immediately comes into their minds? When they hear your name, it is as if a little passport picture of you pops out of their mental files. What does that picture look like? Is it glum, sad, hopeless, and depressed? Or is it happy, joyful, and cheerful? Or is it robot neutrality—a stoic of the Stoics?

The positive leader possesses and projects a happy attitude and appearance. He's not Mr. Happy-Happy-Happy all the time-time-time; he knows there is a time to be sober and serious. But on the whole he is Mr. Optimist rather than Mr. Pessimist. He enjoys his work, he looks forward to each day (or most days), and he tries to find the silver lining on the darkest clouds, a smiling face behind the darkest providence. He faces problems with optimistic hope, trusting God to help him face, overcome, or learn from difficulties.

In *The Happiness Project*, Gretchen Rubin noted that happier people make more effective leaders: "They perform better on managerial tasks such as leadership and mastery of information. They're viewed as more assertive and self-confident than less happy people. They're perceived to be more friendly, warmer, and even more physically attractive."[45]

A sunny character and joy-filled words attract people and empower them. It is much easier to follow such a person than someone who looks like a tornado and who speaks like an undertaker. This is why companies like Google try to make their workplaces happier places by providing game rooms, gyms, and even scooters in the hallways.

Shawn Achor said, "Rarely have I seen an optimistic and motivated worker under the supervision of a pessimistic, apathetic manager. As the leaders go, so go their employees."[46] Same with pastors and churches, parents and children.

Positive Leaders Serve by Challenging

In Scotland, Munro-bagging is a hobby. A Munro is a mountain that is more than three thousand feet high, and Munro-baggers spend their leisure time "bagging" (climbing) these Munros. They plan, organize, train, buy supplies, enlist friends, rise early, drive many hours, and then they climb . . . and climb . . . and climb. After bagging their first Munro, most usually aim for 10, then 100, then 200, until, after many years, they conquer all 283 peaks. And all this while the rest of us are enjoying our Saturday morning sleep ins.

Positive leaders are Munro-baggers rather than sleep-ins. They are not content with accepting the comfortable status quo or with managing gradual decline. They are looking out for, planning, or taking on the next Munro.

But I'm not talking here of personal ambition or careerism. No, the servant leader's primary passion is to help *others* climb higher, grow stronger, and move onward, upward, and outward in their lives. She leads to serve, and she serves by leading.

She doesn't want to leave people where she found them. She wants to help them bag some Munros. She can look back on their past achievements and attainments with pleasure, but she doesn't rest on that. She's seeking new challenges, new Munros to climb with her team.

She studies each individual and asks how she can help him progress, grow, and mature. What aspects of a person's character could be developed? What areas of life could be improved? What service opportunities can be provided for this person? What relationships can be strengthened? What gifts could be developed and utilized? What new challenges could he attempt? What new opportunities would suit him? How can I help him grow?

Gretchen Rubin's happiness formula satisfied her only when she added the italicized words at the end of this statement: "To be happy, I need to think about feeling good, feeling bad, and feeling

163

right, *in an atmosphere of growth.*[47] God has built into all of us this desire for growth, for progress, for development, and so on, and the servant leader will facilitate and encourage that in those she leads.

Robert Greenleaf was one of the first to advocate for servant leadership in business. His website offers the following suggestion to test whether we are servant leaders: "The best test, and difficult to administer, is: Do those served grow as persons? Do they, *while being served*, become healthier, wiser, freer, more autonomous, more likely themselves to become servants?"[48]

Positive Leaders Serve with Confidence

As a teenager, I attended a mountain-climbing church camp in the Scottish Highlands where we were trying to bag a number of Munros. On the second day, we set out on a fairly ambitious trek. About halfway through, the mist and rain enveloped us, separating us into small, detached groups going in different directions, and very soon all of us were lost.

At one point, a bedraggled handful of us decided that the way back to base was over a particular mountain. We started climbing, but when we got about halfway up, the Scottish mist descended, we could hardly see in front of our noses, and we decided to retrace our steps. On the way down, we were relieved to meet our camp leaders on the way up the mountain.

"Oh!" we said. "So we were heading in the right direction after all?"

"I don't know," replied the camp commandant. "We were just following you. You seemed to know where you were going."

Needless to say, we immediately lost any remaining confidence in our leaders and spent the rest of the week (which was filled with similar disasters), doubting, second-guessing, and double-checking all our leaders' plans. Not enjoyable.

A positive leader knows where he's going, how he's going to get there, and what he's going to do when he arrives. Without this, who's going to be inspired to follow his direction and instruction? Doubting, hesitating, prevaricating leaders will replicate themselves in others. But a confident leader inspires people's confidence. And he doesn't just improve their moods; he improves their performances too.

Positive Leaders Serve by Communicating

Weak, negative, fearful leaders hear the phrase "Knowledge is power" and think, *Yes, the more I know and the less they know, the more powerful I'll be.* The positive leader hears "Knowledge is power" and thinks, *How can I empower people by sharing knowledge with them?*

Open, honest communication, especially when it is face-to-face, increases trust, empathy, and clarity. It strengthens the relationship between manager and employee and is the main factor that determines how long someone stays in a job and how productive she is in it.

A lack of communication is the main complaint from employees about their bosses, devastating happiness and productivity: "According to a recent study published in *Human Resource Executive* magazine, a third of U.S. workers spend a minimum of 20 hours per month at work complaining about their boss. The Gallup Poll estimates U.S. corporations lose $360 billion annually due to lost productivity from employees who are dissatisfied with their boss."[49]

Positive Leaders Are Contagious

By giving positive leadership, we bless those with whom we interact directly and even their colleagues, clients, friends, and families. In *Connected*, Nicholas Christakis and James Fowler estimate that there are almost one thousand people within three degrees of us—friends (one degree), our friends' friends (two degrees), and even our friends' friends' friends (three degrees).[50] That means by positively serving and leading the people God has put in our lives, through them we have the ability to positively impact the lives and homes and workplaces of hundreds of people around us.

Sometimes it is as simple as smiling more. Scientists have discovered that people subconsciously mimic the voices, expressions, and body language of those around them and that such physical behaviors make them start feeling the emotions also. If you smile, your brain picks up the changes in your facial muscles and starts producing the happy chemicals usually associated with smiling. That's why comedies always seem funnier in a group setting. One study found that even having one happy player on a team improved not only team morale but also results.[51]

Imagine the impact you could have on your workplace, your clients, your church, your home, and your friends if you begin to implement not just positive leadership but positive faith in every aspect of your life. Some experiments have demonstrated that when three strangers meet it only takes two minutes for the most emotionally expressive person to transfer that emotion to the others.[52] If emotions are so contagious in just a few minutes, imagine the impact over a longer period of time, say in a church, a workplace, or a marriage.

GIVING BY FOLLOWING

But what if the leaders in our lives are not positive servant leaders? Our pastor or elders frustrate us, our parents and teachers irritate us, our coaches exasperate us, and our political leaders infuriate us. To honor, obey, and follow these leaders can sandpaper our minds and hearts. How can we be happy followers when we have such sad excuses for leaders? You're probably not going to like this, but I'm going to ask you to believe that it involves giving to them, even when you're getting nothing from them. The apostle Paul said, "Render therefore to all their due: taxes to whom taxes are due, customs to whom customs, fear to whom fear, honor to whom honor."[53] That is really just an exposition of Jesus' famous words: "Render to Caesar the things that are Caesar's."[54]

I know, it feels much better to give them nothing—apart from abuse. But we need to believe God's Word that it is more blessed to give than to get. How do we give honor, submission, respect, and obedience to those whom God has appointed over us in the home, the workplace, the church, and the state—even when they give nothing back?

Follow Jesus

"Follow Me" was one of the first commands Jesus uttered on earth. We will find it very difficult to cheerfully follow any earthly authority if we do not follow the greatest authority in heaven and on earth. As King of kings, Lord of lords, and Boss of bosses, Jesus demands our first loyalty. We follow Him by bowing to His authority, by handing over the reins of our lives to Him, by trusting Him, and by obeying His Word.

Imitate Jesus

Jesus had bad bosses. His parents made mistakes, His pastors were blind leaders of the blind, the local and national politicians were a bunch of compromisers, the military commanders were brutal bullies, and the king was corrupt. So He led a rebellion against them all? Nope! Instead "Christ also suffered for us, leaving us an example, that you should follow His steps: 'Who committed no sin, nor was deceit found in His mouth'; who, when He was reviled, did not revile in return; when He suffered, He did not threaten, but committed Himself to Him who judges righteously."[55]

Study Christ's life to see how He related to those in authority over Him, even as they sinned in the exercise of it, and use it as an example when you suffer at the hands of unrighteous bosses, leaders, and even Supreme Court justices.

Suffer with Jesus

As you enter into Jesus' painful experiences as a follower, you will also enter into the fellowship of His sufferings.[56] You will understand in a greater way what He suffered for you. The next time your pastor treats you badly, and the next time the other party wins an election by lying and media bias, think about what Jesus suffered at the hands of His leaders and better understand and enjoy what your salvation cost Him.

Serve Jesus

As you'll see in the next chapter, Paul wanted us to imagine Christ standing beside us as we do our work[57] and to present our daily work to Him as an act of worship. Seeing our daily work as our primary sphere of Christian service can transform the most menial and mundane tasks into the most significant and satisfying of activities.

Witness for Jesus

By this I do not mean that we should always be quoting verses to our superiors. No, the best witness is to do our work to the very best of our ability and to demonstrate submission to authority. That's the most powerful witness, all the more so because it is so rare. Such actions not only speak louder than many of our words; they also silence foolish men and their foolish ideas.[58]

Confess to Jesus

What I've described probably doesn't sound like your life so far, does it? You've not given honor to whom honor is due. You have sinned against your bosses and your Boss. So have I. So do I, right up to the present day. We can confess all our sins to Jesus and seek His pardon, however, even for dishonoring and disrespecting those whom God has ordained to be our leaders. There's nothing so demoralizing and draining as guilt. To get a clean conscience can be a great motivator to a fresh start even in the most painful relationships.

Look to Jesus

This is really tough, isn't it? It is radically countercultural and counterintuitive. We need power outside ourselves. And we can have it. We can come to Jesus each day and pray for His help. We look to Him not only as we open our Bibles but also as we open our exam papers, our shops, our factories, and our dishwashers.

Rest in Jesus

As wicked men and women take over the reins of power in our society, we worry about the loss of religious liberty, we worry about being forced to do things against our consciences, we worry about being sued for homophobia, and we worry about the world that our children are going to grow up in. This anxiety can lead to overwork ("I better get as much money as I can before this all goes south") or laziness ("What's the point in even trying to build a career or a business if I'm going to lose everything for believing in traditional marriage?"). Instead we need to rest in Jesus, trust Him with our future, and thereby find the right balance between anxious over-work and lazy despair.

Wait for Jesus

No matter how Jesus-like we are in following the various authorities in our lives, we are still going to suffer grave injustices and prejudices from time to time, and most of them will not be put right in this world. But Jesus will put them right in the world to come. The apostle James warned unjust employers and politicians that there is a final judgment when Jesus will call them to account for their oppression and robbery of the poor and the weak.[59] In the meantime, we sing Psalm 37 in confident faith.

ALL OF GRACE

Although he was writing specifically about giving thanks, happiness researcher Robert Emmons's words apply to all kinds of giving: "At the cornerstone of gratitude is the notion of *undeserved merit*. The grateful person recognizes that he or she did nothing to deserve the gift or benefit; it was freely bestowed."[60] In *Thrive*, Arianna Huffington says, "Gratitude works its magic by serving as an anti-dote to negative emotions. It is like white blood cells for the soul, protecting us from cynicism, entitlement, anger, and resignation."[61]

However little we get in this world, and however much we give, one thing is sure: we get more than we deserve and give less than we've been given. Sin has ripped every entitlement from our grasp, apart from the entitlement to hell and everlasting punishment. The more we grasp this, the more we will ask ourselves two empower-ing and elevating questions, the first asked by the apostle Paul and the second by King David.

How Much Have I Been Given?

"Who makes you differ from another? And what do you have that you did not receive? Now if you did indeed receive it, why do you boast as if you had not received it?"[62]

How Much Can I Give?

"What shall I render to the LORD / For all His benefits toward me?"[63]

Answer these two questions correctly, and you are well on the way to calculating Giving > Getting = Positive+

Chapter Nine

HAPPY WORK

WORK > PLAY = POSITIVE+

"I'M *JUST* A PLUMBER." "I'M *JUST* A HOUSEWIFE." "I'm *just* a secretary." "I'm *just* a salesman." "I'm *just* an accountant."

People say this kind of stuff all the time, especially to pastors. I've lost count of the number of times I've heard it.

What's implied in these statements?

A pastor's work is a divine calling, but mine isn't.
My work is not as important as ministry work.
Pastors and missionaries are worth more to God than I am.
I wish I could serve God more than one day a week.

What's at the root of all this is an unbiblical view of work: the false idea that only ministry callings are divine callings, that only ministry work is real work, that only overtly Christian work is worthwhile work, and that only ministry work is *Christian* work.

Because our work occupies more of our waking time than anything else, such wrong views of work will cast a negative pall over our daily lives, producing discouragement, discontent, envy, and frustration. We then begin to simply clock-watch, living for the weekend or even early retirement. Our jobs and the money we earn from them are necessary evils, means to the end of getting play-time and the toys to fill it. In other words: Play > Work = Positive. Or we might even dream of Play – Work = Positive!

On the other hand, some go to the other extreme and think that work itself will turn life into a positive experience. They become workaholics, devoting themselves to their work to the neglect of rest, leisure, family, and church. By calculating that Work – Play = Positive, they make work their god, a horrific miscalculation.

The biblical equation is Work > Play = Positive. Yes, our work can make a huge positive contribution to our lives and our world. But the Bible includes rest, leisure, and pleasure in the equation, too, not in the primary place but in an important secondary place, as we shall see later.

I want to give you a biblical lens through which to view your work so that you are working on the right equation, thus ensuring that you will arrive at a correct and positive result. Let's begin by viewing work through the lens of Romans 11:36: "For of Him and through Him and to Him are all things, to whom be glory forever. Amen."

All things, yes, even your work!

- Your work is of God.
- Your work is through God.
- Your work is to God.
- Your work is for God's glory.

Let's unpack each of these truths and begin to turn our work into a big positive for us, our neighbors, our churches, and God Himself.

YOUR WORK IS OF GOD

First, we'll examine work in general as God originally gave it. Then we'll delve into *your* work in particular.

Work Is from God

God created work and called Adam and Eve into it. That happened in a perfect prefall world; work is not an evil or a punishment for it. It was part of the "very good" that God saw when He made the world.

Indeed, we can go further and say that God was the first worker, and it was manual labor He chose to do. He created all the materials in the world and worked them into shape. He made Adam from dust and Eve from a male rib. He made things out of things, and He thoroughly enjoyed doing it. "Very good!" He joyfully exclaimed.

God then called Adam and Eve to continue His work. Significantly, the Hebrew word for God's work in Genesis 1–2 is also the word for ordinary human work. God worked as a gardener, then called Adam and Eve to continue the gardening, equipping them for the work in the process. Matthew Henry said, "Skill in common arts and employments is the gift of God; from him are derived both the faculty and the improvement of the faculty."[1]

Work is part of the blessedness of the garden of God, as Tim Keller explains: "Work is as much a basic human need as food, beauty, rest, friendship, prayer, and sexuality; it is not simply medicine but food for our soul. Without meaningful work we sense significant inner loss and emptiness. People who are cut off from work because of physical or other reasons quickly discover how much they need work to thrive emotionally, physically, and spiritually."[2]

Work is one of God's greatest gifts to humanity, part of being distinctively and fully human, a necessary component of human flourishing, and one of the primary ways in which we reflect and relate to God. And that goes for manual labor as much as knowledge work. Remember, in Genesis, God came into the world as a gardener, and in the New Testament, He came as a carpenter! He doesn't ask us to do what He wouldn't do. God was not above these tasks. He ennobled them and elevated them. Just try to survive a couple of weeks without garbage collectors. It would be easier to survive without preachers!

Your Work Is from God

Let's now turn to the particular work that God has given each of us to do. I'm assuming here that the work we're doing is not essentially sinful and forbidden; such work obviously is *not* from God.

But *if* we are doing lawful work and *if* it is the work that God has called us to, our work is *from* God.

That second *if* is a big *IF*, isn't it? How do I know that my work is God's calling for me? I can accept that God gives work, but how do I know that He gave me *this* work? If our work is going to make a positive contribution to our lives, we must answer this question positively.

Let me propose questions to help you decide whether you are doing the work God wants you to do:

Can I glorify God in this job?
Does this work help me live a holy life?
Does it compromise my commitments to God, family, and church?
Does it provide for my needs?
Does it help me be a blessing to others?
Does it make a positive contribution to society?
Does it use my God-given talents?

Do I want to do it?

Is there opportunity to do it?

Timothy Keller sums it up as follows: "The question regarding our choice of work is no longer 'What will make me the most money and give me the most status?' The question must now be 'How, with my existing abilities and opportunities, can I be of greatest service to other people, knowing what I do of God's will and of human need?'"[3]

Pray over this, and seek the counsel of others as you try to discern God's call on your life. If you're already in a job and wondering whether to change careers, you should also use these questions to help you decide. Moses, King David, and Jesus had different God-given vocations at different stages of life. But in a world of unparalleled mobility and opportunity that is characterized by people changing jobs rapidly, for the slightest reason, Christians should be demonstrating countercultural stability, loyalty, and contentment.[4]

That's not to say we should never leave a job. If we decide we're in the wrong job, we're not condemned to stay in it for the rest of our lives. God may use one vocation, even a wrong choice of vocation, to prepare us for other vocations. Moses' mistake in one vocation led to forty years of sheep farming in Midian, but God used it to prepare him for forty years of shepherding His people in the wilderness.

Let's now assume that you are doing lawful work and that it is the work God prepared for you to do. He gave you the work, He designed you for it, He equipped you for it, He gave you a desire for it, and He's called you to perform it today. As such, your work is a reflection of God's wise sovereignty. It is also part of the good works He prepared for you to do before the world began.[5]

Yes, your daily work is good work, part of your holiness.

"But I only clean houses."

"But I only build tables."

Have you forgotten that Jesus was a carpenter for most of His life? It was part of His holiness, part of the way He lived out His life. He was not evangelizing and preaching all the time. He was building tables, and it was as holy as His ministry work. He was as holy as a woodworker as He was as a preacher. Both were ways in which He loved His Father and His neighbors.

One of the Reformers said, "No task will be [seen as] so sordid and base, provided you obey your calling in it, that it will not shine and be reckoned very precious in God's sight."[6]

If we want to have joy in our work, we need to get this sense of divine calling deeply embedded in our hearts and minds. What a difference a sense of God's commissioning would make to our Mondays!

Most people regard their work as a job, a career, or a calling. Those who see their work as a *job* see it just as something they have to do to get money. They usually try to work as little as they can for as much money as they can so they can play as much as they can. The work itself is irrelevant and usually a negative.

Those who view their work as a *career* usually enjoy their jobs much more and invest much more time and energy in them, but again, they don't usually find as much satisfaction in the work as in the promotions and increased pay they get along the way.

Those who see their work as a *calling* usually find the work itself to be rewarding and fulfilling. To them, it is a major part of their lives, rather than something they do to enjoy the rest of life or the perks it can give them.

Shawn Achor wrote in *The Happiness Advantage*: "Unsurprisingly, people with a calling orientation not only find their work more rewarding, but work harder and longer because of it. And as a result, these are the people who are generally more likely to get ahead."[7]

What greater meaning, goal, or vision can we have than doing what God calls and equips us to do? But God doesn't just call and equip; He also enables and empowers so that we do our work in dependence on Him, looking to Him for everything we need in our callings. Our work is not just *from* Him but *through* Him.

YOUR WORK IS THROUGH GOD

You spend your week filing papers, printing reports, chasing bad debts, and putting stamps on envelopes. Then you go to church on Sunday and you see a man leading hundreds in worship and prayer and preaching inspiring sermons. It is pretty obvious who is pleasing God most, isn't it?

Is it?

Not so fast.

God looks on the heart, not the outward appearance.

What does He see?

Through God

Well, He sees that you start your day with prayer as you go to the office. You ask Him to protect you in your travels. You praise Him for safely navigating you through the rush hour. You sit at your desk and begin the mindless filing, but as you do so, you are praying for family and friends. You are interrupted by a boring colleague, but you cheerfully bear with him, listen to his moaning, try to cheer him up, and send him away with a bit of a spring in his step. You sit down for a coffee break and bow your head for a few seconds of thanksgiving. You pray for the Lord's help to make that difficult phone call to a bad debtor. He yells and screams at you again, but you sense the Lord's help as He gives you patience, self-control, gentleness, and peace. Slowly, your soft answer turns away wrath, and a few days later, the long-promised check appears.

Later in the day, you are putting the stamps on the mail and praying for the Lord's blessing on the day's work, that the company would prosper and God would give harmony among the workers. You leave work thanking God for His help throughout the day, thanking Him for a steady income, and asking Him to bless your witness.

Then God looks at the pastor in his office. There's certainly a lot of hustle and bustle. He's reading furiously and typing even more furiously. He lost a couple of hours aimlessly surfing the Internet this morning and a few more hours in a heated online debate about the Millennium. Now he's up against the clock as he tries to pull a sermon together. But he's done it many times before. He knows the sermon websites to check, he's a skilled cutter-and-paster, and by the end of the day he's constructed a fairly polished sermon. He picks the songs he knows that everyone likes and assures himself that after all these years in the ministry, he can easily lead the worship. And sure enough, Sunday comes, he struts his stuff, everybody praises him, and he goes home, not to fall on his knees, but to start reading the latest novel from Amazon.

Not one prayer. Not one contact with heaven. Not one act of dependence. Not one thanksgiving. Not one call to God.

Now, you tell me, who is pleasing God?

You do all that you do each day and no one praises you or encourages you or thinks you are particularly godly. The pastor comes and does his thing, and everyone swoons. You go back to work on Monday without all that encouragement and affirmation, yet you patiently persevere in your calling.

But who is pleasing God?

If you do your work "through Him," in dependence on God, looking to Him alone for guidance, protection, strength, and blessing, you are doing your job with more faith than some men in pulpits!

And don't we need God's help and His blessing on our work?

After all, we're no longer working in Paradise. Sin has brought God's just curse upon the world. The ground brings forth thorns and thistles, and we bring forth sweat, blood, and tears. No matter how hard we try, work is often frustrating, disappointing, unfulfilling, boring, painful, tiring, and fruitless. Work reveals the curse on sin as much as childbearing does.

Just think of the perplexing ethical dilemmas and moral challenges that most Christians are facing in their daily work these days. We need the Lord's help and blessing not just in the church but in the office, in the schools, in the hospital, in the store, and on the building site. Remember, Bezalel, the first person that Scripture records as being filled with the Spirit, was a builder![8]

If we don't do our work through God, we are missing out on one of the major means of sanctification in our lives. Sanctification is much more than "Don't do this or that." It is doing our work in dependence on God and to the glory of God. And as we do so, God shapes us and forms us into who He wants us to be. If worship is one hand God uses to shape the clay of our humanity, then work is the other. God gave us our work to purify and grow us.

Through You

But we don't work only through God; God works also through us. He cares for the world through us. Through our work, we become His eyes, hands, feet, and heart to others.

But has God really called me to clean sinks and change diapers? Is this really God working through me?

Yes, as someone said, "Nothing is wasted in God's economy." Nothing. No act of work He has called you to do is pointless. Everything has significance and value, regardless of whether your brain can calculate it or not. God doesn't just take pleasure in Sunday and in church services while barely tolerating the nine-to-five of

Monday through Friday. He cares about and values the office, the factory, and the sink. More than that, He takes pleasure in our work, probably more pleasure than we do! In *Chariots of Fire*, when Eric Liddell was being pressured to change from a running career to a missionary career, he said, "I believe God made me for a purpose, but He also made me fast. And when I run, I feel His pleasure."[9]

It is wonderful to feel the sense, "This is what I was made for." And when we can't feel it, we call faith to our side to help us believe it. God is using us to advance His work of providence in the world. God channels our work to benefit others. It is one way God loves the world and we love our neighbors. Lutherans often speak of Christians at work being "the fingers of God," or as Tim Keller put it, the "agents of his providential love for others."[10] We are His representatives put here to steward His world.

In Luther's *Large Catechism*, when he explains the prayer for our daily bread, he says that "when you pray for 'daily bread' you are praying for everything that contributes to your having and enjoying your daily bread. . . . You must open up and expand your thinking, so that it reaches not only as far as the flour bin and baking oven but also out over the broad fields, the farmlands, and the entire country that produces, processes, and conveys to us our daily bread and all kinds of nourishment."[11] Or as he put it elsewhere: "God milks the cows through the vocation of the milk maids."[12]

Doesn't that change the way you view the store assistant, the salesperson, the mailman, the businesswoman, and yourself? God is working through them and you. It should also change the way you deal with people. That unbelieving mechanic and that unbelieving nurse are, unbeknownst to them, the way God is working out His care and providence in the world.

YOUR WORK IS TO GOD

Of Him, through Him, and *to Him* are all things.

To Him?

How can my fixing my car be to God? How can my dishwashing be to God? How can my filling out forms be to God? Is it not blasphemy to suggest God is interested in these things? Well, it would be if God had not told us through the apostle Paul that He is: "Whatever you do, do it heartily, *as to the Lord* and not to men, knowing that from the Lord you will receive the reward of the inheritance; *for you serve the Lord Christ.*[13]

Whatever we do, we are doing it to the Lord, we are serving Christ, and He is taking an interest with a view to future reward.

That means we work as if He was our employer, our manager, our boss. We wash dishes as if He was going to eat from them. We unblock drains as if it was His home. We don't work primarily for money (that's a job), for promotions (that's a career), or for a way to fill the time (that's an occupation), but for the Lord (that's a vocation). Whatever we do, it is to Him and for Him we do it. Our work is an act of love to God. That's revolutionary, isn't it?

Again it takes a positive act of faith. We wouldn't believe it unless the Word of God said it. But God has said it and means it. We, therefore, must exercise faith. No matter how unseen our work, He sees. No matter how unrewarded, He will reward it. No matter how ignored, He does not ignore it. No matter how seemingly insignificant, it has huge worth in His eyes. Our work brings the Lord to us and us to the Lord. That's a good paycheck, is it not? I'd rather wash dishes for the Lord than run a multimillion-dollar business without any reference to God.

William Tyndale wrote, "If our desire is to please God, pouring water, washing dishes, cobbling shoes, and preaching the Word 'is all one.'"[14] And Luther—in his typical earthy style—wrote, "God and the angels smile when a man changes a diaper."[15]

Our work has significance now and for eternity. Colossians 3:23–24 says that God will take account of how we work when He is distributing His rewards to His people in eternity. Every minute we work influences eternity.

Knowing that should make us pursue excellence in all we do. The diligent Christian shelf stacker will get a greater eternal reward than the lazy and incompetent Christian CEO. The faithful and loyal secretary who does her work as to the Lord will enjoy a greater reward than the manager who spent his time trying to evangelize when he should have been organizing his staff and inspiring them to greater productivity.

Many Christians live a double life in the sense that they view spiritual value only in overtly Christian work (missions, evangelism, helping the poor), whereas their everyday work, while not non-Christian, seems to have nothing whatsoever to do with Christianity. Churches and preachers must help people unite these two lives. We must tell carpenters, "The best thing you can do for God is to make a good chair." We must tell farmers, "The best thing you can do for the Lord is to grow quality corn." We must tell young moms, "The best thing you can do for the Lord is to care for your kids."

As such, our work becomes a religious act, a prayer, a praise, even a sermon. Yes, we can worship God in the workshop, in the kitchen, and under a car as well as in a cathedral.

Everyday work done "as to the Lord" can be a more religious act than many sermons, acts of charity, or missions. Indeed some preachers, missionaries, and charity workers might do better serving God with excellence in boardrooms and factories.

To drive home God's intense interest in the everyday minutiae of life, remember this little nugget of Solomon's wisdom: "Dishonest scales are an abomination to the LORD, / But a just weight is His delight" (Prov. 11:1). To put it bluntly, an honest day's work delights the Lord; it puts a smile on His face and joy in His heart. In Scotland after the Reformation, this verse was often inscribed above market gateways, not just as a warning but as an inspiration. Despite many Christians thinking that they're doing nothing for the Lord, this verse tells us that if we do a good, honest, hard day's work, we can come home and slump in our favorite chairs knowing that God is absolutely delighted with what we did that day.

YOUR WORK IS FOR THE GLORY OF GOD

The world of work is a theater of God's glory. It is not just beautiful natural landscapes that motivate our worship, but beautiful work as well, even when done by unbelievers. Who can look at an apple and not worship God? Who can look at an Apple iPhone and not worship God? Yes, the simplest natural product and the most sophisticated digital product provoke and promote worship.

Work and Worshiping God

We're used to nature inducing us to worship our Creator, but consider how technology can do this too.

- Technology makes us worship God's wisdom. God's mind conceived of silicon, radio waves, fiber optics, light, electricity, magnetism, space travel, rocket fuel, and much more.
- Technology makes us worship God's creativity. Behind every good invention and ingenious design is the Inventor and the Designer.
- Technology makes us worship God's goodness. How

> thankful we should be that we are living in an age of such lifesaving and life-enhancing technology.
> • Technology makes us worship God's power. It is mind-blowing to think of the amount of energy that technology is consuming every day—hundreds of billions of kilowatts—and yet that's just a little part of God's great power.
> • Technology makes us worship God's patience. What incredible patience and long-suffering that see such good gifts taken, abused, and turned against the Creator and His creatures, and yet He still spares us and our world.

Wherever we turn—the workshop, the operating theater, the garage, and the studio—we gaze on the glory of God's attributes in the daily work of His creatures and what they create. Such focusing on glorifying God in and through our work saves us from the sin of glorifying ourselves and trying to find our identity in our work.

Work and Imaging God

But we not only glorify God by seeing Him and His character in the world of work; we also glorify Him by imaging Him to others. As we work, we want to ask, "What can I do to represent who God is in His power, in His justice, in His mercy, and all the rest? How can I as God's image bearer image Him to other image bearers?"

We can do so by bringing order out of chaotic cupboards, by bringing beauty out of ugly yards, by repairing damaged limbs, by cleaning dirty clothes, by educating ignorant children, by healing sick seniors, and so on. All make visible the invisible image and character of God.

Does that not transform your sink, your classroom, your workbench, and your desk? Indeed, when we take account of the whole teaching of Romans 11:36, it positively transforms every job and every aspect of working life:

As we mow lawns: "Of Him, through Him, to Him, for Him. Glory forever!"

As we change diapers: "Of Him, through Him, to Him, for Him. Glory forever!"

As we study algebra: "Of Him, through Him, to Him, for Him. Glory forever!"

Work and the Purpose of God

A major pharmaceutical company asked Lisa Earle McLeod to shadow hundreds of its salespeople to find out what makes the difference between an average salesperson and a top performer.[16] She didn't know the sales figures of each salesperson, but after two days with one woman, McLeod was sure she'd found one of the stars. When this woman walked into doctors' offices, the receptionists stopped what they were doing and ran to get the doctors. Not a common reaction to most drug sales reps!

When they parted at the Phoenix airport, McLeod wanted to get inside the woman's head a bit and asked her: "What do you think about when you go on sales calls?"

The rep looked around the car as if someone else was listening in a kind of conspiratorial, "I'm going to tell you the big secret right now" way. "I don't tell many people this. But I always think of this one patient. When I first started this job, I was in the waiting room, waiting on one of my doctors, and this little old woman comes up to me, taps me on the shoulder, and says, 'Excuse me, are you the rep that sells this drug?'"

"Yes, ma'am, I am."

"The little old woman turned to me and said, 'I just want to thank you. Before I started taking this I didn't have a life. I couldn't go anywhere. I couldn't travel. Now I can go and visit my grand-children. I can get down on the floor and play with them.'"

This high-powered corporate sales rep started crying and said, "I think about her every day, and that's my purpose."

Despite being initially focused on lots of technical data and stats, McLeod was sure she'd stumbled on the magic ingredient. She went back through hundreds of interviews and found seven reps who alluded to a noble sense of purpose. It wasn't just any sense of purpose, but a *noble* sense of purpose, a sense of purpose that was driven by serving and helping others.

At the end of the study, the pharmaceutical company asked her to identify the top reps. "These seven," she said. And she was 100 percent correct. "And I know your top performer too!" Right again. The Phoenix saleswoman was the company's top sales rep three years in a row in the entire country.

McLeod's conclusion was that the way for companies to increase revenue was not so much behavioral—train reps to write better letters, make more phone calls, and do better presentations. It was much more about motivation and attitude. Salespeople who had a sense of noble purpose, who wanted to give more than get, who truly wanted to make a beneficial difference in their custom-ers' lives, drove more revenue than salespeople focused on quotas, targets, and commissions.

It's that sense of noble purpose—*How can I make a beneficial difference to my customers?*—that can make even the job of selling a glorious and God-glorifying Christian vocation. And that not only results in better performance and results. It also results in greater happiness and job satisfaction. Happy people work harder and lon-ger, are more appreciated as colleagues and bosses, and have much lower rates of conflict, stress, and absenteeism. They also get paid more and get promoted quicker.

A positive attitude toward work and at work stimulates creativity, increases skills, strengthens resilience, boosts health, multiplies relationships, increases income, and maximizes job security and job satisfaction.[17]

WORKVIEW AND WORLDVIEW

Let's wrap up this chapter by briefly considering how such an all-encompassing view of work changes our view of the ministry, leisure, and heaven itself.

Our View of the Ministry

If we accept this biblical view of work, we will stop thinking that gospel ministry is the highest calling. The work that God has given you is the highest calling and is itself a God-given ministry. The ministry is the highest calling only for those whom God has called to ministry (and as Paul said, God usually calls the least of all saints to that work). But if God has called you to another kind of work, that is His highest calling for you.

Anything less than this equalizing of callings is a return to the pre-Reformation elevation of sacred work above secular work. The medieval church viewed the ministry as a primary calling (that was the perfect life), and other work was only a secondary calling (or as some called it, the "permitted life").

Priests were called, but everybody else worked. It was not that the other jobs were evil. They just weren't holy. They were concerned with earthly things and were not divine callings.

Early church fathers also fell into this trap by regarding the contemplative life as the preferred life; the active life was second class. Even after the Reformation, the ministry was often viewed as the ideal, and everything else was second class.

When William Wilberforce was converted in his midtwenties,

he immediately thought he should leave politics and go into the ministry, which he saw as more important than secular work. John Newton helped Wilberforce understand that God was calling him to a public life. He said, "My walk is a public one. My business is in the world; and I must mix in the assemblies of men, or quit the post which Providence seems to have assigned me."[18]

Martin Luther wrote that the work of monks and priests, "however holy and arduous they be, do not differ one whit in the sight of God from the works of the rustic laborer in the field or the woman going about her household tasks, but all works are measured before God by faith alone."[19]

William Perkins, the English Puritan, commented, "The action of a shepherd in keeping sheep, performed as I have said, is as good a work before God as is the action of a judge in giving sentence, or of a magistrate in ruling or a minister in preaching."[20]

This is not to demean the ministry, to bring the ministry down. It is to lift up all other callings to the high and holy level of dignity and significance that God has given them. Remember, God called Adam and Eve not to pray and study the Bible but to be good and godly gardeners.

Our View of Leisure

If we follow the biblical blueprint for work, we will not only avoid a slothful and lazy attitude to our work, we will also avoid the other extremes of workaholism and burnout by adopting God's blueprint for rest, leisure, and pleasure. God has made us with a 6:1 rhythm of work to rest. To paraphrase Exodus 20:9, "Six days you shall labor and do all your work, but the seventh day is a day created by God for holy resting."

We need not feel guilty about taking a day off a week. Indeed, we should feel guilty if we don't, because we are then rebelling against God's created order. It is not a necessary evil but a necessary blessing. It recharges our bodies and gives us time, space, and quiet to rest our minds and lift them to higher and eternal things. Such a rhythm will help us get a healthier perspective on our work and prepare us to do better work. It will help us see that we need Christ's perfect work to rest in as our ultimate hope of happiness in this life and the life hereafter. Yes, our competitors and colleagues may be working every day of the week, but God has commanded us to take one day in seven as a rest day and to have adequate sleep.[21] That's where faith comes to our aid again. God commands it. We believe it. And as we exercise such faith, the positive benefits of God's order flow abundantly into our lives.

Our View of Heaven

A biblical view of work changes our worldview and what we imagine heaven will be like. By faith we see it as a place of holy rest and satisfying work. The primary presentation of heaven in the Bible is as a place of holy rest, a place where we rest from our painful and frustrating labors and rest in worshipful joy at the feet of our Savior. The fact that work was part of the original good creation of God, however, should also lead us to consider the likelihood that work of some nature will also be part of the re-creation, the new heaven and the new earth.

What a joy it will be to finally, fully, and forever experience: "For of Him and through Him and to Him are *all things*, to whom be glory forever. Amen." And to do so with people of every class, culture, country, and color.

Chapter Ten

HAPPY DIFFERENCES

DIVERSITY > UNIFORMITY = POSITIVE+

BECAUSE WE LOVE OURSELVES so much, we tend to love those most like ourselves. We are drawn to people who look like us, talk like us, dress like us, and smell like us, and we tend to ignore, avoid, belittle, criticize, or even hate those who aren't and don't.

We know we shouldn't, and when we're given time to think things through, we can usually, hopefully, reason ourselves to more appropriate attitudes, words, and actions. But our instinct, our natural reflex, is to love people like us and to shun the opposite.

This bias affects all our choices: whom we marry, where we live, what school our children attend, where (and how) we worship, what music we listen to, where we vacation, and on and on. It is a deep, wide, and long *prejudice*, or prejudgment, which one dictionary defines as "an unfavorable opinion or feeling formed beforehand or without knowledge, thought, or reason."[1] Such prejudices can often grow or lapse into a much more subjective, hostile, aggressive attitude toward certain people or people groups.

Of course, not everyone is equally biased. Those who grow up in racially and ethnically mixed communities are usually a bit more accepting of differences than those who were raised in all-white or

193

all-black communities. Unless, of course, these mixed communities were marred by racial tensions, in which case the prejudice is often even worse than usual.

MY STORY

Monocultural

My background is almost entirely monocultural. I spent most of my life in white, middle-class areas of Scotland. I was raised in a 98 percent white area of suburban Glasgow. Of the 180 kids in my high school year group, maybe five of them were of Pakistani origin. There were also maybe five or six Jewish kids. Apart from that, it was all white Scottish kids, half of them middle class and half of them from poorer backgrounds.

Although I regularly played soccer and other sports with a couple of the Asian guys from time to time, and I used to walk to and from school with a Jewish lad, the Asians largely stayed with themselves, as did the Jews. There wasn't any aggressive racism as far as I can remember, but there was certainly a failure to include and involve the Asians in activities, a thoughtless insensitivity, and even failure to oppose racism when it did arise.

Also, whenever any nonracial conflict arose, color was often thrown into the mix. Sometimes in the locker room there was "good-humored" bantering with our Asian defender about his color and culture. I put "good-humored" in quotation marks because there's really nothing humorous about it on reflection, but we all laughed along at the time.

All this is to say that my childhood was largely monocultural, with just a few very minor racial issues along the way. When I left school at age seventeen, I worked for a large Scottish financial services company where, as far as I can recall, there wasn't a nonwhite on a staff of more than four hundred. The pubs and clubs I attended in my unconverted late teens and early twenties were similarly all white. When I went to the university to begin studies for the ministry, there was certainly more of a mix, but not much mixing.

Multicultural

The closest I came to a multicultural environment was living for a couple of years in an area of Glasgow that was more than 60 to 70 percent Pakistani immigrants, so much so that some called it "mini-Pakistan." Instead of making me more multicultural, however, it probably deepened my monocultural bias due to the frequent hostility my sister and I experienced from the teenage Asians who used to hang out at the corner of our street. There were two cultures, but they were living very much side by side, and sometimes side *versus* side.

But I didn't need to think too much about my latent prejudices. I was soon married and able to move back into a safer and more uniform culture. Before too long I was pastoring in the Scottish Highlands, thirteen years in two all-white churches and 99 percent white middle-class communities.

Then I came to America!

Admittedly it wasn't exactly to the most multicultural area of America. Grand Rapids, Michigan, was a stronghold of Dutch immigrants and the Dutch Reformed Church. Still, although there were many similarities with my Scottish Presbyterian background, there were significant differences, especially in church services. It was the first time I had even a faint sense of being in the minority. It irritated me a bit. *Why can't everyone be more like me?*

The seminary where I taught had a good number of international students from almost every continent, and their diverse learning and preaching styles began to challenge me and reveal a little of my barely hidden sense of cultural superiority. *Why can't everyone be more like me?*

As I ventured forth into other parts of America for teaching and preaching engagements, I became increasingly aware of the latent prejudice that was in my heart and beginning to bubble up in my mind. Different colors, different cultures, different speaking styles, different clothes, different worship. *Why can't everyone be more like me?*

Anti-immigration

I've always leaned right in my politics and tended to disagree with the UK government's immigration policies that have produced large and rapidly growing Muslim populations in most English cities. I also witnessed the post-2001 flood of Eastern European immigrants that swept many British people out of their low-paid jobs. When I came to America, I swallowed a lot of the right-wing rhetoric against immigration. Although some of that was justly targeted against illegal immigration, it was often difficult to distinguish it from a generalized opposition to all immigration.

This all came to a head one day in Walmart as I waited impatiently behind a line of cheerful migrant workers from Mexico as they slowly checked out their goods.

Wouldn't it be much better if they weren't here?

Yes, that's the question that arose in my mind. Followed by, *What right do they have to be here?* Which suddenly provoked an intense inner dialogue:

Hey, you're an immigrant yourself, Murray!

Yes, but I'm not a Mexican immigrant.

What's the difference?

Well, I'm white and speak proper English.

So what? Does that make you better than them?

Well, yes. . . . I mean, no. . . . I mean . . .

It was an unforgettable moment of painful self-discovery. I had to face the facts. I was prejudiced. Racist even. It had been there all along, but it was being exposed in all its hideous vile reality.

What was I really saying? I was saying my color was better, my culture was better, my clothes were better, my hairstyle was better, and my children were better. I was better than them and superior to them. I was a *good* immigrant, and they were *bad* immigrants.

But I was saying even more than that. I was saying that my happiness would be increased if they weren't here. Their being there at that time in that line was reducing my joy. If only I could get rid of them, I'd be a happier person. As I reflected on the horror of this self-discovery, I began to realize that the Walmart cashier's checkout line had not just been a one-off. It revealed my worldview. It took one of my deepest presuppositions out of the ugly depths of my heart and mind, stripped it, and exposed it: *I'm better than you, and I'd be happier if you were not here or if you were more like me.*

This was one of the most humbling and convicting moments of my life. For days, weeks, and months afterward I began to see the evil pride and self-love reflected in this belief, this principle by which I'd been unwittingly living my life.

Have you ever had a Walmart moment? Have you ever recognized thoughts and attitudes that you wish you didn't have, thoughts and attitudes about your superiority and another's inferiority that you didn't want anyone else to know?

I've left this chapter until last partly because I didn't want you to discover on page one what a horrible person I am. But I also put it last because it is probably going to be the hardest chapter for some readers to swallow.

None of us like to admit that we have sinful prejudices, and even fewer of us want to deal with them and drive them out of our lives. Part of that is not wanting to accept how sinful we are. But part of it is that it is really, really hard to believe we can be happier and our lives can actually be enhanced and improved by embracing and pursuing more diversity than uniformity. Can diversity really be a positive in our lives?

The Joy of Diversity

There's something deep within us that says, "The more people are like me and the more people like me I can gather around me, the happier I'll be." What I've increasingly discovered since the Walmart reverse epiphany is that the opposite is the case. The more I've listened, talked, and walked with diverse and varied people, the more joy I've experienced. Although there have been times when my attempts to reach out have been met with indifference and even hostility, that's been the exception rather than the rule.

"But," some might say, "we're losing our country!"

It is certainly true that our society is rapidly diversifying. International mobility, favorable immigration policies, increased urbanization, and accelerating population growth among minority groups mean that the majority white culture is proportionately shrinking in size and influence. According to the US Census Bureau's 2008 projections:

- By 2023 the majority of children will be minorities, and by 2042 the majority of our population will be minorities.
- The non-Hispanic white population will lose population in the 2030s and 2040s and by 2050 will only be 46 percent of the population (66 percent in 2008).
- The Hispanic population will triple from 46.7 million to 132.8 million between 2008 and 2050, meaning one in three US residents will be Hispanic.
- The black population will increase from 41.1 million to 65.7 million between 2008 and 2050.

- American Indians, Alaska Natives, Native Hawaiian and other Pacific Islander populations will also double in size.

But is that "losing our country"? *Our* country? It is not *our* country. It is God's, just like every other country. And if He sees fit to change the demographics, who are we to oppose Him? We're here only because He changed the demographics in the past.

And what about losing? Does change automatically mean loss? Why can't it be a gain?

These changes do not need to be bad news. We're not going to change the statistics, but we can by God's grace change our hearts and minds about these statistics, about our changing communities, so that diversity is not a negative but a positive, not a curse but a blessing, not a threat but an opportunity.

I'll come back to the pluses of diversity later, but I want to be crystal clear here before going any further: I'm not talking about moral diversity. That's what the world often means by diversity—the idea that all moralities are equal and valid and that there's no such thing as immorality. Neither am I talking about the world's promotion of diversity or multiculturalism that often calls us to accept everyone's beliefs and practices regardless of whether they align with biblical values. What I'm talking about is primarily racial diversity, but much of what I say will also apply to the kind of cultural and ethnic diversity that does not contradict scriptural standards.

I've already discussed what I believe lay at the root of my cultural and racial sense of superiority—proud self-love that believes happiness can be found only by people being and becoming more like me. But, I hasten to add, racism and culturalism are not limited to white Protestants! Since I've begun to venture forth into unfamiliar territory, I've encountered racism going in the opposite direction too. One African American pastor told me that he voted for President Obama only because of Michelle: "She's a real black, unlike Obama who's only half black!" Although things are much improved over the past hundred years or so, the awful history of race-based chattel slavery and Jim Crow segregation has left a painful legacy of animosity, suspicion, and resentment that continues to impact daily life in America.

EMBRACING AND PURSUING DIVERSITY IN OUR PERSONAL LIVES

But how can we stop our sinful and self-destructive prejudice? Indeed, how can we embrace the diversity God designed and turn it into a constructive positive in our lives? Let's examine several ways we can do this as individuals, in our families, and in our places of work. Then we'll explore the church's opportunity to show God's mind and heart on this.

Confess

First, let's ask God to reveal to us our passionate *self-love* and the huge obstacle it is to *other-love*, especially the love of others who are different from us. Ask Him to show you the pride that makes you think you are superior to someone because you are of a different and, in your eyes, a better race. As God shows you this gruesome reality, confess the latent and patent prejudice that is in your heart—whether it is a white heart, a yellow heart, a brown heart, or a black heart.

Equalize

Soak in the Bible's equality themes: all peoples are created equally in the image of God,[2] all peoples have the same human father,[3] all peoples are to be judged on the same level by God,[4] all believers are saved equally by the grace of God,[5] all believers have equal standing before God, all believers have equal place in the church of God,[6] and all believers live forever with God.[7] Let these revolutionary truths penetrate and saturate your soul.

Break Barriers

Believe in Jesus Christ, the barrier breaker and bridge builder. God sent Jesus Christ to smash the walls that divide people from people and people from God. It could even be argued that the two points of application in His first synagogue sermon were about racial integration.[8]

He smashed national barriers by sending the gospel to the nations to unite the nations. He smashed racial barriers by making a Samaritan woman one of His first converts and a Samaritan man one of His best examples of love. He smashed gender barriers by making women some of His closest friends and by defending them from abusive men. He smashed age barriers by welcoming children into His arms of blessing and by condemning any who hindered or harmed His little ones. He smashed social barriers by eating and drinking with the worst of sinners. He smashed ceremonial barriers by touching lepers, healing them, and sending them into the temple. He smashed class barriers by rejecting the rigid caste system of His day, embracing rich and poor, educated and uneducated among His disciples.

Above all He smashed the barrier between God and sinners, the massive barrier that sinners had built out of their sins to keep God out of their lives. But Jesus died for these sins and dismantled that wall, brick by brick, as He shed His blood to bring us to God. What a barrier breaker! What a bridge builder!

What an example and inspiration to continue this barrier-breaking and bridge-building work among all peoples. As African American pastor Dolphus Weary wrote, "Proclaiming the gospel of

Jesus Christ and working for racial reconciliation [are] two sides of the same coin."[9] Although Weary engaged in social action on behalf of blacks, he insisted that racial reconciliation is ultimately a spiritual issue: "If we only work on the social aspects of racism and never introduce the gospel, then we'll never see complete transformation."[10]

Study

Study other people groups. Find out the background of the racial makeup of our society. Read Civil War history, read civil rights history, read biographies of Native Americans. So much of our prejudice is based on ignorance. If we knew the history of minority communities, we would build a lot more sympathy and understanding for them and their plight. But don't just study the past. Find out the present statistics that reflect the educational, moral, religious, economic, and judicial factors that contribute to the just grievances of minority communities.

In "How Racism Is Bad for Our Bodies," Jason Silverstein highlighted how discrimination increases the risk of depression, the common cold, hypertension, cardiovascular disease, breast cancer, and mortality.[11] One study of thirty thousand people found that black people experienced six times more stress than white people, which not only damages the body and mind but also pushes people to cope in unhealthy ways. The study showed that just the fear of racism increased blood pressure, heart rate, and so on. Little wonder that current life expectancy among African Americans is only that of white Americans forty years ago.

Reach Out

Reach out to other races and ethnic groups. Listen to their stories; feel their pain; taste their tears. Ask them to help you understand their sensitivities, their feelings, their concerns, and their perspectives.

Ask yourself, "Is there anything I can do today in my interactions with people that will make them feel more loved, more accepted, more valued?" It might be just an extra smile and thank you at the checkout. Maybe you can do or say something positive online. Or how about an encouraging word to a colleague or even a complete stranger?

Admire

Every culture has strengths and weaknesses. It is common to see the strengths of our culture and the weaknesses in others. With a bit of effort, however, we can find and admire values and practices in other cultures that are better than our own. Think, for example, of the resilience and patience of the African American community.

Stephen Liggins, who is involved in training African church leaders via Moore College's international outreach program, said that African Christians taught him how to evangelize better, pray more fervently, and minister more holistically.[12]

Closer to home, Scott Moore, a white church planter in an all-black neighborhood, said, "There are jewels, if you will, in marginalized communities that are missing from the Church's crown. Without these jewels, the Church sparkles less." Speaking more of the culture that is the 'hood than the color of it, he picked out two jewels that we need to take away from these communities:

"People in the 'hood know how to celebrate." Instead of taking graduations, vacations, and birthdays for granted, in the 'hood people celebrate these events in joyful community-wide ways. "The streets are full. Children are everywhere. Smoke from a hundred grills permeates the air. Laughing echoes through the streets. It is a celebratory taste of heaven."

"People in the 'hood instinctively understand covenantal commitment." Although families are often painfully broken, in other ways their commitment to one another is sacrificial and heroic.

"I have seen friends in the neighborhood sacrifice greatly so that those they love can survive. I have seen a man give his last dollars, without a single hesitation, so that his brother could pay the rent. I have seen a man take a jail sentence so his friend wouldn't have to. . . . Men are willing to put themselves in harm's way to protect and vindicate those they love. They are willing to bleed so that others won't have to, or because others they love have already bled. And these decisions are made instantly and naturally. It is rooted in both their commitment and courage."

He concluded: "I'm convinced that if the 'hoods of America are left unreached, the Great Commission will remain unfulfilled. The Church needs the 'hood and has much to gain from the treasures that can be plentifully mined there. When a river floods and becomes destructive, we don't eliminate or neglect the river. Rather, we use our resources and ingenuity to redeem, redirect, and use its force."[13]

Befriend

Befriend a minority family in your neighborhood. In most American contexts, that will be either an African American family or a Hispanic family. Do this for your benefit, but be sure that this will also make a huge statement to your children and to your other neighbors about how you view and treat all people equally. And if you are African American or Hispanic, why not reach out to a white family?

Teach

Teach your children to respect other races and cultures. Help them recognize the prejudice that is in their hearts and seek God's help in fighting against it. Children will absorb racism from the surrounding culture, but even the most protected homeschooled kids are born with racist hearts and it only takes opportunity for it to erupt. Encourage them to defend minorities and to oppose racism. It is not enough not to be racist, because racism can be a sin of omission as well as commission. Dolphus Weary observed: "You don't have to be a member of a racist group to practice racism. You don't even have to feel prejudice against an entire race to practice racism. All you have to do is watch someone from another race being treated unjustly and remain silent."[14]

EMBRACING AND PURSUING DIVERSITY IN THE CHURCH

Due to the spiritual, social, and cultural benefits of biblical diversity, the church should take a leading role in exemplifying and pursuing this. We have a long way to go. According to one 1987 study, 92.5 percent of churches in the United States are segregated, meaning they have less than 20 percent from minority races. Although there has been a growing awareness among churches that this must change, the overall statistics barely budged when the study was updated in 2007.[15]

Educate

Teach your congregation about biblical diversity. Thread this biblical theme throughout sermons, Sunday school lessons, and Bible studies. Or why not make a special study of the Bible's teaching about God's plan to bless the nations through Jesus and His plan to break down the walls of partition between the most hostile people groups—not just in heaven but also on earth?

Promote

Promote books and sermons by minority preachers and teachers. Don't always quote from white Americans, but acquaint yourself with a wider range of writing and preaching. Invite minority preachers and speakers to your congregation and conferences. Support and promote transracial adoptions and interracial marriages.

Join

Although the ideal is racially integrated churches reflecting the diversity of our populations, that's not going to happen overnight. As we work toward this goal, though, we can work together with African American and Hispanic churches in the meantime. Why not hold joint conferences on things we do agree on? Or at least have joint meetings from time to time?

"How many Christians do you know who don't look like you?" Dolphus Weary pointedly asked in *Crossing the Tracks*. Weary challenges churches to reach out to congregations of different racial composition and provides two pages of ideas for how racially different and divided churches can partner together in kingdom work. According to Weary, when Christians who don't look like each other come together in the ways he proposes, powerful things happen:

- They address a real need in their community.
- They show the world what racial reconciliation looks like by coming together as brothers and sisters in Christ and living out the unity Christ desires.
- Because of that unity they offer a compelling witness to the world that Jesus is Lord of a united people, answering Jesus' prayer in John 17.[16]

Grow

Cherish growth in diversity as much as numerical growth. Even be prepared to sacrifice numerical growth to experience a growth in the diversity of our congregations. Bill Hybels said that if he had to do everything over again, he would make racial integration a Willow Creek value from the very beginning. When asked if he would do it, knowing that he would never be able to grow Willow so far and so fast, he said, "Absolutely." The interviewer pressed him: "You would be willing to reach less people just so your church could be a picture of diversity?" Hybels replied, *The corporate witness of racially diverse churches in America would be more powerful than a number surge in any one congregation.*[17]

Train

Identify potential leaders in minority communities, and train them for taking on leadership roles in the church and other Christian institutions. And if you are faced with the choice of two equally capable and qualified candidates, one from the majority community and one from the minority, why not appoint the person from the community that has been underrepresented in the past?

That's not so much about making up for the past; it is also about inspiring for the future. Seeing members of their own community in leadership positions can have a hugely inspiring impact on future generations. For example, the *New York Times* reports that "a performance gap between African-Americans and whites on a 20-question test administered before Mr. Obama's nomination all but disappeared when the exam was administered after his acceptance speech and again after the presidential election. The inspiring role model that Mr. Obama projected helped blacks overcome anxieties about racial stereotypes that had been shown, in earlier research, to lower the test-taking proficiency of African Americans."[18]

Change

Work to reduce merely cultural practices that are standing in the way of other cultures or races coming to worship in your church. This will not be smooth or easy. J. D. Greear said, "Multi-ethnic churches can only thrive when people are, so to speak, 'comfortable being uncomfortable.'"[19]

While making sure that our practices are based on biblical principles, we should ask if there is a way of putting these principles in different clothes. The churches with the thinnest cultural layers will experience the most integration, whereas churches with tradition closer to the center of their worship and practice create less room for those who are different.[20]

If we want to fulfill God's plan of the church being a "house of prayer for all nations"[21] we will have to accept the necessity of change. But we must fight the reflex that all change equals total loss. As J. D. Greear wrote, "My white culture needs the influence of my Asian or African American brothers and sisters, just like they need influence from my culture. We are actually *lacking* something when our cultures fail to rub shoulders and borrow from each other."[22]

Identify

Help Christians see themselves and other Christians' identity as being first and foremost "in Christ." I am not primarily Scottish, Presbyterian, or white. Before and above all that, I am in Christ. Similarly don't see others as African Americans or Hispanics who happen to be Christians. Rather see them as Christians who happen to be African American or Hispanic.

Be Patient

Be compassionately patient with those who are different. If we are in the majority community, remember that the minority communities have not enjoyed our longstanding privileges and opportunities. Instead, they have suffered many years of oppression, prejudice, and injustice. If we work to eliminate these great evils in our hearts, churches, and communities, many of the lesser problems will die out in the process.

Celebrate

Rejoice in what God is already doing among the nations and races of the world. Although the church's influence is weakening in the Western world, it is growing at astonishing rates in Africa, Latin America, and Asia. Although Europeans comprised 70 percent of the world's Christian population at the beginning of the twentieth century, one hundred years later Europeans were only 28 percent, while Latin American and African were 48 percent of the Christian population. In one hundred years the Christian population in Africa grew from 10 million to 360 million. These mighty world- and church-transforming works of God should be celebrated.[23]

Hope

Despite all the legislation, education, sermons, and dollars, so much racial reconciliation work remains to be done in society and in the church. But if we keep preaching, believing, and living the gospel, we should still have huge hope. The gospel smashes superiority and inferiority complexes. The gospel doesn't deny or exploit guilt but deals with it. The gospel humbles both white supremacy and black power. The gospel gives vengeance over to God. The gospel replaces hate with love. The gospel gives powerful hope.

ADVANTAGES OF DIVERSITY

For many people, the rapidly changing color of our population and the call to welcome racial diversity and to promote reconciliation can be very unsettling and uncomfortable. "Can't I just deal with racism in my heart and leave everything else well enough alone? I'll repent of my secret sins and let everything else carry on as normal with friendships, family, business, and church."

Simple answer? No.

At least not if you really want to have positive faith and live optimistically in a negative culture. Although it looks daunting and discomforting, and it is at first, the pursuit of this kind of diversity will enrich you and those around you in numerous ways. *Diversity will make you happier than uniformity.* Yes, there will be a cost, there will be loss, and there will be pain, but such cost is relatively minor compared with the following gains.

Personal Sanctification

Attacking the sin of prejudice attacks one of the deepest and most pervasive sins in the human heart. By weakening prejudice (and its cousins—racism, nationalism, and culturalism), you will weaken the roots of many other sins as well. You will need the power of God's Spirit to do this work, but as He works you will experience His faith-confirming power in unforgettable and unmistakable ways.

Resources

As you develop relationships with other people from other cultures and colors, you will discover the unique gifts and graces that God has placed in these communities. These challenge all of us, but they are also a fund to draw from. The beautiful loyal relationship between African Americans and their pastors is one from which white congregations could certainly learn.

As the American church increasingly faces minority status in an increasingly hostile secular environment, there is much the wider church can learn from the historical experience of African American Christians who know what it is like to try to retain their faith and morality not only as a minority, but in a place that questioned even their freedom and right to exist.

Thabiti Anyabwile, an African American from Atlanta now

pastoring in Washington DC, called evangelicals to "learn to be the moral minority from a much older moral minority," that is, African American Christians. He explained:

1. *Learn to suffer with dignity and grace.* Because of its privilege, white evangelical churches don't know how to joyfully accept the plundering of its possessions and persons. If true persecution comes, it will need to learn this lesson in spades. There are two models: Jesus and the Black Church. Jesus' model is perfect; the Black Church's example is proximate, near at hand. One you read in the scripture, the other you can read in history texts or even access in conversation.

2. *Learn to do theology from the underside.* Privilege affords a person the ability to think about life and God from "above." It allows a person to form conclusions in abstraction, detached from the grit and grime of suffering and need. But you can't do that if you're in a "persecuted minority" status. . . . In many respects that's the great difference between theology done in Black and White circles. Most of African-American theology gets worked out in the crucible of suffering and under-privilege.

3. *Learn to hope in God.* When you're the majority community wielding power in society, you don't have to hope in God in quite the same way as you do when you're the minority and oppressed community. There's a sense in which it becomes easy to trust in chariots, horses, and armies rather than the name of the Lord our God. But true persecution strips you of every support but God. Persecution brings you to

your knees, but that's where you find power. That's one part of the legacy of the Black Church. When life was at its worst, it was a praying church. Despite injustice, persecution and the threat of death on every hand, African-American Christians put their hope in a God they were sure would bend the arc of history toward justice and deliverance.[24]

Love

In "A New Day for Multiracial Churches," Michael Emerson highlighted how white Americans currently have about *twenty times* the wealth of black and Hispanic Americans. Yet because our churches are still largely segregated, there is limited opportunity for those with the most to lovingly help those with the least: "[Instead] members of groups with the least are busy trying to meet the needs of others in their group, which, because the group has less, are typically bigger needs, trying to be met with less."[25] Because separation also makes it almost impossible for us to understand and sympathize with another group's needs, we miss out on the power of love, compassion, and persuasion to overcome group divisions and inequalities.

On the other hand, Emerson points out how integrated multiracial churches produce fundamental differences: Friendships patterns change. Through national surveys we find that people in multiracial congregations have significantly more friendships across race than do other Americans. For example, for those attending racially homogenous congregations, 83 percent said most or all of their friends were the same race as them. . . . But for those attending multiracial congregations, there is a dramatic difference. Only 36 percent of people attending racially mixed congregation[s] said most or all of their friends were the same race as them.[26]

Witness

The racial divisions in our culture are known all over the world. Imagine if the Christian church in America led the way in reuniting black and white. What a testimony to the power of the gospel over intractable problems. But we don't need to wait for church-wide actions; we can begin on our own individual level and demonstrate to the world that we are Jesus' disciples by the love we have one to another.

J. D. Greear points to Rodney Stark in *The Rise of Christianity*, who "lists racial integration as one of the things that made the early church distinct from other religious groups and led to its rapid growth. Local churches were the one place in the Roman Empire where differing races actually got along. Their racial harmony gave them a chance to explain that Jesus was not only a Jew, but the Lord of *all* humanity, the Savior of *all* races."[27]

Also, many young African Americans are turned off to Christianity by what they perceive as the racism of a white man's religion. If we can demonstrate that this is everyman's religion and it is not biased, it takes away one of the excuses that African American pastors increasingly encounter as they work among their young people.

A passion for racial integration in our personal lives and local churches will fuel worldwide mission as well. The more we embrace the different races and nationalities in our locality, the greater our burden for the unreached peoples of the world will grow.

Imitation

By smashing barriers and building bridges we are imitating our Lord and Savior, Jesus Christ, and imaging Him to the world. We are also contributing to the defeat of the evil barrier builder and bridge breaker, the Devil.

Welcome

Many black people will not come to churches unless other black people are there. The more diverse churches are, the more diverse they will become. Jemar Tisby, of the Reformed African American Network, said that the more multicultural a church is, the easier it is for its people to engage people across cultural and racial gaps as they grow in comfort and skill at interacting with varied cultures and ethnicities. Tisby also said that "multi-ethnic churches make it easier for different people—folks with purple hair and earrings in their eyebrows, folks who can't afford a suit and tie, folks who have never been to church and don't know how to pray, folks of a different color—to feel at home. This, in turn, makes you bolder and more confident to invite people to church."[28]

Reformation

A multiethnic church always has to ask what parts of its worship and practice are principle and what's preference. Doing that challenges people to go back to the Bible. By using biblical diversity as a lens through which to view the church, churches are helped to focus on the essential truths, and what is merely culture or preference falls away.

Fulfill the Plan of God

A primary plotline of the Bible is bringing glory to God by bringing back together various races in one common salvation. J. D. Greear stated, "The redemption that Jesus purchased for us was not merely an individual salvation; it was also an interpersonal, intercultural, interracial reconciliation."[29] He added,

> From Genesis 12 to Revelation 7, God brings back together what sin has driven apart. The Pentecost event of Acts 2 is intentionally multicultural. Mark recounts Jesus' vision of the church as

distinctly multicultural: "My house shall be a house of prayer *for all nations*" (Mark 11:18). Paul calls the racial integration of the church evidence of the "manifest wisdom of God" (Eph. 3:10). . . .

Revelation 7:9 records people from *every* nation, tribe, people, and language worshiping in unity around the throne of Jesus. What sin had marred, Christ repairs. The fracturing dissonance of racial segregation is overcome, and can only ever be overcome, through the unifying power of Christ.[30]

Glory for God

A number of psalms connect the glory of God with the spread of the gospel among the nations. John Piper said,

There is a beauty and power of praise that comes from unity in diversity that is greater than that which comes from unity alone. . . . More depth of beauty is felt from a choir that sings in parts than from a choir that sings only in unison. Unity in diversity is more beautiful and more powerful than the unity of uniformity. . . . the strength and wisdom and love of a leader are magnified in proportion to the diversity of people he can inspire to follow him with joy. If you can lead only a small, uniform group of people, your leadership qualities are not as great as if you can win a following from a large group of very diverse people.[31]

What glory will accrue to Jesus when people see His multicolored followers!

Foretaste

God's original plan was and is to bless the nations through the Jewish nation and the Jewish Messiah. That remains His plan, and it will be accomplished as the book of Revelation confirms. We have the opportunity, however, to bring heaven to earth, to get a little foretaste of heaven before we get there. Who hasn't enjoyed the amazing experience of worshiping with a much more diverse group at a national Christian conference? It's special, isn't it? Well, imagine if we could do that every Sunday! What a positive faith experience that would be.

DIVERSE DIVERSITY

Before I leave this subject, let me encourage you to travel a bit farther down the diversity road, still avoiding the unbiblical diversity that sees all moralities and immoralities as equally valid.

We've been focusing on cultural and racial diversity. But we can legitimately pursue many other diversities as well. What about intellectual diversity? Why do we tend to gravitate toward those who have the same level of education that we do? Why do we avoid those with more or less education than we have? The more educated are not all elitist snobs; they have their own weaknesses and struggles too. But especially consider the less educated. I've found levels of spirituality and theological discernment among farmers and mechanics that I've not come across in many pastors and professors. And that's what Jesus leads us to expect too.[32]

What about financial diversity? Again, I'm thinking especially of the enrichment that can come to our lives from spending time in the homes, churches, factories, offices, and sport fields of the less well-off. They often have a level of community that would make the most gated communities seem like a high-security prison.

What about vocational diversity? Some of my best friends are in manual trades. I love being with them, seeing their perspective on life and benefiting from faith that has been honed on the building sites of our cities and the production lines of our factories.

What about enhancing your life with the diversity of physical ability or inability? The parents of children with special needs tend to gravitate toward other similar parents. However, if you befriend and support such parents, you will find immeasurable blessing from the work that God is doing in their lives through their precious children.

Biblical diversity is a positive, not a negative. It is an addition, not a subtraction. It is an advantage, not a disadvantage. It is an essential element of a positive faith. It makes for happy Christians. Unless we embrace it, every encounter with diversity will be a negative, a threat, an enemy. It is not going away in our hyperconnected and hypermobile world; it is only increasing. You are fighting a losing battle by opposing it. Why not give up the battle? Consider biblical diversity a friend, an ally, a help in the battle for a positive faith, and find that it results in a more optimistic you, no matter how pessimistic the culture around you becomes.

CONCLUSION

GRAND TOTAL = POSITIVE FAITH
= THE HAPPY CHRISTIAN

AS WE CLOSE THIS ten-lesson math curriculum, I trust that your grand total column is showing a big positive number and that you are already beginning to live more optimistically and happily in our gloomy negative culture.

I want to encourage you to work on these ten formulas every day or at least the ones that will produce the highest returns for you until they become automatic, habitual, ingrained, and instinctive; until they transform the way you view yourself, your church, your media, your relationships, your job, your world, your past, present, and future, and even your sin and your suffering.

Sin and suffering?

Yes, we have to face the fact that even though we want to accentuate the positive and change many minuses into pluses, in this fallen and sin-sick world there are going to be negatives we just cannot change that will remain stubbornly strong and painful.

Sin will continue to plague us and frequently defeat and humiliate us. Some relationships will never be repaired. Some memories will never fade. Some diseases will never be healed. Some habits will never be conquered.

Sometimes, these negatives will threaten to overwhelm us.

They will multiply and add up so fast and so high that we cannot get our positive calculator out quickly enough or believe deeply enough to keep ahead of the deluge of red ink. We'll be tempted to give up the fight and succumb again to a background hum of trundling low-grade depression or perhaps even worse.

As I hope I've made clear throughout, *positive faith*, in contrast to *positive thinking*, does not deny the reality and pain of sin and suffering. Negative feelings of sadness, anger, and fear can be appropriate and helpful in the right place and proportion. Barbara Fredrickson wrote, "Some sources of negativity are simply inevitable in the commerce of daily life. They are called forth by the facts of the circumstances and are commensurate with those facts. This sort of negativity helps you stay healthy, productive, and grounded in reality."[1]

Instead of reacting to hard things with a fixed smile, positive faith takes it head-on, looks it straight in the eye, and uses the powerfully positive truths of the gospel to not only persevere in the face of sin and suffering but also draw positive good out of them.

How can that be?

We'll consider sin first, then suffering.

SIN

When the Holy Spirit starts working in our hearts, the first thing He does is convict us of sin.[2] As the prodigal son and many of us have discovered, that is often an excruciating process as we are brought face-to-face with what we've done or not done and with who we are. It's not just that we've committed sins; it's that we are sinful. It's not just that we've done wrong; it's that we've failed to do what's right. It's not just that we've fallen short of our standards or human standards; it's that we've fallen far short of God's standards.

It's not just that we've broken one or two of God's commandments; it's that they all lie in a broken and shattered heap. It's not just that we've sinned; it's that we've loved sinning and sometimes still do. It's not just that we've offended men and women; it's that we've offended God. It's not just that we've deceived others; it's that we've deceived ourselves.

This deep uncovering and revealing work of God's Spirit can go on for many months and perhaps years. Even after we've been converted to Christ, the Holy Spirit continues His convicting work so that we have regular, recurring, and painful times of conviction as we discover how deep, wide, long, and evil our sin is.

But why? Why is this traumatic spiritual experience necessary? What good can possibly come out of it? Why doesn't God just show us His love in Christ, bring us into it painlessly, and keep us in it without any further spiritual agony? What possible benefit can there be in this? It certainly doesn't feel beneficial. Consider some of the good results of sin that is repented of and forgiven:

We are humbled. When we fall into sin, we realize our
   pathetic weakness and vulnerability. We are not as strong
   and impregnable as we thought we were.
We are sensitized. We often fall into sin when we are
   spiritually hard and cold, but when we are humbled and
   broken, our spiritual senses are revived and restimulated,
   making us tender and sensitive again to God's Word and
   Spirit.
We are silenced. We so easily get arrogant, self-confident,
   and full of ourselves, with an opinion on everyone and
   everything. But when we are convicted of our sin, we talk
   less favorably of ourselves and less judgmentally of others.
We are drawn nearer. Having wandered slowly and
   imperceptibly away from the Lord, we are now shocked

to see how far we have traveled from Him, how distant we have become. We find ourselves longing for the nearer presence of the Lord again as He begins to woo us back to Himself.

We are dependent. Sin is usually the result of relying on our own strength and wisdom and failing to pray, "Lead me not into temptation, but deliver me from evil." When we are convicted by God's Spirit, we learn to depend on the Lord like a little baby on her mother. Looking away from ourselves, we do nothing without seeking God's help and blessing.

We are careful. Often our sin comes about when we have been spiritually careless. We've played with temptation. We've walked too close to the edge, then fallen over. Now our scars and memories make us much more cautious about letting even the first thought of sin lodge in our minds and hearts. We run away from the edge of the cliff.

We hate sin. When we see the evil of sin and the misery it produces, we no longer view it as harmless or humorous. We hate it with a passion and want to kill it at the roots.

We fight the Devil. Looking back on our sin, we see the role the Devil played. He was well disguised, for sure, but now we see him unmasked in all his hideous ugliness. We resolve to go to war with him and never again to let him seduce us.

We are disciplined. When we retrace our steps, we recognize that we had become irregular and halfhearted in our Bible reading, prayer, family worship, and church attendance. We now realize how much we need to use these divine means to keep us on the right track and become much more regular and disciplined in our daily and weekly use of these resources.

We love Christ. Whether or however we loved Jesus before,

we love Him all the more now. He who has been forgiven much, the same loves much.

We are thankful. We are even more thankful for Christ's atoning work and gracious salvation. We love His cross; we love His mercy; we love His love. And we're even thankful for the Holy Spirit who pained us for our sin.

We are equipped. Having experienced the power of the gospel to forgive and restore, we are better able to draw alongside others and skillfully apply the gospel to their sinful failings and faults.

We long for heaven. Oh, to be free from sin. Oh, to never want to sin. Oh, to be with and like Jesus.

I would even argue that one of the greatest helps to interpreting and understanding the Bible is a deep sense of my own sin:

- When I feel my sinfulness, I'm much more motivated to search the Scriptures for grace to help in my time of need.
- When I'm convicted of my sin, I doubt my wisdom and rely more on the Holy Spirit.
- When I see my sin, I understand the character of God better—His frightening holiness and His refreshing love.
- When I'm confronted with my sinful inability, I have no doubts about my need of God's grace.
- When I grasp how bad my best deeds are, salvation by faith without works becomes fascinating and utterly compelling.
- When I'm utterly condemned, all new perspectives on justification look ridiculous, and I get a far deeper insight into the old but ever new perspective of justification by faith alone.
- When I mourn my spiritual deadness, the resurrection of Christ is not only a doctrine but my only source of life.

- When I sense my immeasurable guilt, I have no difficulty whatsoever in grasping the existence and eternality of hell.
- When I absorb the enormity of my spiritual enmity, substitution is no longer a theory of the atonement but my only and enthralling hope.
- When I see the untrustworthiness of my heart and mind, the inerrancy of Scripture becomes a matter of life or death.
- When I perceive the deceitfulness of my heart, I understand so much better how to minister the Word to other similar hearts.
- When I behold the ugliness and vileness of my sin, my eyes are opened to behold more of the glory and beauty of Christ.

A deep sense of sin gives insights into the deep things of the Bible.

Now, let me emphasize that *all sin is evil*. No sin is worth it. It is always better that we don't sin. However, God can turn even sin for good. This is why Jesus said, "Blessed are those who mourn, for they shall be comforted."[3] The mourning is essential, but it is not the end; it is not the destination. Comfort is. And part of that comfort is seeing how God can bring spiritual benefit from even our worst sins, even the benefit of a clearer grasp of Scripture.

SUFFERING

What about disease? What about bereavement? What about injustice? We must not deny or downplay the agony of these experiences. We shouldn't expect even the strongest believers to just brush off these kinds of burdens as if they were feathers. Even Jesus wept over lost cities and dead friends.

If we take just physical suffering, for example, there's no question that it is much easier to maintain a happy outlook and a positive faith when our bodies are fit, healthy, and functioning well. Indeed, one of the quickest ways into negative faith, even positive unbelief, is to abuse the bodies that God has given us through overdoing work or underdoing sleep, exercise, and good food. God has so made us that the body and soul are mysteriously tied together, dependent on each other, and each to some degree determining the health of the other. The majority of people I've counseled with depression have ended there through overwork, overstress, undersleeping, and underexercising. A Christian psychologist friend told me that he always prescribes three pills as a vital part of his treatment plan for depressed patients: good food, good exercise, and good sleep!

I know that when I'm not sleeping enough or when I'm not getting daily exercise, negative thought patterns quickly set in and I start spiraling downward. My tense and weary body drags down my mind and soul. But a few good nights' sleep and regular exercise will usually turn me around again so that I can live with a more positive and God-glorifying faith. As the apostle Paul teaches us, our bodies are for the Lord, members of Christ, temples of the Holy Spirit, and bought with a price. Therefore, he says, "glorify God *in your body and in your spirit*, which are God's."[4]

Some studies have shown that regular exercise is as effective as antidepressant medication. It helps us physically and psychologically by reducing anxiety and stress, by improving sleep, and by increasing confidence. Sonja Lyubomirsky says that multiple surveys and experiments show that "exercise may very well be the most effective happiness booster of all activities."[5]

But what if health is no longer an option? What if our bodies are sick, diseased, disabled, and even dying? That will happen to most of us, even to those of us who have cared most for our bodies. We are mortal. We will weaken and sicken. Can we really call such sufferers to be happy Christians, to exercise positive faith?

I'm thinking especially of one of my friends who was recently diagnosed with multiple sclerosis, aged twenty-two. Because he was misdiagnosed for seven years, he is already losing power in his legs, and his hopes of beating the odds are massively reduced. Can I give him this book? Or would that just add insult to injury? Can I expect him to be a happy Christian in the midst of such devastating suffering? Yes, because God is able to work even the worst suffering together for our good and His glory.

He does this by helping us find a redemptive perspective, which, Donald Miller explained, is really about creating two lists rather than one: "Normally when something hard happens we start a running mental list of all the negative consequences. And that's fine and normal. Finding a redemptive perspective, however, is about creating a second list, a list of the benefits of a given tragedy. And there are always benefits."[6] Although we must never deny the painful negatives of life, we must seek God's help to put and keep positive truths in the foreground of our minds.

Post-Traumatic Growth

Christians aren't the only ones who believe that good can come out of suffering. One of the most remarkable illustrations of this is found in the growing body of research into post-traumatic growth (PTG) among military personnel. Until recently the focus and headlines have all been about post-traumatic stress disorder (PTSD), an emphasis that produces additional problems, as Martin Seligman illustrated:

> If all a soldier knows about is PTSD, and not about resilience and growth, it creates a self-fulfilling downward spiral. Your buddy was killed yesterday in Afghanistan. Today you burst into tears, and you think, I'm falling apart; I've got PTSD; my life is

ruined. These thoughts increase the symptoms of anxiety and depression—indeed, PTSD is a particularly nasty combination of anxiety and depression—which in turn increases the intensity of the symptoms. Merely knowing that bursting into tears is not a symptom of PTSD but a symptom of normal grief and mourning, usually followed by resilience, helps to put the brakes on the downward spiral.[7]

In the course of his research, Dr. Seligman questioned seventeen hundred people who had experienced one or more of "the fifteen worst things that can happen in a person's life: torture, grave illness, death of a child, rape, imprisonment, and so on." He noted, "To our surprise, individuals who'd experienced one awful event had more intense strengths (and therefore higher well-being) than individuals who had none. Individuals who'd been through two awful events were stronger than individuals who had one, and individuals who had three—raped, tortured, and held captive for example—were stronger than those who had two."[8]

This, of course, is not to see good in the trauma itself but to highlight how trauma can produce positive growth in many areas of life. For example, after the March 11, 2004, train bombings in Madrid, "many residents experienced positive psychological growth. So too do the majority of women diagnosed with breast cancers," said Shawn Achor.[9] The positives included increased spirituality, compassion, self-confidence, life-satisfaction, and greater intimacy in their relationships.[10]

If such growth outcomes are possible for non-Christians, how much more possible should they be for Christians who have so many more spiritual resources to draw on? Suffering Christians are called not just to survive, bumping along the bottom of the graph with greatly reduced happiness, motivation, and hope. Neither are we called to merely recover to pretrauma levels of functioning. Rather, we are called to thrive and flourish, to climb higher than our normal default levels of faith, hope, and love, and to do so via the ladder of suffering: "We also glory in tribulations, knowing that tribulation produces perseverance; and perseverance, character; and character, hope. Now hope does not disappoint, because the love of God has been poured out in our hearts by the Holy Spirit who was given to us."[11]

Of course, this is not easy, smooth, or without setbacks. But the long-term graph should reveal not a downward slide or even a flat line but an upward swing from the deepest of dips.

Storytelling

Psychologists who have studied how people respond to trauma say that the key to profiting from pain and flourishing after suffering is the story we tell ourselves when we are facing hard times. Shawn Achor distinguished between optimistic storytellers who view difficulty as local and temporary (i.e., "it's not so bad, and it will get better") and pessimists who view these events as more global and permanent (i.e., "it's really bad, and it's never going to change"). He explained further: "Their beliefs then directly affect their actions; the ones who believe the latter statement sink into helplessness and stop trying, while the ones who believe the former are spurred on to higher performance."[12]

One way to help us tell a better and brighter story is to challenge ourselves with questions when we feel ourselves sinking. Questions such as these can help us reinterpret painful events and see them in a more positive light:

What good could come from this?
What can I learn from this about myself, about others?
How can I grow through this?

Spiritual Growth

In addition to seeing hard times as opportunities to grow in character, Christians want to use them to grow spiritually—to deepen sanctification, appreciate Christ's sufferings, strengthen spiritual graces, increase evangelistic zeal, drive us to the promises of God, and make us long for the world to come. We also have the huge help of the Holy Spirit in all this.

We agree that the key is the story we tell ourselves. But Christians don't have to make up a story that may or may not be true and that may or may not have a happy ending. We simply have to connect by faith with the already written redemptive story of God. It is the truest of all stories and has the happiest of all endings for all its characters. If unbelievers can get so much benefit out of suffering, how much more should believers!

Why not go back through the previous list of "benefits" from the conviction of sin and calculate which of these fruits that suffering has produced in your life? Just like sin, suffering humbles us, sensitizes us, silences us, draws us, makes us dependent, increases carefulness, fans hatred for sin, motivates us to oppose the Devil, drives us to the Bible and our knees, stimulates love for the Christ who suffered for us, provokes thankfulness for the good days and for the good that God draws out of the bad days, makes us better comforters and encouragers, and above all, makes us long for heaven. As the apostle Paul said, "The sufferings of this present time are not worthy to be compared with the glory which shall be revealed in us."[13] But we don't need to wait until heaven to see and enjoy the fruit of affliction. Though "no chastening seems to be joyful for the present, but painful; nevertheless, afterward it yields the peaceable fruit of righteousness to those who have been trained by it."[14]

That's a beautiful balance, isn't it? The apostles do not downplay sin or suffering. Neither do they view them apart from the sovereign power and wisdom of God, who is able to make the most and the best of our least and our worst.

The Stockdale Paradox

Let me illustrate this with the Stockdale Paradox, named after Admiral Jim Stockdale, who was held captive for eight years during the Vietnam War and tortured more than twenty times before finally making it home. According to Stockdale, it was mainly optimists who did not survive the POW camps. Strange, isn't it?

He explained: "They were the ones who said, 'We're going to be out by Christmas.' And Christmas would come, and Christmas would go. Then they'd say, 'We're going to be out by Easter.' And Easter would come, and Easter would go. And then Thanksgiving, and then it would be Christmas again. And they died of a broken heart."

In contrast to this false optimism, Stockdale attributed his survival to realistic faith: "I never lost faith in the end of the story, I never doubted not only that I would get out, but also that I would prevail in the end and turn the experience into the defining event of my life, which, in retrospect, I would not trade." He concluded, "You must never confuse faith that you will prevail in the end—which you can never afford to lose—with the discipline to confront the most brutal facts of your current reality, whatever they might be."[15]

The suffering apostle Paul put it this way: "As dying, and behold we live; as chastened, and yet not killed; as sorrowful, yet always rejoicing; as poor, yet making many rich; as having nothing, and yet possessing all things."[16] Both sides together at the same time. Sorrowful and rejoicing. Mourning and being comforted.

This distinguishes positive faith from mere optimism and enables faith to trump optimism. This produces a happy Christian in the gloomiest times. We confront the brutal reality of our lives, our families, our churches, and our society. But at the same time, we keep steady faith in the Word of God, especially its sure promises of personal perseverance and the ultimate triumph of faith and the church of Christ. Optimism is not faith, but faith is optimistic. Especially when faith looks beyond the horizon of this world and time. And that's where I want to end this spiritual math course.

HEAVEN

Let's leave this class and go along the corridor to the art department. There we find a studio with a sculptor at work. He's thinking, imagining, creating, concentrating, inventing, innovating, improvising, beautifying, loving, hammering, smoothing, decorating, styling, and polishing.

What's His name?

It is God. It is God at work on His latest masterpiece.

What's the masterpiece?

Look closely. It's *you*!

Yes, believer, you are God's masterpiece! Paul said that you are God's "workmanship,"[17] but the Greek word can also be translated "His masterpiece," or "His poem."[18]

Think of how much time and talent the poet pours into every word she crafts, every line she composes. God is lavishing even greater time and talent on you each and every day. He is weaving together the seemingly disconnected rhythms and rhymes of your life into an epic poem of grace. He is tapping away on the block of your humanity to produce an outstanding living statue of grace.

I remember a cartoon from my childhood in which a sculptor was tapping away on a block of ugly stone for days, months, and years, without any sign of progress. As he aged through the years, the mocking crowds grew larger as this poor little man tip-tapped away with patient care. And still, for all his work, just the odd chip of stone had fallen to the ground. The block was largely unchanged ugliness.

But one day, when the jeering crowd was particularly large and hostile, the sculptor leaned on his stool, took a little silver hammer, and gave the block one faint tap on the top. A crack started moving down and out, breaking into multiple tributaries. Little chips began to fall away, then larger blocks, until at last an avalanche of material was cascading to the ground.

The dust settled, jaws dropped, eyes popped, and voices gasped: "It's a masterpiece!"

That's what we have to look forward to. What a day that will be! I imagine it will be something like the day we finished school. Do you remember that? What joy, when we could hand back the books, put away the calculator, file the papers, and enter a new world of freedom, joy, maturity, and opportunity.

Well, thankfully, such a day also awaits those of us who have spent our lives in the school of Christ, learning how to calculate these ten formulas. Sometimes we got the answers right and flourished. We experienced all the spiritual, physical, mental, emotional, social, ecclesiastical, and vocational benefits of a positive and happy faith. Other times, we failed and ended up with red ink all over our lives.

The day is coming, however, when we will graduate from this class and leave this testing spiritual math behind. Because we are going to a world where there will be no negatives in our minds, our bodies, our relationships, our churches, our work, our society, or our world. We will no longer battle to live an optimistic life in a negative culture, because everything and everyone will be positive.

The most negative person, the most depressed person, and the saddest believer will be happy, happy, happy all day and every day.

The negatives of our lives will be left behind, and we will enjoy life in the new heaven and new earth with new bodies, new minds, new emotions, new relationships, and new experiences.

All things new! All things positive! All things happy!

ACKOWLEDGMENTS

Thank you, yes *you*, for reading this book. I know, it's a bit unusual to start acknowledgments by thanking the readers, but without Christian readers, there would be no Christian books. I hope reading this made you happier and that you've been inspired to encourage others to join the ranks of happy Christians.

If you did read through to the end, you will have noticed how much I quoted from books written by positive psychologists. I'm deeply grateful to these men and women for their multiple and manifold labors that have produced so much excellent research dedicated to increasing human happiness. I would encourage you to read these books, most of which have been written in a popular and accessible style.

Thank you also to Thomas Nelson. This is now the second book that we've published together, and both times have been fantastic experiences. I've learned so much from every stage of the process as I've worked with your wonderfully gifted editors: Joel Miller, Kristen Parrish, and Janene MacIvor. Joel, I'll greatly miss you as you exercise your gifts in new territories, but I want you to know again how much you changed my life.

Thanks to Chad Cannon and Erica Reid and the many others involved behind the scenes at Nelson: in management, accounts, design, marketing, distribution, and so on. Thank you to all of you for being such indispensible links in the long chain from first-typed word to book-in-hand. And skillfully connecting all these links together is Brian Hampton. Brian, thank you for all that you do, and for all you have done for me. Deeply appreciated.

Then my dear friends and agents Crosland Stuart and D. J. Snell of Legacy Management. What can I say? You, too, have been life transformers and tremendous encouragers to me these past few years. I value your friendship and counsel more than I can ever express. You are truly happy Christians, and that's not just because you live in Florida!

I'm grateful to all the happy Christians I've known and been inspired by over the years, but none more so than my beloved wife, Shona. Yes, Shona, you fought with pregnancy-related depression over the years, we've had some painful trials along the way, and you've had to survive being married to me for twenty-three years! But despite all that, to me and many others you are still the happiest Christian in the world! Your Christian joy energizes me every day of life. Our happy marriage has made me a much happier Christian.

Ultimately all our thanksgiving returns to the ultimate source of all good, our great and gracious God—Father, Son, and Holy Spirit. I offer this book as a praise to You, for You have made me so deliriously happy with Your wonderful salvation. I dedicate this book to You and pray that You will use it to beautify Your people with holy happiness and happy holiness, so that many others will be irresistibly drawn to You and the grace of the gospel in Jesus Christ.

NOTES

Introduction: The Happiest People in the World

1. Proverbs 23:7, author's paraphrase.
2. Nehemiah 8:10.
3. Romans 5:20.
4. Bradley Wright, *Upside: Surprising Good News about the State of Our World* (Bloomington, MN: Bethany, 2011), 18–19.
5. Aaron Ben-Zeev, "Are Negative Emotions More Important than Positive Emotions?" *In the Name of Love* (blog), *Psychology Today*, July 18, 2010, http:// www.psychologytoday.com/blog/in-the-name-love/201007/are-negative-emotions -more-important-positive-emotions.
6. R. F. Baumeister et al., "Bad Is Stronger than Good," *Review of General Psychology* 5 (2001): 323.
7. Shiv Malik, "Adults in Developing Nations More Optimistic than Those in Rich Countries," *Guardian*, April 14, 2014, http://www.theguardian.com/politics/2014 /apr/14/developing-nations-more-optimistic-richer-countries-survey.
8. You can read more of this history in Shawn Achor's book, *The Happiness Advantage* (New York: Random House, 2010), 9–11.
9. Achor, *The Happiness Advantage*, 9.
10. Jessica Colman, *Optimal Functioning: A Positive Psychology Handbook* (Jessica Colman, 2010), Kindle edition, 77–84. Colman is summarizing M. E. P. Seligman and M. Csikszentmihalyi, "Positive Psychology: An Introduction," *American Psychologist* 55, no. 1 (2000): 5–14.
11. 2 Corinthians 6:10, emphasis added.
12. Colleen Stanley, "Optimism Is a Selling Skill," *Eyes on Sales*, February 10, 2011, http://www.eyesonsales.com/content/article/optimism_is_a _selling_skill_is_your_sales_glass_half_empty_or_half_full/.
13. T. Bryan and J. Bryan, "Positive Mood and Math Performance," *Journal of Learning Disabilities* 24 (1991): 490–94.
14. E. Diener et al., "Dispositional Affect and Job Outcomes," *Social Indicators Research* 59 (2002): 229–59.

15. D. Danner et al., "Positive Emotions in Early Life and Longevity: Findings from the Nun Study," *Journal of Personality and Social Psychology* 80 (2001): 804–13.
16. Gallup-Healthways Well-Being Index (2008).
17. Barbara Fredrickson, "The Role of Positive Emotions in Positive Psychology," *American Psychologist* 56, no. 3 (March 2001): 218–26. B. L. Fredrickson and C. Brainigan, "Positive Emotions Broaden the Scope of Attention and Thought-Action Repertoires," *Cognition and Emotion* 19 (2005): 313–32.
18. S. Kopelman, A. S. Rosette, and L. Thompson, "The Three Faces of Eve: Strategic Displays of Positive, Negative, and Neutral Emotions in Negotiations," *Organizational Behavior and Human Decision Processes* 99 (2006): 81–101.
19. S. Lyubomirsky, L. King, and E. Diener, "The Benefits of Frequent Positive Affect: Does Happiness Lead to Success?" *Psychological Bulletin* 131 (2005): 803–55.
20. Nehemiah 8:10; see Matthew 6:33.
21. Deuteronomy 33:1–28.
22. Deuteronomy 33:29.
23. 2 Corinthians 6:10.
24. Proverbs 23:7, author's paraphrase.
25. "Right Direction or Wrong Track," *Rasmussen Reports*, July 2, 2014, http://www.rasmussenreports.com/public_content/politics/mood_of_america/right_direction_or_wrong_track.
26. Mark Penn and Donald A. Baer, "Americans Are No Longer Optimists," *Atlantic*, July 1, 2014, http://www.theatlantic.com/politics/archive/2014/07/has-america-entered-an-age-of-impossibility/373744/.
27. Michelle Cottle, "The Purpose Driven Life a Decade Later," *Newsweek,* December 3, 2012.

1 HAPPY FACTS

1. S. Lyubomirsky, K. M. Sheldon, and D. Schkade, "Pursuing Happiness: The Architecture of Sustainable Change," *Review of General Psychology* 9 (2005): 111–31.
2. Ibid.
3. Sonja Lyubomirsky, *The How of Happiness* (New York: Penguin, 2007), 22.
4. Gretchen Rubin, *The Happiness Project* (New York: Harper, 2011), 12.
5. Ibid., 3.
6. Proverbs 23:7, author's paraphrase.
7. Romans 12:2.
8. Jessica Colman, *Optimal Functioning* (Jessica Colman, 2010), Kindle edition, 822.
9. Ibid. Colman says: "The 'ABC' process was developed by two of the world's leading cognitive therapists, Dr. Steven Hollon and Dr. Arthur Freeman, along with Dr. Martin Seligman."
10. Ibid., 829, 870. For the Disputation and Energization points, Colman references Martin Seligman, *Learned Optimism* (New York: Alfred A. Knopf, Inc., 1991).
11. Ibid., 885.
12. Ross Pomeroy, "Belief in Angry God Associated with Poor Mental Health," *RealClearScience.com* (blog), April 16, 2013, http://www.realclearscience.com/blog/2013/04/belief-in-punitive-god-associated-with-poor-mental-health.html.
13. N. R. Silton, K. J. Flannelly, K. Galek, and C. G. Ellison, "Beliefs about God and Mental Health Among American Adults," *Journal of Religious Health*, April 10, 2013.

14. Shawn Achor, "The Happy Secret to Better Work," TED.com, May 2011, http://www.ted.com/talks/shawn_achor_the_happy_secret_to_better_work.html.
15. Matthew Syed, "'I Have Never Been Happier,' Says the Man Who Won Gold but Lost God," *Times*, June 27, 2007, http://www.thetimes.co.uk/tto/sport/athletics/article2375163.ece.
16. Matthew Syed, "'I Have Never Been Happier' Says the Man Who Won Gold but Lost God," Richard Dawkins Foundation, June 26, 2007, http://old.richarddawkins.net/articles/1340-39-i-have-never-been-happier-39-says-the-man-who-won-gold-but-lost-god.
17. Norman Vincent Peale, *The Power of Positive Thinking* (New York: Simon & Schuster, 2003), 1.
18. Ibid., 8.
19. Ibid., 82.

2 HAPPY MEDIA

1. Shawn Achor, *The Happiness Advantage* (New York: Random House, 2010), 94.
2. Miguel Jiron, "Sensory Overload," Interacting with Autism Project, 2012, https://vimeo.com/52193530.
3. Achor, *The Happiness Advantage*, 01–02.
4. Philippians 4:8.
5. John Milton, *Paradise Lost*, in *Bartlett's Familiar Quotations*, 16th ed. (Boston: Little, Brown, 1992), 256.
6. Philippians 4:6–7.
7. Philippians 4:8.
8. Philippians 4:7, 9.
9. E. Littell, *Littell's Living Age*, vol. 22 (Boston: E. Littell & Co., 1849), 477.
10. Bradley Wright, *Upside: Surprising Good News about the State of Our World* (Bloomington, MN: Bethany, 2011), 36.
11. Ibid., 38.
12. Ibid., 201, 204–5.
13. Ibid., 207–8.
14. Barbara Fredrickson, *Positivity* (New York: Random House, 2009), 37.
15. Martin Seligman, *Flourish* (New York: Simon & Schuster, 2011), Kindle edition, 1113–20.
16. Cited in Julie Beck, "How to Build a Happier Brain," *Atlantic*, October 23, 2013, http://www.theatlantic.com/health/archive/2013/10/how-to-build-a-happier-brain/280752/.
17. Norman Vincent Peale, *The Power of Positive Thinking* (New York: Simon & Schuster, 2003), 60.
18. Gretchen Rubin, *The Happiness Project* (New York: Harper, 2011), 282.
19. Rolf Dobelli, "News Is Bad for You—and Giving It Up Will Make You Happier," *Guardian* (UK), April 12, 2013, http://www.guardian.co.uk/media/2013/apr/12/news-is-bad-rolf-dobelli?CMP=twt_gu.
20. Achor, *The Happiness Advantage*, 53.
21. Philippians 4:9.
22. Romans 3:23.
23. John 3:17.
24. Philippians 3:10.

25. Romans 7.
26. Romans 8.
27. Ecclesiastes 3:4.
28. Quoted in Wright, *Upside*, 15.
29. John Ortberg, foreword to *Upside*, 12.
30. Acts 5:41.
31. Matthew 5:12.
32. Fredrickson, *Positivity*, 37.
33. S. J. Lopez and M. C. Louis, "The Principles of Strengths-Based Education," *Journal of College and Character*, 10(4) (2009): 1–8.
34. Matthew 25:14–30.
35. Martin Seligman, *Flourish* (New York: Simon & Schuster, 2011), Kindle edition, 696–702.
36. Barbara Fredrickson, "Open Hearts Build Lives," National Center for Biotechnology Information, http://www.ncbi.nlm.nih.gov/pmc/articles/PMC3156028/; Robert Schneider, "Long-term Effects of Stress Reduction on Mortality in Persons > or = 55 Years of Age with Systemic Hypertension," *American Journal of Cardiology* 95 (2005): 1060–64; Herbert Benson and William Proctor, *Relaxation Revolution: The Science and Genetics of Mind Body Healing* (New York: Scribner, 2011), 59; Bruce Barrett et al., "Meditation or Exercise for Preventing Acute Respiratory Infection: A Randomized Trial," *Annals of Family Medicine* 10 (2012): 337–46; Fadel Zeidan et al., "Brain Mechanisms Supporting the Modulation of Pain by Mindfulness Meditation," *Journal of Neuroscience* 31 (2011): 5540–48; J. David Creswell et al., "Mindfulness-Based Stress Reduction Training Reduces Loneliness and Pro-Inflammatory Gene Expression in Older Adults," *Brain, Behavior, and Immunity* 26 (2012): 1095–1101.
37. Psalm 119:11.
38. 1 Peter 3:15.
39. Romans 8:6.
40. Psalm 1:1–3; 104:34.
41. Cited in Brian Johnson, "The Happiness Hypothesis," *Experience Life.com*, March 2013.

3 HAPPY SALVATION

1. John 19:30.
2. Samuel Johnson, *The Works of Samuel Johnson*, vol. 2 (New York: Alexander V. Blake, 1838), 679.
3. 1 Peter 1:12.
4. Hebrews 2:1–3.
5. 1 John 1:9.
6. Isaiah 26:3.
7. Psalm 37.
8. Shawn Achor, *The Happiness Advantage* (New York: Random House, 2010), 128.

4 HAPPY CHURCH

1. Isaiah 1:11–17.
2. Matthew 6:1–18; Matthew 23.
3. Matthew 13:24–30.

4. 2 Corinthians 13:5.
5. Matthew 13:30.
6. Ephesians 5:27.
7. Psalm 92:12–15.
8. Matthew 13:33.
9. Sonja Lyubomirsky, *The How of Happiness* (New York: Penguin, 2007), 117–19.
10. John 1:14.
11. Philippians 2:5–8.
12. 2 Corinthians 8:9.
13. Luke 7:47.
14. Zechariah 3:1–2; Revelation 12:10.
15. Luke 11:34–36.
16. Ephesians 5:27; Jude 24.
17. Hebrews 10:25.
18. "Social Groups Alleviate Depression," Canadian Institute for Advanced Research, March 19, 2014, http://www.cifar.ca/social-groups-alleviate-depression.
19. Shawn Achor, *The Happiness Advantage* (New York: Random House, 2010), 174.
20. Todd Essig, "Bodies Matter," *Forbes*, February 28, 2013.
21. Cited in Joshua Shenk, "What Makes Us Happy," *Atlantic*, June 1, 2009, http://www.theatlantic.com/magazine/archive/2009/06/what-makes-us-happy/307439/?single_page=true.
22. From the abstract of E. Diener and M. Seligman, "Very Happy People," *Psychological Science* 13 (January 2002); 81–84, http://www.ncbi.nlm.nih.gov/pubmed/11894851.
23. Achor, *The Happiness Advantage*, 176.
24. Mihaly Csikszentmihalyi, *Finding Flow* (New York: Basic Books, 1997), 43.
25. Cited in Anneli Rufus, "15 Signs You'll Live Forever," *Daily Beast*, July 27, 2010.
26. Ibid.
27. L. F. Berkman, L. Leo-Summers, and R. I. Horwitz, "Emotional Support and Survival After Myocardial Infarction," *Annals of Internal Medicine* 117 (1992): 1003–9.
28. J. House, K. Landis, and D. Umberson, "Social Relationships and Health," *Science*, 241 (1998): 540–44, http://www.ncbi.nlm.nih.gov/pubmed/3399889.
29. J. W. Pennebaker and R. C. O'Heeron, "Confiding in Others and Illness Rate Among Spouses of Suicide and Accidental Death Victims," *Journal of Abnormal Psychology* 93 (1984): 473–76.
30. Tom Valeo, "Good Friends Are Good for You," WebMD.com, http://www.webmd.com/balance/features/good-friends-are-good-for-you.
31. D. Spiegel, J. R. Bloom, H. C. Kraemer, and E. Gottheil, "Effect of Psychosocial Treatment on Survival of Patients with Metastatic Breast Cancer," *Lancet* 2 (1989): 888–91.
32. Dan Buettner, "New Wrinkles on Aging," *National Geographic*, November 2005, 2–27.
33. Cited in Wayne A. Meeks, *The Moral World of the First Christians* (Philadelphia: Westminster John Knox Press, 1986), 57.
34. Cited in Claudia Wallis, "The New Science of Happiness," *Time*, January 9, 2005, http://content.time.com/time/magazine/article/0,9171,1015902-4,00.html.
35. Martin Seligman, *Flourish* (New York: Simon & Schuster, 2011), Kindle edition, 423.

NOTES

5 HAPPY FUTURE

1. Galatians 4:4.
2. Romans 8:28.
3. Gretchen Rubin, *The Happiness Project* (New York: Harper, 2011), 289.
4. Arianna Huffington, *Thrive* (New York: Harmony, 2014), 197.
5. Ibid.
6. Ibid., 199.
7. Isaiah 51:1.
8. 1 Samuel 7:12.
9. Rubin, *The Happiness Project*, 101.
10. 1 John 1:7.
11. Psalm 103:12.
12. 1 Corinthians 10:13.
13. Dane Stangler, "The Economic Future Just Happened," *Kauffman Foundation*, June 6, 2009, http://www.kauffman.org/what-we-do/research/2009/08/the-economic-future-just-happened.
14. Interview with Clayton Christensen, "How Hard Times Can Drive Innovation," *Wall Street Journal*, December 15, 2008, http://online.wsj.com/news/articles/SB122884622739491893.
15. Facts and Figures: Suicide Deaths, American Foundation for Suicide Prevention, http://www.afsp.org/understanding-suicide/facts-and-figures.
16. John Tierney, "What Is Nostalgia Good For?" *New York Times*, July 8, 2013, http://www.nytimes.com/2013/07/09/science/what-is-nostalgia-good-for-quite-a-bit-research-shows.html?smid=tw-share&_r=1&.
17. Bradley Wright, *Upside: Surprising Good News about the State of Our World* (Bloomington, MN: Bethany, 2011), 44.
18. Romans 8:18–25; Psalm 96:10–13.
19. Psalm 130:5–6.
20. John Bunyan, *Pilgrim's Progress*, pt. 1 (New York: Charles E. Merrill, 1910), 200.
21. Julian L. Simon, ed., *The State of Humanity* (Cambridge, MA.: Blackwell Publishers, 1995), 7.
22. Wright, *Upside*, 30.
23. Sandra Blakeslee, "Placebos Prove So Powerful Even Experts Are Surprised; New Studies Explore the Brain's Triumph Over Reality," *New York Times*, October 13, 1998, http://www.nytimes.com/1998/10/13/science/placebos-prove-so-powerful-even-experts-are-surprised-new-studies-explore-brain.html.
24. 1 Peter 3:15.
25. Hermann Nabi et al., "Low Pessimism Protects Against Stroke," *Stroke. ahajournals.org*, September 28, 2009, http://stroke.ahajournals.org/content/41/1/187?cited-by=yes&legid=strokeaha;41/1/187.
26. "Positive Thinking: Stop Negative Self-Talk To Reduce Stress," Mayoclinic.com, March 4, 2014, http://www.mayoclinic.org/healthy-living/stress-management/in-depth/positive-thinking/art-20043950?pg=1.
27. Shawn Achor, *The Happiness Advantage* (New York: Random House, 2010), 97–98.
28. 1 John 3:3.
29. B. L. Fredrickson and C. Branigan, "Positive Emotions Broaden the Scope of Attention and Thought Action Repertoires," *Cognition and Emotion* 19 (2005): 313–32.

30. Winifred Gallagher, *Rapt* (New York: Penguin, 2009), Kindle edition, 609–10.
31. Achor, *The Happiness Advantage*, 97–98.
32. L. S. Nes and S. C. Segerstrom, "Dispositional Optimism and Coping: A Meta -analytic Review," *Personality and Social Psychology Review* 10 (2006) 10: 235–51.
33. Hebrews 6:19; 10:34.
34. Norman Vincent Peale, *The Power of Positive Thinking* (New York: Simon & Schuster, 2003), 95–96.
35. Romans 8:14–39.
36. Ephesians 6:17; 1 Thessalonians 5:8.
37. Sonja Lyubomirsky, *The How of Happiness* (New York: Penguin, 2007), 102.
38. C. S. Dweck, *Mindset: The New Psychology of Success* (New York: Ballantine, 2006), 7.
39. 1 Peter 3:15.
40. Cited in Lyubomirsky, *The How of Happiness*, 104.
41. C. Feudtner, "Hope and the Prospects of Healing at the End of Life," *The Journal of Alternative and Complementary Medicine*, 11(1), (2005): S-23-S 30. C. R. Snyder, "Hope Theory: Rainbows in the Mind," *Psychological Inquiry*, 13 (4), (2002): 249–75.

6 HAPPY WORLD

1. John Murray, *Collected Writings, vol 2, Systematic Theology* (Edinburgh: Banner of Truth, 1991), 96.
2. Steve DeWitt, *Eyes Wide Open* (Grand Rapids: Credo House, 2012), 18.
3. Matthew 5:45.
4. Acts 14:17.
5. Psalm 145:9; Acts 14:15–17.
6. John 1:9.
7. Romans 2:4.
8. Matthew 5:43–48.
9. Romans 1:20.
10. Romans 2:4.
11. 2 Peter 3:9.
12. Romans 1:20; Luke 12:48.
13. DeWitt, *Eyes Wide Open*, 74.
14. Ibid., 62.
15. Ibid., 67.
16. Psalms 65:5–13; 104:13–24; 145:9, 15–16. Especially look at the chorus of Psalm 136.
17. DeWitt, *Eyes Wide Open*, 70, 182.
18. John Calvin, *Institutes of the Christian Religion*, ed. John T. McNeill (Philadelphia: Westminster Press, 1960), 274–75 [Inst. 2.2.15–16].
19. Herman Bavinck, *Our Reasonable Faith* (Grand Rapids: Eerdmans, 1956), 37.
20. Psalm 19; Romans 1:19–21.
21. Romans 2:14–15.
22. 1 Peter 2:14; Romans 13:3–4; 1 Timothy 2:1–2; Isaiah 45.
23. Martin Seligman, *Flourish* (New York: Simon & Schuster, 2011), Kindle edition, 1321–28.

24. Ibid.
25. DeWitt, *Eyes Wide Open*, 116.
26. Ibid., 121.
27. Ibid., 124, 64.
28. John Piper, *The Pleasures of God* (Colorado Springs: Multnomah, 2000), 97–98.
29. DeWitt, *Eyes Wide Open*, 140.

7 HAPPY PRAISE

1. Sam Crabtree, *Practicing Affirmation* (Wheaton: Crossway, 2011).
2. Genesis 7:1.
3. Job 1:8.
4. Luke 7:9.
5. John 1:47.
6. Matthew 15:28.
7. Matthew 5:48.
8. Jessica Colman, *Optimal Functioning* (Jessica Colman, 2010), Kindle edition, 612–25.
9. Crabtree, *Practicing Affirmation*, 18.
10. Romans 1:8.
11. Crabtree, *Practicing Affirmation*, 18.
12. Erik Raymond, "Help for Pastors: How to Bottle Pastoral Encouragement," *Ordinary Pastor.com,* September 29, 2010, http://www.ordinarypastor .com/?p=5067.
13. Crabtree, *Practicing Affirmation*, 32.
14. Acts 11:23.
15. Crabtree, *Practicing Affirmation*, 20.
16. Ibid., 71.
17. Arie Elshout, *Overcoming Spiritual Depression* (Grand Rapids: Reformation Heritage Books, 2006).
18. Z Di Blasi et al., "Influence of Context Effects on Health Outcomes: A Systematic Review," *The Lancet*, vol. 357 (2001): 757–762.
19. Martin Seligman, *Flourish* (New York: Simon & Schuster, 2011), Kindle edition, 1213–19.
20. Ibid., 1217.
21. Crabtree, *Practicing Affirmation*, 21.
22. Ibid., 63–65.
23. *Online Etymology Dictionary*, http://etymonline.com/.
24. Shawn Achor, *The Happiness Advantage* (New York: Random House, 2010), 58. Martin Seligman, *Flourish* (New York: Simon & Schuster, 2011), Kindle edition, 1217, 60–61.
25. Tony Schwartz, *"Be Excellent at Anything* (New York: Free Press, 2010), 129.
26. Chad Burton and Laura King, "The Health Benefits of Writing about Intensely Positive Experiences," *Journal of Research in Personality* 38 (April 2004): 150–63, http://www.sciencedirect.com/science/article/pii/S0092656603000588.
27. Achor, *The Happiness Advantage*, 194.
28. Acts 9:26–28; 11:25–26.
29. Tony Schwartz, "Why Appreciation Matters So Much," *Harvard Business Review*, January 23, 2012, http://blogs.hbr.org/schwartz/2012/01/why-appreciation-matters -so-mu.html.

30. Shelly Gable et al., "Will You Be There for Me When Things Go Right?" *Journal of Personality and Social Psychology,* vol. 91, no. 5 (2006): 904–17.
31. Proverbs 11:25.
32. Crabtree, *Practicing Affirmation,* 42.
33. C. S. Lewis, *Reflections on the Psalms* (New York: Houghton Mifflin, 1964), 94.
34. Acts 20:1–2, emphasis added; cf. Acts 14:21–22; Colossians 2:1–2; 1 Thessalonians 2:12.
35. Seligman, *Flourish,* Kindle edition, 2825–28.
36. Tim Challies, "Discipline," *Challies.com,* February 17, 2010, emphasis in original, http://www.challies.com/christian-living/discipline.
37. Westminster Confession of Faith 16.7, Evangelical Presbyterian Church in England and Wales, www.epcew.org.uk/wcf/XVI.html.
38. Matthew 19:17.
39. Roy Baumeister, "Bad Is Stronger than Good," *Review of General Psychology* 5 (2001): 323–70, http://www.csom.umn.edu/Assets/71516.pdf.
40. Robert Sutton, "Bad Is Stronger than Good: Evidence-based Advice for Bosses," *Harvard Business Review,* September 8, 2010, http://blogs.hbr.org/sutton/2010/09/bad_is_stronger_than_good_evid.html.
41. Romans 5:20.
42. Augustine cited in Eugene H. Peterson, *A Long Obedience in the Same Direction* (Downers Grove: InterVarsity Press, 2012), 53.

8 HAPPY GIVING

1. "Will Generation 'Gimme' Work for the American Dream?" Fox News video, November 29, 2011, http://video.foxnews.com/v/1300268927001/will-generation-gimme-work-for-the-american-dream/#sp=show-clips.
2. Jake Halpern, "The New Me Generation," *Boston.com,* September 30, 2007, http://www.boston.com/news/globe/magazine/articles/2007/09/30/the_new_me_generation/.
3. Acts 20:35.
4. 1 Corinthians 16:2; 2 Corinthians 9:7.
5. James 1:17.
6. 2 Corinthians 8:9.
7. 2 Corinthians 8:7, author's paraphrase.
8. Ecclesiastes 11:1.
9. 2 Corinthians 9:7.
10. 2 Corinthians 8:1–5.
11. Elizabeth Dunn et al., "Spending Money on Others Promotes Happiness," *Science,* vol. 319, no. 5870 (March 2008): 1687–88. Abstract here: http://www.sciencemag.org/content/319/5870/1687.abstract.
12. Hebrews 13:16.
13. Psalm 116:12.
14. Jeff Schapiro, "Christians Who Tithe Have Healthier Finances than Those Who Don't," *Christian Post,* May 15, 2013, http://www.christianpost.com/news/study-christians-who-tithe-have-healthier-finances-than-those-who-dont-95959/.
15. Dunn et al., "Spending Money on Others Promotes Happiness," *Science,* 1687–88.
16. Elizabeth Landau, "Study: Experiences Make Us Happier than Possessions," CNN.com, February 10, 2009, http://www.cnn.com/2009/HEALTH/02/10/happiness.possessions/.

17. S. G. Post, "Altruism, Happiness, and Health: It's Good to Be Good." *International Journal of Behavioral Medicine*, 12 (2), (2005): 66–77.
18. Matthew D. Lieberman, *Social: Why Our Brains Are Wired to Connect* (New York: Crown, 2013), Kindle edition, 3489–93; Lara B. Akin et al., "Prosocial Spending and Well-being," Harvard Business School working paper (2010), www.hbs.edu.
19. John Wilson and Marc Musick, "The Effects of Volunteering on the Volunteer," *Law and Contemporary Problems*, 62 (1999): 141–68; Camille Noe Pagan, "How Volunteering Boosts Your Brain," *Prevention*, November 2011, www.prevention .com; "Doing Good Is Good for You: 2013 Health and Volunteering Study," *UnitedHealth Group*, http://www.unitedhealthgroup.com/~/media/UHG/ PDF/2013/UNH-Health-Volunteering-Study.
20. Sonja Lyubomirsky, *The How of Happiness* (New York: Penguin, 2007), 89.
21. R. A. Emmons, *Thanks! How the New Science of Gratitude Can Make You Happier* (New York: Houghton Mifflin, 2007).
22. Joyce Bono et al., "Building Positive Resources: Effects of Positive Events and Positive Reflection on Work-Stress and Health," *Academy of Management Journal* 56 (2012): 1601–27.
23. Barbara Fredrickson, *Positivity* (New York: Random House, 2009), 187.
24. B. L. Fredricksen et al., "What Good Are Positive Emotions in Crises?" *Journal of Personality and Social Psychology* 84 (2003): 365–76.
25. Lyubomirsky, *The How of Happiness*, 95.
26. Martin Seligman, *Flourish* (New York: Simon & Schuster, 2011), Kindle edition, 572–74.
27. R. A. Emmons and C. M. Shelton, "Gratitude and the Science of Positive Psychology," in *Handbook of Positive Psychology*, eds. C. R. Snyder and S. J. Lopez (New York: Oxford University Press, 2005), 459–71.
28. R. A. Emmons and Michael McCullough, eds., *The Psychology of Gratitude* (Oxford: Oxford University Press, 2004), Kindle edition, 152–73, emphasis in original.
29. R. A. Emmons and M. E. McCullough, "Counting Blessings Versus Burdens: An Experimental Investigation of Gratitude and Subjective Well-being in Daily Life," *Journal of Personality and Social Psychology* 84 (2003): 377–89.
30. Cited in Lyubomirsky, *The How of Happiness*, 98–99.
31. Barry Schwartz, *The Paradox of Choice* (New York: HarperCollins, 2004), Kindle edition, 1142–52.
32. Ibid., Kindle edition, 2943–3125.
33. Philippians 4:11.
34. 1 Thessalonians 5:18.
35. Romans 2:14–15.
36. Lyubomirsky, *The How of Happiness*, 64–65.
37. Ibid., 65, emphasis in original.
38. Ibid.
39. John Gottman, *The Seven Principles for Making Marriage Work* (New York: Three Rivers Press, 1999), 2, 260.
40. 1 Corinthians 16:15.
41. Philippians 2:3–7.
42. Carrie Fisher, *Wishful Drinking* (New York: Simon & Schuster, 2008), 153.

43. Lyubomirsky, *The How of Happiness*, 172–73.
44. Luke 7:47.
45. Gretchen Rubin, *The Happiness Project* (New York: Harper, 2011), 70.
46. Shawn Achor, *The Happiness Advantage* (New York: Random House, 2010), 85.
47. Rubin, *The Happiness Project*, 282, emphasis added.
48. Robert Greenleaf, "What Is Servant Leadership?" Robert K. Greenleaf Center for Servant Leadership, emphasis in original, https://www.greenleaf.org/what-is-servant-leadership/.
49. Travis Bradberry, "A Bad Boss Can Send You to an Early Grave," *Philanthropy Journal*, January 30, 2009, http://www.philanthropyjournal.org/resources/managementleadership/bad-boss-can-send-you-early-grave-0.
50. Nicholas A. Christakis and James Fowler, *Connected* (New York: Little, Brown, 2009), 28–30.
51. P. Totterdell, "Catching Moods and Hitting Runs. Mood Linkage and Subjective Performance in Professional Sports Teams," *Journal of Applied Psychology* 85 (2000): 848–59.
52. H. Friedman and R. Riggio, "Effect of Individual Differences in Nonverbal Expressiveness on Transmission of Emotion," *Journal of Nonverbal Behavior* 6, (1981): 96–104.
53. Romans 13:7.
54. Mark 12:17.
55. 1 Peter 2.21–23.
56. Philippians. 3:10.
57. Ephesians 6:6–7; Colossians 3:23.
58. 1 Peter 2:15.
59. James 2:5–7.
60. Emmons and McCullough, *The Psychology of Gratitude*, Kindle edition, 152–73, emphasis in original.
61. 1 Corinthians 4:7.
62. Psalm 116.12.

9 HAPPY WORK

1. Matthew Henry, Commentary on Exodus 31:6, www.biblestudytools.com.
2. Tim Keller, *Every Good Endeavor* (New York: Dutton, 2012), 37.
3. Ibid., 67.
4. 1 Corinthians 7:17.
5. Ephesians 2:10.
6. John Calvin, *Institutes of the Christian Religion*, ed. John T. McNeill (Philadelphia: Westminster Press, 1960), 274–75 [Inst. 3.10.6].
7. Shawn Achor, *The Happiness Advantage* (New York: Random House, 2010), 78.
8. Exodus 31:3.
9. Cited in *Chariots of Fire* (1981), IMDb, www.imdb.com/title/tt0082158/quotes.
10. Keller, *Every Good Endeavor*, 20–21.
11. Cited in Ibid., 69–70.
12. Ibid., 71.
13. Colossians 3:23–24, emphasis added.
14. William Tyndale, cited by Os Guinness, *The Call* (Nashville: Thomas Nelson, 2003), 34.

15. Martin Luther, cited by Os Guinness, *The Call*, 34.
16. Dave Ramsey, "Selling by Serving with Lisa Earle McLeod," *Entreleadership Podcast*, http://www.daveramsey.com/entreleadership/podcast.
17. "Don't Bother with the Gym Today," *Daily Mail*, May 11, 2003, http://www .dailymail.co.uk/health/article-2323054/Dont-bother-gym-today-Positive-outlook -life-making-friends-good-diet-exercise.html; James Clear, "How Positive Thoughts Build Skills, Boost Health, and Improve Work," *Lifehacker*, June 28, 2013, http:// lifehacker.com/how-positive-thoughts-build-skills-boost-health-and-i-600484130; "Happiness Improves Health and Lengthens Life," *U.S. News and World Report*, March 3, 2011, http://www.usnews.com/science/articles/2011/03/03/happiness -improves-health-and-lengthens-life; "Unhappy People Don't Do as Well Economically as Those with a Positive Attitude," *Techyville*, December 10, 2012, http://www.techyville.com/2012/12/uncategorized/unhappy-people-dont-do-as- well-economically-as-those-with-a-positive-attitude/; Meg Carter, "Happiness Means Creativity," *Fast Company*, July 1, 2013, http://www.fastcocreate. com/1683288/happiness-means-creativity-one-companys-bet-on-positive -psychology.
18. "William Wilberforce: Anti-slavery Politician," *Christianity Today*, August 8, 2008, http://www.christianitytoday.com/ch/131christians/activists/wilberforce.html.
19. Cited in Os Guinness, *The Call*, 33.
20. Ibid., 34.
21. Psalm 127:2.

10 HAPPY DIFFERENCES

1. Dictionary.com, s.v. "prejudice," http://dictionary.reference.com/browse/prejudice ?s=ts, accessed November 3, 2014.
2. James 3:9.
3. Acts 17:26.
4. Romans 2:11.
5. Galatians 3:28.
6. Ephesians 2:11–18.
7. Revelation 5:9.
8. Luke 4:18–27.
9. Dolphus Weary, *Crossing the Tracks* (Grand Rapids: Kregel, 2012), 53.
10. Ibid., 32.
11. Jason Silverstein, "How Racism Is Bad for Our Bodies," *Atlantic*, March 12, 2013, http://www.theatlantic.com/health/archive/2013/03/how-racism-is-bad-for-our -bodies/273911/.
12. Stephen Liggins, "What We Can Learn from African Christians," Matthias Media, April 8, 2013, http://matthiasmedia.com/briefing/2013/04/what-we-can-learn-from -african-christians/.
13. Scott Moore, "Why We Need the 'Hood," Reformed African American Network, April 8, 2013, http://www.raanetwork.org/2013/04/why-we-need-the-hood/.
14. Weary, *Crossing the Tracks*, 70.
15. Mark Caves and Shauna Anderson, "Continuity and Change in American Congregations: Introducing the Second Wave of the National Congregations Study," *Sociology of Religion* 69 (2008).
16. Weary, *Crossing the Tracks*, 165–66.

17. Cited in J. D. Greear, "Why Pursue Racial Integration in Our Churches (A Practical Answer)," *Between the Times*, March 19, 2013, emphasis in original, http://betweenthetimes.com/index.php/2013/03/19/why-pursue-racial-integration-in-our-churches-a-practical-answer/.
18. Sam Dillon, "Study Sees an Obama Effect as Lifting Black Test-Takers," *New York Times*, February 22, 2009, http://www.nytimes.com/2009/01/23/education/23gap.html?_r=0.
19. J. D. Greear, "Challenges to Racial Integration—Cultural Preferences," *Between the Times*, April 9, 2013, http://betweenthetimes.com/index.php/2013/04/09/challenges-to-racial-integration-cultural-preferences/.
20. Thabiti Anyabwile, "The Current Battle for Richmond," *Pure Church*, March 26, 2013, http://thegospelcoalition.org/blogs/thabitianyabwile/2013/04/04/the-current-battle-for-richmond/.
21. Isaiah 56:7; Mark 11:17.
22. J. D. Greear, "Racial Integration: Of Marbles, Soup, and Beef Stew," *Between the Times*, April 2, 2013, emphasis in original, http://betweenthetimes.com/index.php/2013/04/02/racial-integration-of-marbles-soup-and-beef-stew/.
23. Dana L. Robert, "Shifting Southward: Global Christianity Since 1945," *International Bulletin of Missionary Research* 24.2 (April 2000): 50, Philip Jenkins, "Believing in the Global South," *First Things*, December 2006, 13.
24. Thabiti Anyabwile, "Learning to Be the Moral Minority from a Moral Minority," *Pure Church*, February 4, 2013, http://thegospelcoalition.org/blogs/thabitianyabwile/2013/02/04/learning-to-be-the-moral-minority-from-a-moral-minority/.
25. Michael Emerson, "A New Day for Multiracial Congregations," *Yale University Reflections*, Spring 2013, http://reflections.yale.edu/new-day-multiracial-congregations.
26. Ibid.
27. J. D. Greear, "Why Pursue Racial Integration in Our Churches (A Practical Answer)," *Between the Times*, March 11, 2013, emphasis in original, http://betweenthetimes.com/index.php/2013/03/19/why-pursue-racial-integration-in-our-churches-a-practical-answer/.
28. Jemar Tisby, "The Joyful Pursuit of Multi-Ethnic churches," *Gospel Coalition*, November 13, 2012, http://thegospelcoalition.org/blogs/tgc/2012/11/13/the-joyful-pursuit-of-multi-ethnic-churches/.
29. J. D. Greear, "Why Pursue Racial Integration in Our Churches (A Biblical Answer)," *Between the Times*, March 12, 2013, http://betweenthetimes.com/index.php/2013/03/12/why-pursue-racial-integration-in-our-churches-a-biblical-answer/.
30. Ibid., emphasis in original.
31. John Piper, *Bloodlines* (Wheaton, IL: Crossway, 2011), 196.
32. Matthew 11:28.

CONCLUSION: GRAND TOTAL = POSITIVE
FAITH = THE HAPPY CHRISTIAN

1. Barbara Fredrickson, *Positivity* (New York: Random House, 2009), 170.
2. John 16:8.
3. Matthew 5:4
4. 1 Corinthians 6:20, emphasis added.
5. Sonja Lyubomirsky, *The How of Happiness* (New York: Penguin, 2007), 245.

NOTES

6. Donald Miller, "Happy People Seem to Do This Well," *Storylineblog.com*, http://storylineblog.com/2013/06/27/happy-people-seem-to-do-this-well/.
7. Martin Seligman, *Flourish* (New York: Simon & Schuster, 2011), Kindle edition, 2546.
8. Ibid., 2578.
9. Shawn Achor, *The Happiness Advantage* (New York: Random House, 2010), 109.
10. Ibid., 110.
11. Romans 5:3–5.
12. Achor, *The Happiness Advantage*, 123.
13. Romans 8:18.
14. Hebrews 12:11.
15. Cited in Jim Collins, *Good to Great* (New York: HarperCollins, 2001), 83–86.
16. 2 Corinthians 6:9–10.
17. Ephesians 2:10.
18. *poi?ma* (workmanship): "a piece of literary workmanship." John MacArthur, *The MacArthur New Testament Commentary on Ephesians* (Chicago: Moody Press, 1986), 63.

SCRIPTURE INDEX

SUBJECT INDEX

SUBJECT INDEX

SUBJECT INDEX

SUBJECT INDEX

ABOUT THE AUTHOR

DR. DAVID MURRAY is professor of Old Testament and Practical Theology at Puritan Reformed Theological Seminary and pastor of the Free Reformed Church in Grand Rapids. He was ordained to the ministry in 1995 and pastored two churches in Scotland for twelve years. Murray is the author of *Jesus on Every Page*, *Christians Get Depressed Too*, and *How Sermons Work*. He regularly speaks at conferences in North America and beyond. David and his wife, Shona, have five children, and they love camping, fishing, boating, and skiing in the Lake Michigan area.